Quiz
BOOK

THE  TIMES

Quiz
BOOK

OLAV BJORTOMT

Published by Times Books

An imprint of HarperCollins Publishers
Westerhill Road
Bishopbriggs
Glasgow G64 2QT
www.harpercollins.co.uk
times.books@harpercollins.co.uk

First edition 2016

ISBN 978-0-00-819029-3

10 9 8 7 6 5 4 3 2 1

© Times Newspapers Ltd 2016
www.thetimes.co.uk

The Times® is a registered trademark of Times Newspapers Ltd

A catalogue record for this book is available from the British Library.

Printed and bound in Great Britain by Clays Ltd., St Ives plc.

If you would like to comment on any aspect of this book, please contact us at the given address or online.
E-mail: puzzles@harpercollins.co.uk
 facebook.com/collinsdictionary
 @collinsdict

Contents

Introduction   6

How to use this book   11

Quizzes   13

Quizzes by subject   444

Image Credits   445

Introduction

It started with a call to come down to the features department back in the summer of 2005. Mike Harvey, a former news editor turned features editor who had absolutely terrified me during my time as a graduate trainee on the newsdesk, said he wanted me to do the T2 quiz from now on.

He had heard from fellow staff members of my sterling performances at the celebrity-studded PEN quiz and thought that I could inject some life into the little bit of the T2 back page occupied by five questions every day, since it appeared that someone – any one on the features staff – had just been using a bunch of boring old quiz books to compile it. Also, I had noticed the cardinal sin of the same questions being repeated; it was as if nobody cared.

So I took it upon myself to bring out some really interesting questions. To mould a new and fascinating T2 quiz. But when I say "interesting" (the origin of the Harrington jacket name; the origin of the phrase "banana republic"), I thought, wow, this'll knock the socks off those readers who by now must be so angered by the dullness of the existing quiz that such questions would be an instant panacea.

I could not have been more wrong. The reaction was instantaneous and it was devastating. Reader emails poured in asking how had this insanely, obscure trivia nonsense taken the place of the normal quiz? They asked: why? I had totally misjudged its then tone. So action on the editing side had to be taken. Jonathan, my "controller" on T2 as it were, took it upon himself to regulate then quiz's content.

The problem was Jonathan was Australian and general knowledge culture can vary wildly from country to country.

Therefore, we exchanged several emails where I had to explain the cultural import of things like "Alcock and Brown" – who made the non-stop first transatlantic flight in 1919 – because Jonathan flatly rejected the question as he had never heard of them. Rejected questions followed in their dozens: I understood why on some occasions; other times, I fumed at the assumptions made.

The difficult beginnings of my quiz were also fraught with rudimentary factual errors – naively, I never bothered to verify every question; trusting my own noggin to be faithful and to be true. This was disastrous behaviour on my part. One example? I said Z in the NATO Phonetic Alphabet stood for Zebra. Idiot. Of course, it is Zulu.

But things settled down; the rejections dwindled from a flood to a trickle after a few months, and apart from one telephone call from Mike about two years later, in which he mentioned off-handed how "bloody difficult" the quiz was, no more complaints about the quiz's perceived fairness were received.

Other incidents stick out in the memory. The Mayor of Alnwick once hunted me down because she was convinced that Alnwick and not Morpeth was the county town or administrative centre of Northumberland. In that instance, however, I was correct (and for once, I'd actually been there).

I never complained when the quiz was "rested" for the sake of an advert taking its allotted space – an advert that sometimes, if I recall correctly, wanted to cure male impotence – but apparently enough fans complained about its frequent absences for such rests to stop and for the quiz to do its then five-a-day thing.

Another odd thing was a mysterious sub-editor's insistence that the fifth question always be a sports one – he or she just kept on inserting his own questions. Their sports question just kept on turning up in place of whatever general knowledge question I had intended for that spot. I never bothered to ask why – I was paid regardless. Although this was not my innovation, it is one that I took over and stays with the quiz to this day, and one that has greatly increased my sports knowledge and appreciation of sporting life.

Of course, the following book only has 20 question quizzes (the Qs I have chosen for these quizzes are my absolute favourites, culled from the tens of thousands I have written over the past decade). The quiz has grown from five questions to ten (from February 2014) and then to 15 per day and 20 on a Saturday with an added daily picture question (from February 2015). The jumps in growth have been thanks to editor enthusiasm, first from online news editor Pat Long, then from the actual editor in chief John Witherow – though admittedly, I was terrified that he would have some sort of problem with the quiz (thankfully, all I got was enthusiasm – I was later told that John had become addicted to the daily quiz during a cruise and so "could I do more questions?" "Err, okay").

Alas, once I could just do the five questions every morning for publication the very next day: whatever popped into my head, in fact. Ninety-five questions per week demands a far more efficient and wide-ranging operation. In fact, I'd estimate that the quiz takes me up 10-12 hours to compile: filing three quizzes on Friday and three more on Monday.

While I could once rely on whatever novel I was reading, film I had just seen or album I was listening to, now I had to comb sources properly (though the mighty Wikipedia is always my first port of call); make sure I was covering all the quiz subjects (because when I don't, I get letters asking "where is the science?", "where is the classical music?") and try to never, ever repeat a question (though I invariably do, every three months on average). Even if I may fail on occasion, the overall aim is to always be interesting.

I keep two text files for maintenance, one headlined "times2quizzes (master)", which contains every quiz I've ever done for *The Times* (with over 26,000 questions); the other: "times2 questions reserve", which is a file containing containing 742 pages with an average of 20-25 questions per page. These are questions that might go into the quiz one day, if most of them weren't too long or incredibly, unbelievable hard by far. Meanwhile new questions are written for this file every day.

So when I compile the quizzes, I have good base of existing material to work from, though the urge is always to use new stuff or whatever morning inspirations I've had. The aim is to cover each core quiz subject: film, literature, history, current affairs, art, geography, politics, theatre, sport, with an unconscious emphasis on arts and books because that is what I truly love. Then, when the final 15/20 is done, the verification starts.

Checking the questions can change the quiz irrevocably. Because verification is a serious business: it often takes longer to check the quiz than write it. Aside from vast chunks of wording being rewritten, what cannot be double or triple sourced must be excised.

Therefore I always take these opportunities to insert a much easier question in place of what has been rejected (on average, this happens about three times per quiz). So the quiz I started with – believe it or not, people will gasp – was much harder than the one that ends up in the newspaper (of which about 75 per cent has survived). Then there are the queries about what I have written, in which vocabulary and phrasing are interrogated so thoroughly, it might bring out a burst of inane giggles just to read the emails exchanged between myself and the times2 puzzles desk.

The process has no doubt helped me in my life as what has been termed a "professional" quizzer, however. Since the quiz went to 10 questions I have won two European individual titles and one

World individual title in the big wide world of quizzing. Checking sources thoroughly, nay obsessively, has helped me become a champion quizzer, searing thousands of facts on my brain.

And when an error slips through? There is hell to pay. I sometimes wish I had never been born, such is the probably deserved opprobrium I have been showered with by disgusted Times readers. But others are quick to shower the quiz with love when it stirs a half-forgotten memory of a place they had once lived or an obscure autoimmune disorder-type disease that needs as much public exposure as it can get. Even, if such knowledge has been turned into a mere quiz question.

All of the questions you will find within these pages are, I hope, either challenging, interesting or enlightening. Some questions – if fortune has favoured my setting – might even satisfy all three requirements.

So, please, enjoy…

Olav Bjortomt

How to use this book

The answers to each quiz are printed at the end of the following quiz. For example, the answers to Quiz 1 appear at the bottom of Quiz 2. The exception to this rule is the last quiz, the answers to this quiz appear at the end of Quiz 1.

QUIZZES

QUIZZES

1   7X is the secret formula in which drink?

2   Cleeve Cloud is the highest point of which English hills?

3   Who succeeded George Washington as US President?

4   Which British composer wrote *Eight Songs for a Mad King* (1968)?

5   Who took the famous 1963 photograph of Christine Keeler sitting astride an Arne Jacobsen chair?

6   Peter O'Toole played King Henry II in which two films?

7   In a nursery rhyme, whose "wife could eat no lean"?

8   Who founded the High Holborn toy shop *Noah's Ark* in 1760?

9   Roger Delgado first played which *Doctor Who* villain in 1971?

10   William Huskisson MP died after being run over by which steam locomotive?

11   Which "Fabergé of the Footwear" designed Queen Elizabeth II's coronation shoes?

12   Henry Laurens is the only American to have been imprisoned in which UNESCO World Heritage Site?

13   The Egyptian goddess Heqet was depicted with the head of which amphibian?

14   On which website is a person's followers measured in Wheatons (500,000 = 1 Wheaton)?

15   Which African nation is the Francophone country with the largest population?

16   Which distinguishing features are absent in a person who has the disorder adermatoglyphia?

17   Which Austrian-born philosopher reportedly once threatened Karl Popper with a red-hot poker?

18 Which world light heavyweight boxing champion won TV's *Superstars* in 1974?

19 Which athlete broke Wyndham Halswelle's 53-year-old Scottish 300 yards record in 1961?

20 What is the pictured temple complex?

Answers to QUIZ 215 – Film

1	Errol Morris	**12**	Agnès Jaoui
2	*Miller's Crossing*	**13**	*Plan 9 from Outer Space*
3	*A Little Night Music*	**14**	Jacques Rivette – Suzanne
4	*Frozen*		Schiffman is often credited
5	Henry Fonda		as a co-director
6	*The Danish Girl*	**15**	Billy
7	James Horner	**16**	Carmen Miranda
8	Rex Harrison	**17**	*Bridge of Spies*
9	Chris Rock	**18**	*Sweet Smell of Success*
10	Kevin O'Connell	**19**	Mr. Big (in *Sex and the City*)
11	*Foreign Correspondent*	**20**	Takashi Miike

QUIZ 2 – General Knowledge

1   Which female singer had a no. 4 hit in 1974 with *Y Viva Espana*?

2   What is the British equivalent of the Swiss savoury spread Cenovis?

3   Who proposed "the Easyway" of quitting smoking?

4   Which musician found fame thanks to his *Reggae Reggae* sauce?

5   HMV's very first store was opened by which composer in 1921?

6   Which bone derives its name from the Latin for 'little key'?

7   Beatrice Portinari was the muse of which Italian poet?

8   Which Dane published his theory of the orbital behaviour of electrons in 1912?

9   The dentist Alfred P. Southwick was inspired to invent which chair in 1881?

10   Located near St Petersburg, what is the largest lake in Europe?

11   Which 2011 comedy film centres on the run-up to Lillian Donovan's wedding day?

12   The Scotsman, Thomas Sutherland, founded which banking corporation in 1865?

13   Inspired by the Sanremo Festival, Marcel Bezençon conceived which event in 1955?

14   Which protrusion is also known as the laryngeal prominence?

15   Which substance, named from the Latin for 'cheese', makes up about 80 per cent of the proteins in cow milk?

16   Butch McGuire's bar in Chicago claims to have added which flavoured stirrer to the Bloody Mary cocktail?

17   Winston Churchill observed that which sport is "the best passport in the world"?

18 Which England cricketer was Muttiah Muralitharan's record 709th Test wicket?

19 In 1985, what became the first side in European football to have won all three major UEFA club competitions?

20 Who is the pictured conductor?

Helga Esteb / Shutterstock.com

Answers to QUIZ 1 – General Knowledge

1 Coca-Cola
2 Cotswolds
3 John Adams
4 Peter Maxwell Davies
5 Lewis Morley
6 *Becket* and *A Lion in Winter*
7 Jack Sprat
8 William Hamley
9 The Master
10 Stephenson's *Rocket*
11 Roger Vivier
12 The Tower of London – during 1780–81
13 Frog
14 Twitter
15 Democratic Republic of the Congo
16 Fingerprints
17 Ludwig Wittgenstein
18 John Conteh
19 The future Lib Dem leader Menzies 'Ming' Campbell
20 Angkor Wat in Cambodia

QUIZ 3 – Art

1 Which Georges Seurat painting features 48 people, 8 boats, 3 dogs and 1 monkey?

2 In Edwin Landseer's 1839 painting, who are *Dignity and Impudence*?

3 Gerhard Richter's 15-painting *October 18, 1977* cycle portrays which group?

4 Chinese sculptor Lei Yixin designed which $120m Washington, DC memorial?

5 *War Horse* and *Walking Madonna* are sculptures by which Dame, who died in 1993?

6 Which US artist was born Emmanuel Radnitzky in 1890?

7 Which artist married Saskia van Uylenburg in 1634?

8 What is the name of Turner Prize-winning potter Grayson Perry's female alter-ego?

9 David Mach crafted his gorilla sculpture, *Silver Streak*, from which everyday objects?

10 Daniel Day-Lewis played which Irish painter and writer in the film *My Left Foot*?

11 Which Flemish painter's *Portinari Altarpiece* is in the Uffizi?

12 The English graphic artist Donald McGill (1875–1962) famously designed which items?

13 Which two artists shared the Yellow House, Arles, for nine torrid weeks in 1888?

14 Who "started painting in blue" when he learned of Carlos Casagemas' suicide?

15 *Blam* (1962) and *As I Opened Fire* (1964) are paintings by which Pop artist?

16 Which art movement was called *Jugendstil* in German?

17 In 1993, which sculptor became the first female winner of the Turner Prize?

18 Who wrote the hoax biography *Nat Tate: An American Artist 1928–1960*?

19 Which US painter married the photographer Alfred Stieglitz in 1924?

20 Which American artist created the pictured piece?

shalunts / Shutterstock.com

Answers to QUIZ 2 – General Knowledge

1 Sylvia
2 Marmite
3 Allen Carr
4 Levi Roots (born Keith Tanyue)
5 Edward Elgar
6 Clavicle (from *clavicula*)
7 Dante Alighieri
8 Niels Bohr
9 Electric chair
10 Lake Ladoga
11 *Bridesmaids*
12 The Hongkong and Shanghai Banking Corporation (HSBC)
13 Eurovision Song Contest
14 Adam's apple
15 Casein
16 Celery stick
17 Polo
18 Paul Collingwood
19 Juventus – it won the 1977 UEFA Cup, 1984 European Cup Winners' Cup and 1985 European Cup
20 Gustavo Dudamel

QUIZ 4 – General Knowledge

1   Which painter killed Ranuccio Tomassoni in a brawl following a tennis game?

2   On hearing Handel's 'Hallelujah Chorus', who reputedly said: "He is the master of us all"?

3   *Let Them Talk* was which British actor's debut blues album?

4   A deipnosophist excels in conversations that take place where?

5   The architect Frank Matcham (1854–1920) famously designed which buildings?

6   Who wrote the 1963 report "The Reshaping of British Railways"?

7   Which soap opera is Godfrey Baseley's most famous creation?

8   Brunei is entirely surrounded by which Malaysian state?

9   Tenzin Gyatso is the 14th man to hold which title?

10   Who did Hartley Booth succeed as MP for Finchley in 1992?

11   Who was US President when the British set fire to the White House in the War of 1812?

12   Which 1984 novel centres on Soviet submarine commander Marko Ramius?

13   What was the nickname of the metal-eating French entertainer Michel Lotito?

14   Dating back to 2000 BC, the Swastika Stone sits on the edge of which Yorkshire moor?

15   Nicolas-Jacques Pelletier was the first person to be executed using which device?

16   Mae Questel last voiced Betty Boop in which 1988 film?

17   Newstead Abbey was the ancestral home of which poet, who died in 1824?

18   What is the smallest metropolitan area in the US to host a major professional sports franchise?

19 Which Irish jockey won the 1986 Prix de l'Arc de Triomphe on Dancing Brave?

20 Name the pictured music group –

Kobby Dagan / Shutterstock.com

Answers to QUIZ 3 – Art

1 *A Sunday on La Grande Jatte – 1884* aka *A Sunday Afternoon on the Island of La Grande Jatte*
2 Jacob Bell's pet bloodhound Grafton & terrier Scratch
3 The Baader-Meinhof group or Red Army Faction
4 Martin Luther King, Jr. National Memorial
5 Elisabeth Frink
6 Man Ray
7 Rembrandt van Rijn
8 Claire
9 Metal coat hangers
10 Christy Brown
11 Hugo van der Goes
12 Saucy seaside postcards
13 Paul Gauguin & Vincent van Gogh
14 Pablo Picasso
15 Roy Lichtenstein
16 Art Nouveau
17 Rachel Whiteread
18 William Boyd
19 Georgia O'Keeffe
20 Jeff Koons – it is titled *Balloon Dog*

1 According to legend, which Italian city was founded at 12 o'clock noon on March 25, 421 AD?

2 The 2015 Spike Lee film *Chi-Raq* is based on which play by Aristophanes?

3 Which chain of "Mexican Grill" restaurants was launched by Steve Ells in Denver in 1993?

4 Which US president's New York City memorial is the largest mausoleum in North America?

5 The naturalist Georges-Louis Leclerc, comte de Buffon, called which animal the "proudest conquest of Man"?

6 In which country is Europe's highest peak, Mount Elbrus?

7 Aged 22, who became conductor of the attendants' band at Worcester and County Lunatic Asylum in Powick in 1879?

8 What is the oldest of the natural sciences?

9 Marillenschnaps is an Austrian brandy made from which fruit?

10 First performed in 1978, *Talent* was the first play by which English comedienne?

11 Peercoin, Monero, Ethereum, Nxt, Ripple and DigitalNote are types of what?

12 Which portrait of Shakespeare was the first painting to enter the National Portrait Gallery's collection?

13 Launched in 1963 by Hoffmann-La Roche, what was the pharmaceutical industry's first billion dollar drug?

14 Who is the director of *Star Wars: The Force Awakens*?

15 Founded in 2014, which Spanish political party is led by Pablo Iglesias?

16 The name of which fashion brand, formed in Aosta in 1987, is a variation of the Finnish word for the Arctic Circle?

17 Which US game designer created *Magic: The Gathering*, the first modern trading card game?

18 A two-time French Open singles winner, which retired German tennis star married Barbara Hutton in 1955?

19 Who won a record ninth Stanley Cup as head coach with the Detroit Red Wings in 2002?

20 Name the pictured dog breed –

Answers to QUIZ 4 – General Knowledge

1	Caravaggio	12	*The Hunt for Red October* by Tom Clancy
2	Joseph Haydn		
3	Hugh Laurie	13	Monsieur Mangetout
4	Dinner tables	14	Ilkley Moor
5	Theatres	15	Guillotine – in 1792
6	Dr. Richard Beeching	16	*Who Framed Roger Rabbit?*
7	*The Archers*	17	Lord Byron
8	Sarawak	18	Green Bay (NFL's Green Bay Packers)
9	Dalai Lama		
10	Margaret Thatcher	19	Pat Eddery
11	James Madison	20	Duran Duran

QUIZ 6 – Literature

1 Which Scottish novelist wrote *Ice Station Zebra* and *The Guns of Navarone*?

2 Which 1977 Stephen King novel centres on the aspiring writer Jack Torrance?

3 Which 18th century writer said: "No man but a blockhead ever wrote, except for money"?

4 Who is the hunter hero of the Zulu trilogy, *Marie* (1912), *Child of Storm* (1913) and *Finished* (1917)?

5 Samuel Butler's translation of which epic poem opens: "Sing, O goddess, the anger of Achilles, son of Peleus"?

6 Which children's author wrote and illustrated the 1990 book *Oh, the Places You'll Go!*?

7 Marie Kondo is the Japanese author of the 2011 book *The Life-Changing Magic of...* what?

8 *The Overloaded Ark* (1953) was which naturalist's first book?

9 Alden Pyle is the title character of which 1955 Graham Greene novel?

10 Anastasia "Ana" Steele is the female protagonist of which literary trilogy?

11 Which US novelist wrote *Housekeeping*, *Gilead* and *Home*?

12 Author of *The Snowman*, which Norwegian crime writer created Harry Hole?

13 Which French-Swiss woman of letters wrote the 1807 novel *Corinne*?

14 Which Brothers Grimm fairy tale is known as *Dornröschen*, meaning Little Briar Rose?

15 *Rupert of Hentzau* was the 1898 sequel to which Ruritanian adventure novel?

16 The Prancing Pony pub in Bree features in the works of which writer?

17 In the Charles Dickens novel, which beadle invents Oliver Twist's name?

18 Rebecca West's travelogue *Black Lamb and Grey Falcon* is about which former country?

19 Which Charlotte Brontë novel ends with the title character marrying the tutor Louis Moore?

20 Which illustrated manuscript is pictured?

Answers to QUIZ 5 – General Knowledge

1	Venice	13	Valium (diazepam)
2	*Lysistrata*	14	J.J. Abrams
3	Chipotle	15	Podemos (meaning 'We can')
4	Ulysses S. Grant	16	Napapijri
5	The horse	17	Richard Garfield
6	Russia	18	Gottfried von Cramm
7	Edward Elgar	19	Scotty Bowman – who won
8	Astronomy		five Stanley Cups with the
9	Apricot		Montreal Canadiens and
10	Victoria Wood		one with the Pittsburgh
11	Cryptocurrency		Penguins
12	Chandos portrait	20	Affenpinscher

QUIZ 7 – General Knowledge

1 In 1922, who enlisted in the ranks of the RAF under the name John Hume Ross?

2 Novelist Peter Carey described which art critic as "Australia's Dante"?

3 Which Prime Minister died in 1827 after 119 days in office?

4 Which TV cops often infuriated their boss Captain Harold Dobey?

5 What was found by the Canadian merchant ship *Dei Gratia* on December 4, 1872?

6 Clive Sinclair launched which electric vehicle in 1985?

7 Which bodybuilder won his first Mr. Olympia title in 1970?

8 Which "Coma Scale" is named after a British city?

9 Which scientists published *Molecular Structure of Nucleic Acids* in April 1953?

10 In a 1950 Disney film, Lady Tremaine is which girl's stepmother?

11 Hans Werner Henze's 1968 oratorio *The Raft of the Medusa* is a requiem for which revolutionary?

12 Designed by Zaha Hadid, the MAXXI modern art gallery is in which capital city?

13 Whose weapons of torture include a dish-drying rack, soft cushions and the "comfy chair"?

14 Which British singer had a 2014 no.1 with *Money on My Mind*?

15 Dieter Schwarz bought the rights to which supermarket name from a retired schoolteacher?

16 Which moon of Jupiter has the smoothest surface of any known solid body in the Solar System?

17 Which artist supposedly said: "In the future, everyone will be world-famous for 15 minutes"?

18 Godfrey Rampling, late father of the actress Charlotte, won Olympic gold in which sport?

19 Whose completed Test career batting average of 60.73 is the highest by any English cricketer?

20 Which famous dog is pictured?

Answers to QUIZ 6 – Literature

1   Alistair MacLean
2   *The Shining*
3   Samuel Johnson
4   Allan Quatermain – in novels by H. Rider Haggard
5   *The Iliad*
6   Dr. Seuss
7   *Tidying*
8   Gerald Durrell
9   *The Quiet American*
10 *Fifty Shades* trilogy by E.L. James
11 Marilynne Robinson
12 Jo Nesbø
13 Madame de Staël or Germaine de Staël
14 *Sleeping Beauty*
15 *The Prisoner of Zenda* by Anthony Hope
16 J.R.R. Tolkien
17 Mr. Bumble
18 Yugoslavia
19 *Shirley*
20 The Book of Kells – in the Old Library Building, Trinity College Dublin

1   What was the alliterative nickname of the notorious Hoa Lo Prison?

2   What breed is the fictional dog Lassie?

3   What is the largest instrument of the violin family?

4   Redblush is a variety of which fruit, known in Spanish as *toronja*?

5   Which US novelist is known for her "Grant County" series?

6   Which future Oscar-winner played surfer Scott Irwin on *Home and Away* in 1997?

7   Kelpers are natives of which South Atlantic islands?

8   Who was Soviet Azerbaijan's leader 1969–82, later serving as third president of Azerbaijan, from 1993 to 2003, when his son Ilham succeeded him?

9   Which 10cc song features the lyrics: "I don't like cricket, oh no, I love it"?

10 The Lincolnshire physician Dr Francis Willis famously treated which king?

11 The Kempler video shows the assassination of which Israeli Prime Minister?

12 Who holds the titles Baron Carrickfergus and Earl of Strathearn?

13 The Rogers Commission identified the O-ring seal failure that caused which disaster?

14 Christopher Marlowe wrote about the "troublesome reign and lamentable death of" which king?

15 The Trojan Room coffee pot inspired the first example of which video camera?

16 The Paris shop Deyrolle famously specialises in which hobby?

17 The 2015 Huracán was which carmaker's successor to the Gallardo?

18 In its early years, which tabletop game had a fierce rivalry with Newfooty?

19 The Old Harrovian, Charles Alcock, created which cup competition in 1871?

20 Which American historical site is pictured?

Answers to QUIZ 7 – General Knowledge

1 Lawrence of Arabia aka T.E. Lawrence
2 Robert Hughes
3 George Canning
4 Starsky & Hutch
5 The *Mary Celeste*
6 Sinclair C5
7 Arnold Schwarzenegger
8 Glasgow Coma Scale (GCS)
9 James D. Watson and Francis Crick
10 Cinderella
11 Ernesto "Che" Guevara
12 Rome
13 The Spanish Inquisition in the Monty Python sketch
14 Sam Smith
15 Lidl – from Ludwig Lidl, a former business partner of Dieter Schwarz's father Josef
16 Europa
17 Andy Warhol
18 Athletics (4 x 400m relay in 1936)
19 Herbert Sutcliffe
20 Laika – the first animal to orbit the Earth

QUIZ 9 – Film

1   Who played Bellatrix Lestrange in the *Harry Potter* films?

2   Which movie gunfighters fought Eli Wallach's Mexican bandit leader Calvera?

3   Which *Star Trek* movie saw the crew travel back in time to 1980s San Francisco?

4   Which 2012 film is based on the novel *These Foolish Things* by Deborah Moggach?

5   Teenage film truant Ferris Bueller took his *Day Off* in which US city?

6   Which Vittorio De Sica work won the first *Sight & Sound* greatest film poll in 1952?

7   The Ghanta Awards recognise the worst in film produced by which movie industry?

8   *Knife in the Water* (1962) was which French-Polish director's first feature-length film?

9   Lauren Bacall was the last of the 16 Hollywood icons mentioned in which song to die, 24 years after its release?

10   Giulietta Masina (1921–94) was the wife and muse of which film director?

11   Which movie character was trained by Mickey Goldmill?

12   Vin Diesel plays Dominic Toretto in which movie franchise?

13   Starring Esther Williams, which 1952 film tells the story of Australian swimmer Annette Kellerman?

14   Robert De Niro played the Jewish gangster Noodles in which Sergio Leone film?

15   Starring Gregory Peck, the 1959 film *Beloved Infidel* was based on which US writer's life?

16   Which language in a 2009 movie was created by Paul Frommer?

17 Fred Sexton created the titular statuette for which John Huston film?

18 What was the movie inspiration for Maurice Micklewhite's stage name Michael Caine?

19 The Xquisite strip club is the setting for which 2012 Steven Soderbergh film?

20 Who is the pictured Scottish actress?

Answers to QUIZ 8 – General Knowledge

1 'Hanoi Hilton'
2 Collie or Rough Collie
3 Double bass
4 Grapefruit
5 Karin Slaughter
6 Heath Ledger
7 Falkland Islands
8 Heydar Aliyev
9 *Dreadlock Holiday*
10 George III
11 Yitzhak Rabin
12 Prince William, Duke of Cambridge
13 Space shuttle *Challenger* disaster
14 Edward II
15 First webcam
16 Taxidermy
17 Lamborghini
18 Subbuteo
19 FA Cup
20 The Alamo or the Church of San Antonio de Valero mission

1 Which Grand Prince of Moscow became Tsar of Russia in 1547?

2 A "leapling" is a person born on which date?

3 The Mildenhall Treasure was found in which county in 1942?

4 In the title of a Frances Hodgson Burnett novel, who is Sara Crewe?

5 Which corporation makes the *Hayabusa* motorcycle and *Burgman* scooters?

6 In a Benny Hill no.1 song, who is *The Fastest Milkman in the West*?

7 What is unusual about the Korean octopus dish *Sannakji*?

8 Who was shot dead at Pete Maxwell's ranch home on July 14, 1881?

9 Anthony Marriott and Alistair Foot wrote which long-running 1971 stage farce?

10 The Jeffersonian Institute is home to the Medico-Legal Lab team in which US TV drama?

11 Which saint is credited with staging the first nativity scene (*presepio*) in 1223?

12 Opened in 2002, the Bawabet Dimashq in Damascus is the world's largest what?

13 Which shark species is the second largest fish?

14 Which Penzance-born chemist invented the miner's safety lamp?

15 Which island was called "this cursed rock" by Napoleon?

16 Trevor Philips, Michael De Santa and Franklin Clinton are the playable characters in which 2013 game?

17 In a standard deck of cards, what is the only one-eyed king?

18 Llanwrtyd Wells hosts an annual marathon pitting man against which animal?

19 In 1959, which "Super Bowl of Stock Car Racing" was first won by Lee Petty?

20 Name the pictured Italian sweet bread loaf –

Answers to QUIZ 9 – Film

1	Helena Bonham Carter	12	*The Fast and the Furious* series
2	*The Magnificent Seven*	13	*Million Dollar Mermaid* or
3	*Star Trek IV: The Voyage Home*		*The One Piece Bathing Suit*
4	*The Best Exotic Marigold Hotel*	14	*Once Upon a Time in America*
5	Chicago	15	F. Scott Fitzgerald
6	*Bicycle Thieves*	16	Na'vi – from the film *Avatar*
7	Bollywood	17	*The Maltese Falcon*
8	Roman Polanski	18	The film of Herman Wouk's
9	*Vogue* by Madonna		novel *The Caine Mutiny*
10	Federico Fellini	19	*Magic Mike*
11	Rocky Balboa	20	Tilda Swinton

1   The Torre Agbar dominates the skyline of which city in Spain?

2   Which French fashion house was founded in 1952 by Gaby Aghion?

3   Which peninsula was designated as the first Area of Outstanding Natural Beauty in 1956?

4   Car engineer George Carwardine designed which lamp in 1933?

5   Which two US Presidents both died on July 4, 1826?

6   What is the smallest member state of the United Arab Emirates?

7   Which disease is caused by the parasite *Plasmodium falciparum*?

8   Who composed the 1846 opera *Attila*?

9   Which TV show was based on the Sookie Stackhouse/Southern Vampire books?

10 Which 1813 battle was Europe's largest battle prior to World War One?

11 Which limestone partition in the Old City of Jerusalem is also known as the *Kotel*?

12 Containing the filament and anther, what is the male sex organ of a flower called?

13 The Mond process extracts and purifies which transition metal?

14 Which book of the Old Testament is named after the son of Nun?

15 Known for his hit single *Let Her Go*, Mike Rosenberg uses which stage name?

16 What became the richest art museum in the world when it inherited $1.2bn in 1982?

17 In 1899, the Nottingham grocer Frederick Gibson Garton invented which sauce?

18 Who lost his WBA featherweight title to Steve Cruz in June 1986?

19 What is the northernmost city to have hosted a summer Olympic Games?

20 Which much-maligned car model is pictured?

Answers to QUIZ 10 – General Knowledge

1   Ivan the Terrible or Tsar Ivan IV
2   February 29
3   Suffolk
4   *A Little Princess*
5   Suzuki
6   Ernie
7   The *nakji* baby octopus is served alive
8   Billy the Kid
9   *No Sex Please, We're British*
10 *Bones*
11 St Francis of Assisi
12 Restaurant
13 Basking shark – after the whale shark
14 Sir Humphry Davy
15 Saint Helena
16 *Grand Theft Auto* V
17 King of Diamonds
18 Horse
19 Daytona 500
20 Panettone

1   Which 6th Earl of Leicester defeated Henry III at the Battle of Lewes in 1264?

2   Which Earl of Essex was beheaded on Tower Hill on July 28, 1540?

3   Which airmail pilot won the $25,000 Orteig Prize in 1927?

4   The Year of the Five [Roman] Emperors (193 AD) ended with which man in power?

5   Which Carthaginian general defeated a Roman army at Cannae in 216 BC?

6   The 1881 "Gunfight at the OK Corral" took place where in Arizona?

7   Daniel Lambert (1770–1809) was famous for what reason?

8   Which empire's government was known as the "Sublime Porte"?

9   Played on film by Vincent Price, Matthew Hopkins took what job title in 1644?

10 Which organisation was formed in 1930 as the female branch of the Hitler Youth?

11 Marie Antoinette was the 15th child of which Holy Roman Emperor?

12 William III's top general, Frederick Herman, Duke of Schomberg, was killed at which 1690 battle?

13 The Pratzen Heights was a vital area of high ground in which 1805 battle?

14 Author of *The Tudor Revolution in Government* (1953), which historian was born Gottfried Rudolf Ehrenberg?

15 Which battle spawned the famous epitaph beginning: "Go tell the Spartans"?

16 In honour of the sun god Aton, the Egyptian ruler Amenhotep IV renamed himself what?

17 The *Mayaguez* incident was the last official battle of which war?

18 Which Norman king was the husband of Matilda of Flanders?

19 Pope Clement VII refused King Henry VIII's request to do what?

20 Which infamous Dutchwoman is pictured?

Answers to QUIZ 11 – General Knowledge

1 Barcelona
2 Chloé
3 Gower Peninsula
4 Anglepoise lamp
5 Thomas Jefferson, John Adams
6 Ajman
7 Malaria
8 Giuseppe Verdi
9 *True Blood* – from the novels by Charlaine Harris
10 Battle of Leipzig or Battle of the Nations
11 Wailing Wall or Western Wall or The Buraq Wall
12 Stamen
13 Nickel
14 Joshua
15 Passenger
16 J. Paul Getty Museum
17 HP Sauce
18 Barry McGuigan
19 Helsinki – in 1952
20 Austin Allegro

QUIZ 13 – General Knowledge

1   Which English poet published *The Destruction of Sennacherib* in 1815?

2   KaiKai and Kiki are the emblems of which Japanese artist's production company?

3   Deemed the fairest, which Greek goddess won 'The Judgement of Paris'?

4   The fortified wine, vermouth, derives its name from the German for which herb?

5   Who were Ron Nasty, Dirk McQuickly, Stig O'Hara and Barry Wom?

6   What positive attribute is a common name for the plant *Lunaria annua*?

7   In 1664, Jérôme Hatt founded which brewery in Strasbourg?

8   Who became 'The Red Knight' in his first cartoon outing?

9   What did John Cockcroft and Ernest Walton "split" in 1932?

10   Nicknamed "The Big O", who had a 1964 no.1 with *It's Over*?

11   Which Lars von Trier film features a fox who says "chaos reigns"?

12   In 1976, which Toronto building became the world's tallest free-standing structure?

13   Which late Italian fashion designer lived at 1116 Ocean Drive, Miami Beach?

14   In 1900, who was born the fourth daughter of Lord Glamis, later the 14th Earl of Strathmore and Kinghorne?

15   In 1965, 61-year-old retired bus driver Kempton Bunton confessed to stealing which portrait?

16   What are Madame Jeanette, Trinidad Scorpion 'Butch T' and Carolina Reaper?

17   What is the only country whose name ends in the letter Q?

18 In 1928, the USSR organised which communist alternative to the Olympic Games?

19 Pakistan's Sohail Abbas is the highest international goal scorer in the history of which sport?

20 Identify the famous couple in the picture –

Answers to QUIZ 12 – History

1 Simon de Montfort
2 Thomas Cromwell
3 Charles Lindbergh – it was for the first nonstop aircraft flight between New York and Paris
4 Septimius Severus or Severus
5 Hannibal
6 Tombstone
7 He was the heaviest person of his day, weighing over 50 stone at one time
8 Ottoman Empire
9 "Witch Finder General"
10 League of German Girls or Band of German Maidens

or *Bund Deutscher Mädel* (BDM)
11 Francis I
12 Battle of the Boyne
13 Battle of Austerlitz
14 G.R. Elton or Geoffrey Rudolf Elton
15 Battle of Thermopylae (480 BC)
16 Akhenaton
17 Vietnam War
18 William the Conqueror
19 Annul his marriage with Catherine of Aragon
20 The reputed spy Mata Hari aka Margaretha Geertruida MacLeod, née Zelle

1   Which fictional serial killer was first dubbed 'The Chesapeake Ripper'?

2   The *Doni Tondo* (c.1507) is which artist's only finished panel painting?

3   Which people wish to found a homeland called Khalistan?

4   Maenads were the female followers of which Greek god?

5   Which TV cook was born Phyllis Nan Sortain Pechey?

6   What is the smallest member state of the EU?

7   What is *La Tapisserie de la Reine Matilde* more familiarly called?

8   The bikini takes its name from an atoll in which Pacific republic?

9   Which snake, *Eunectes murinus*, is the largest species of boa?

10 What is the stage name of Kiwi musician Ella Maria Lani Yelich-O'Connor?

11 Steve Jobs wore black turtlenecks designed by which Japanese fashion icon?

12 Where does the Bundle of Kent transmit electrical impulses?

13 Which 1948 Cole Porter musical features the song *Tom, Dick or Harry*?

14 Charles Grey, 2nd Earl Grey, had an illegitimate daughter with which duchess?

15 Which Austrian (1870–1937) founded the school of individual psychology?

16 Who is the only US President not to have lived in the White House?

17 Which colourless flammable gas – C_2H_4 – is the simplest alkene?

18 Which Romanian tennis star was the first professional athlete to sign with Nike?

19 Which boxer won BBC Sports Personality of the Year in 1967 and 1970?

20 What is the pictured Russian street?

Answers to QUIZ 13 – General Knowledge

1   Lord Byron aka George Gordon Noel, sixth Baron Byron
2   Takashi Murakami – the company is called Kaikai Kiki
3   Aphrodite
4   Wormwood
5   The Rutles
6   Honesty
7   Brasseries Kronenbourg
8   *Mr. Benn*
9   The atom or atomic nucleus
10 Roy Orbison
11 *Antichrist*
12 CN Tower
13 Gianni Versace
14 Queen Elizabeth The Queen Mother or Elizabeth Angela Marguerite Bowes-Lyon
15 Goya's *Portrait of the Duke of Wellington*
16 Chilli pepper cultivars
17 Iraq
18 Spartakiad
19 Field hockey (348 goals)
20 Arthur Miller and Marilyn Monroe

QUIZ 15 – Popular Music

1   Wilson Phillips and En Vogue both had US hits in 1990 with which song title?

2   Which US rock 'n' roll musician (b.1935) is nicknamed "The Killer"?

3   *Boy, October, War* – what comes next?

4   Which Canadian musician was the mother of Rufus and Martha Wainwright?

5   Martin Scorsese's film *The Last Waltz* documented which group's final concert?

6   Which band had hits in 1965 with *For Your Love* and *Heart Full of Soul*?

7   *Justified* was which US singer's 2002 debut solo studio album?

8   Which US band had a 1965 no.1 with *Mr. Tambourine Man*?

9   Who formed the band N.E.R.D with Chad Hugo and Shay Haley?

10   Which Canadian reggae fusion band has topped the singles chart with *Rude*?

11   Which rock band frontman released the debut solo album *Pictures at Eleven* (1982)?

12   Which rapper founded the record label GOOD (Getting Out Our Dreams) Music in 2004?

13   Which Canadian rapper released the 2013 single *Hold On, We're Going Home*?

14   The Greek-born singer Yannis Philippakis is the frontman of which British indie band?

15   *Bang* was released in 1989 as the lead single from which Russian rock band's self-titled debut album?

16   *Those Were the Days* was a 1968 no.1 for which Welsh singer?

17 Which English rock band was named after a 1966 novel by Willard Manus?

18 *Praise & Blame* is a 2010 album by which Welsh singer?

19 Which football anthem is New Order's only UK number one single?

20 Name the pictured English rock band –

Avis De Miranda / Shutterstock.com

Answers to QUIZ 14 – General Knowledge

1	Hannibal Lecter	**12**	In the heart
2	Michelangelo	**13**	*Kiss Me, Kate*
3	Sikhs	**14**	Georgiana Cavendish, Duke of Devonshire
4	Dionysus		
5	Fanny Cradock	**15**	Alfred Adler
6	Malta	**16**	George Washington
7	Bayeux Tapestry	**17**	Ethene or ethylene
8	Marshall Islands	**18**	Ilie Nastase
9	Green Anaconda	**19**	Henry Cooper
10	Lorde	**20**	Nevsky Prospekt, St. Petersburg
11	Issey Miyake		

QUIZ 16 – General Knowledge

1   What links Moss in *The I.T. Crowd*, Harold Macmillan and an E.M. Forster novel title?

2   Which Poet Laureate wrote the play *Epsom Wells* (1672)?

3   How was the 1st Marchioness of Pembroke (1504–1536) better known?

4   Which scientist was *Time* magazine's "Person of the [20th] Century"?

5   Which game bird is scientifically known as *Coturnix coturnix*?

6   Who succeeded the assassinated US president James Garfield?

7   What is the longest British river at 219 miles long?

8   The New Mexico town Hot Springs renamed itself after which radio show?

9   What online retailer was originally called Cadabra.com?

10 Manzanilla and Palo Cortado are varieties of which wine?

11 Which mysterious prisoner was buried under the name of 'Marchioly' in 1703?

12 What did Paul Hogan say tasted "like an angel crying on your tongue"?

13 Which TV and audio products company has a museum in Struer, Denmark?

14 Which book series centres on the Baudelaire orphans, Violet, Klaus and Sunny?

15 Which mathematician built the first reflecting telescope in 1668?

16 Which Trinidadian-born rapper launched the perfume Pink Friday in 2012?

17 Which type of single-celled organism derives its name from the Greek for 'change'?

18 Who owned the legendary racehorse Red Rum?

19 Which British wheelchair athlete won his first London Marathon in 2002?

20 What is the nickname of the pictured dinosaur?

Evikka / Shutterstock.com

Answers to QUIZ 15 – Popular Music

1 *Hold On*
2 Jerry Lee Lewis
3 *The Unforgettable Fire* (studio albums by U2)
4 Kate McGarrigle
5 The Band
6 The Yardbirds
7 Justin Timberlake
8 The Byrds
9 Pharrell Williams
10 Magic!
11 Robert Plant of Led Zeppelin
12 Kanye West
13 Drake
14 Foals
15 Gorky Park
16 Mary Hopkin
17 Mott the Hoople
18 Tom Jones
19 *World in Motion* (released under the name Englandneworder)
20 Deep Purple

1   Who succeeded Duncan I as King of Scotland in 1040?

2   Which murderous duo sold their victims to the Edinburgh doctor, Robert Knox?

3   The Chorleywood process is a method of making which common food?

4   Hart's Rules is a set of conventions used by which people?

5   What are High Spy, Barf, Knott Rigg and Whiteside?

6   Achilles was dipped in which river to make him invulnerable?

7   Elvis Presley was born in which Mississippi town in 1935?

8   The murder victim Susie Salmon narrates which novel from beyond the grave?

9   Who traced the source of an 1854 cholera outbreak in Soho to the Broad Street pump?

10 What did Guy de Maupassant call "this tall skinny pyramid of iron ladders, this giant and disgraceful skeleton"?

11 Which BBC TV drama centres on the Shelby crime family?

12 What are the Bowyer, Constable, Beauchamp, Martin, Salt and White?

13 In 1980, the Herbert Johnson 'Poet' was chosen to adorn the head of which movie hero?

14 An adult's third molars are known by which common name?

15 Residents of the Italian village of Campodimele are famous for being what?

16 Which Caribbean luxury resorts operator was founded by Gordon "Butch" Stewart in 1981?

17 First published in 1966, what is the bestselling chess book of all time?

18 Which Olympic champion athlete won 41 LPGA titles and 10 majors in golf?

19 What is the nickname of the Australian men's national rugby league team?

20 The pictured Veil Nebula is in which constellation?

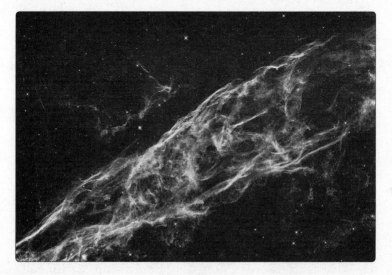

Answers to QUIZ 16 – General Knowledge

1 The first name Maurice
2 Thomas Shadwell
3 Anne Boleyn
4 Albert Einstein
5 Common quail
6 Chester A. Arthur
7 Severn
8 *Truth or Consequence*
9 Amazon
10 Sherry
11 The Man in the Iron Mask
12 Foster's lager
13 Bang & Olufsen
14 *A Series of Unfortunate Events* by Lemony Snicket (aka Daniel Handler)
15 Isaac Newton
16 Nicki Minaj
17 Amoeba
18 Noel Le Mare
19 David Weir
20 Dippy the diplodocus – in the Natural History Museum

1 Though not the final section, what is the last *Canterbury Tale*?

2 Which famous comedienne was the niece of Nancy Astor?

3 Who is friends with Bill Badger, Algy Pug and Edward Trunk?

4 What type of devastating mudflow is named from the Javanese for "lava"?

5 Bariatrics is the branch of medicine that deals with what condition?

6 Which former Prime Minister died at 10 Downing Street in 1908?

7 Formed in 1676, what is The Queen's Body Guard in Scotland?

8 What are Dorabella, Troyte, Ysobel and W.N.?

9 Both André Cassagnes and Arthur Granjean have been credited with which invention, originally called "The Magic Screen"?

10 Which Australian-born author is the subject of the film *Saving Mr. Banks*?

11 The Mariel Boatlift was a 1980 mass emigration to the US from which country?

12 Leper's squint, oeil-de-boeuf and bull's-eye are types of which architectural feature?

13 Iyaric is a dialect spoken by members of which religion?

14 Where would you find relatively empty regions called Kirkwood gaps?

15 Charles Marlow falls in love with Kate Hardcastle in which 1773 play?

16 Based in Glattbrugg, Switzerland, what is the world's largest HR services company?

17 What is the nickname of the *Gangs of New York* movie villain William Cutting?

18 What follows "The Flop" and "The River"?

19 Which championship game is Canada's largest single day sporting event?

20 Nicknamed "La Stupenda", which opera singer is pictured?

Answers to QUIZ 17 – General Knowledge

1 Macbeth
2 William Burke and William Hare
3 Bread
4 Printers & publishers
5 Fells in the English Lake District
6 Styx
7 Tupelo
8 *The Lovely Bones* by Alice Sebold
9 John Snow
10 Eiffel Tower
11 *Peaky Blinders*

12 Some of the towers that form the Tower of London
13 Indiana Jones – it is his fedora/wide brim fur felt hat
14 Wisdom teeth
15 Long-lived (living more than 20 years longer than average)
16 Sandals Resorts
17 *Bobby Fischer Teaches Chess*
18 Babe Didrikson or Mildred Ella Zaharias
19 The Kangaroos
20 Cygnus

1   Sir Thomas Beecham called which London venue a "giant chicken coop"?

2   Alfred Fielding and Marc Chavannes created which packaging material?

3   What number is denoted by the word myriad?

4   Lady Godiva rode nude through the streets of which city?

5   Which English photographer married Catherine Deneuve in 1965?

6   Which children's TV show featured The Soup Dragon and Froglets?

7   Craster in Northumberland is famed for which fish delicacy?

8   Who was the oldest member of the pop group The Jackson 5?

9   Unani, Ayurveda and Siddha are alternative forms of what?

10   Who first appeared together in the 1915 story *Extricating Young Gussie*?

11   A luxury brand of General Motors, what is the oldest active American car make?

12   Which artist painted the Uffizi's *Ognissanti Madonna* (c.1310)?

13   In humans, which dark pigment is the main determinant of skin colour?

14   Named after a British physicist, what is the SI derived unit of absorbed dose?

15   Who did Suetonius claim sang the *Sack of Ilium* during the Great Fire of Rome?

16   A photo of which 1970 meeting is the most requested reproduction from the US National Archives?

17   Whistled by Brother Bones, what is the Harlem Globetrotters' signature song?

18   The Canadian dentist William George Beers is known as the father of which sport?

19   Wearing the Star of David on his trunks, which boxer defeated Max Schmeling in 1933?

20   Name the pictured king –

Mauvries / Shutterstock.com

Answers to QUIZ 18 – General Knowledge

1   *The Parson's Tale*
2   Joyce Grenfell
3   Rupert the Bear
4   Lahar
5   Obesity
6   Henry Campbell-Bannerman
7   Royal Company of Archers
8   Four of Elgar's 14 *Enigma Variations*
9   Etch-A-Sketch
10   P.L. Travers, creator of Mary Poppins
11   Cuba
12   Window
13   Rastafari movement
14   The asteroid belt
15   *She Stoops to Conquer* by Oliver Goldsmith
16   Adecco
17   "Bill the Butcher"
18   "The Turn" (as in Texas Hold 'Em poker)
19   The Grey Cup championship game in Canadian football
20   Joan Sutherland

1 *College Boy*, composed by Derek New, is the theme tune of which quiz show?

2 The time travel TV drama *Outlander* is based on novels by which US author?

3 The 2009 BBC TV drama *Desperate Romantics* centred on which art movement?

4 Norm Peterson and Cliff Clavin propped up the bar in which sitcom?

5 Which flop TV show was set in the fishing village of Los Barcos?

6 Who were Danny Wilde and Lord Brett Sinclair in a 70s TV show?

7 Who played Hawkeye Pierce in the TV series *MASH*?

8 The US sitcom *All in the Family* was based on which BBC TV show?

9 Which 2012 TV drama adapted Shakespeare's *Richard II*, *Henry IV parts 1 & 2* and *Henry V*?

10 Which TV role links David Threlfall and, in its US remake, William H. Macy?

11 Which US sitcom centres on Sheldon, Leonard, Howard, Raj, Penny, Bernadette and Amy?

12 Which TV drama features Kit Harington in the role of Jon Snow?

13 In *Doctor Who*, the Torchwood Institute was founded by which queen?

14 Storybrooke, Maine, is the town setting for which fairy tale TV drama series?

15 South Africa's Henry Cele played the title role in which 1986 TV miniseries?

16 Who replaced Jason Dawe as a *Top Gear* presenter in 2003?

17 Which actor hosted the US TV show *Man v. Food*?

18 Phil Leotardo (Frank Vincent) was the final antagonist of which TV drama?

19 Fred Armisen and Carrie Brownstein star in which Oregon-based TV sketch show?

20 Name the pictured TV weather presenter –

Featureflash Photo Agency / Shutterstock.com

Answers to QUIZ 19 – General Knowledge

1 Royal Festival Hall
2 Bubble Wrap (in 1957)
3 10,000
4 Coventry
5 David Bailey
6 *The Clangers*
7 Kippers
8 Jackie Jackson
9 Medicine
10 Jeeves and Bertie Wooster
11 Buick
12 Giotto
13 Melanin
14 The gray – after Louis Harold Gray
15 Emperor Nero
16 Elvis Presley meeting Richard Nixon
17 *Sweet Georgia Brown*
18 [Modern] Lacrosse
19 Max Baer
20 King Willem-Alexander of the Netherlands

1 The 1944 ballet *Fancy Free* features a score by which US composer?

2 Which baron married Maria Kutschera on November 26, 1927?

3 Who painted *An Experiment on a Bird in the Air Pump* (1768)?

4 Who was the last Norman King of England?

5 Who wrote and directed the 2001 TV film *Perfect Strangers*?

6 Aged 18, Fiona Butler posed for which iconic poster in 1976?

7 What is a male hawk, especially one used in falconry, called?

8 The red Budget box was created for which Chancellor in 1859?

9 Named from a cockatoo, 'galah' is Australian slang for what?

10 What surgical first was performed by Argentine cardiologist Dr Rene Favaloro in 1967?

11 Which Basque Country city is the capital of Guipúzcoa, Spain's smallest province?

12 Which Cuban cigar brand derives its name from the Taino word for 'tobacco'?

13 Alain Delon, John Malkovich and Matt Damon have all played which con artist?

14 Which US mobile phone maker pioneered the "flip phone" with the MicroTAC in 1989?

15 Who gathered 100 nude models in Berlin's Neue Nationalgalerie for her artwork *VB55*?

16 The Shah-e Cheragh mosque is which Iranian city's most important pilgrimage site?

17 What would you do with Onionskins, Commies, Chinas and Aggies?

18 The "Maroons" (Queensland) play the "Blues" (New South Wales) in which rugby league series?

19 Which athlete was the first man to win consecutive Olympic 1500m titles?

20 What is the pictured particle accelerator?

Answers to QUIZ 20 – TV

1	*University Challenge*	11	*The Big Bang Theory*
2	Diana Gabaldon	12	*Game of Thrones*
3	Pre-Raphaelite Brotherhood	13	Queen Victoria
4	*Cheers*	14	*Once Upon a Time*
5	*El Dorado*	15	*Shaka Zulu*
6	*The Persuaders!*	16	James May
7	Alan Alda	17	Adam Richman
8	*Till Death Do Us Part*	18	*The Sopranos*
9	*The Hollow Crown*	19	*Portlandia*
10	Frank Gallagher in *Shameless*	20	Carol Kirkwood

1   What is Berlin's only remaining city gate?

2   What medical journal was founded by Thomas Wakley in 1823?

3   Dick Bruna created which cartoon rabbit in 1955?

4   What holy city was called *Yathrib* in pre-Islamic times?

5   The Airedale is the largest breed of which group of dogs?

6   What did the USA buy from Spain for $20 million in 1898?

7   Which British pop group's second no.1 was the 1977 single *Angelo*?

8   What is the largest artery in the human body?

9   In Greek mythology, who were Clotho, Lachesis and Atropos?

10   Which Brazilian actor learnt Spanish to play Pablo Escobar in the Netflix series *Narcos*?

11   Which Swiss watchmaker introduced the Carrera in 1963 and Monaco in 1969?

12   Which cellist became principal conductor of the Hallé Orchestra in 1943?

13   In 1821, Pierre Berthier discovered which aluminium ore near a village in Provence?

14   Which former member of The Humblebums is nicknamed "The Big Yin"?

15   Who formed the Second Triumvirate with Octavian and Lepidus?

16   *The Troubled Man* is the last novel to feature which Swedish inspector?

17   23 Kirkgate, Thirsk is home to The World of... which vet?

18   Who won his first Grand Slam singles title at the 1933 US Championships?

19 Which Formula One team won its first Constructors'
Championship in 1974?

20 Which ocean liner is pictured?

Rocky Grimes / Shutterstock.com

Answers to QUIZ 21 – General Knowledge

1   Leonard Bernstein
2   Georg von Trapp
3   Joseph Wright of Derby
4   Stephen (of Blois)
5   Stephen Poliakoff
6   The Athena 'Tennis Girl' poster
7   Tercel
8   William Ewart Gladstone
9   An idiot or a fool
10 Coronary or heart bypass surgery
11 Donostia–San Sebastián
12 Cohiba
13 Tom Ripley – Patricia Highsmith's fictional character
14 Motorola
15 Vanessa Beecroft
16 Shiraz
17 Play marbles – they are types of marble
18 State of Origin series
19 Sebastian Coe – in 1980 and 1984
20 The Large Hadron Collider at CERN

1 Referring to their hands, which monkeys derive their name from the Greek for 'maimed'?

2 Which fir tree is named after a Scottish botanist who died in Hawaii in 1834?

3 What is the largest living marsupial?

4 Which farm animals belong to the genus *Capra*?

5 Which gamebird's "Grey" species has the Latin name *Perdix perdix*?

6 The Lammergeier (*Gypaetus barbatus*) is known by which other name?

7 A lithophyte is a type of plant that grows where?

8 The Samoyed dog breed developed in what vast region?

9 *Ciconia ciconia* is the Latin name for which long-necked large bird?

10 Which extinct animal appears twice on the Tasmanian Coat of Arms?

11 "Aurelian" is a term for people interested in which creatures?

12 A zedonk is a rare cross between which two animals?

13 A member of the woodpecker family, the wryneck feeds mostly on what?

14 The Tarpan is an extinct subspecies related to which domesticated animal?

15 A 'binky' is a twisting jump made by which animal being joyful?

16 Which species of penguin is second only in size to the emperor penguin?

17 Which amphibian and "aquatic Panda" is called the *wawa yu*, or crying baby fish, by locals in China?

18 What is the world's largest living structure composed of living entities?

19 Panama disease is a type of Fusarium wilt that threatens which fruit plants?

20 Which weasel family member is pictured?

Answers to QUIZ 22 – General Knowledge

1	Brandenburg Gate	12	John Barbirolli
2	*The Lancet*	13	Bauxite – discovered near Les Baux
3	Miffy		
4	Medina, Saudi Arabia	14	Billy Connolly
5	Terrier	15	Mark Antony
6	The Philippines	16	Kurt Wallander
7	Brotherhood of Man	17	James Herriot
8	Aorta	18	Fred Perry
9	The Fates or Moirae	19	McLaren – then named 'McLaren-Ford'
10	Wagner Moura		
11	TAG Heuer	20	RMS *Queen Elizabeth* 2 or QE2

1   The American G.I. Chris Scott is a major character in which musical?

2   The "Radiant Baby" was the trademark of which US street artist (1958–90)?

3   Which general created and first hoisted Argentina's national flag?

4   Who is the only canine member of Enid Blyton's Famous Five?

5   According to Sir John Seeley, what was "acquired in a fit of absence of mind"?

6   In 1885, what was first tested on the nine-year-old boy Joseph Meister?

7   Symantec is the world's largest maker of what type of software?

8   Which Elvis Presley hit was simply *O Sole Mio* with a new lyric?

9   What symbol links the flags of Vietnam, Somalia and Suriname?

10 In which play does Martin Dysart evaluate the boy Alan Strang?

11 Rosemarie Frankland was the first British winner of which title?

12 *Shark Tank* is the American version of which BBC Two show?

13 Which Allen Ginsberg poem opens: "I saw the best minds of my generation destroyed by madness"?

14 In geology, what term is used for soil at or below the freezing point of water for two or more years?

15 Which Dutch company is Europe's largest brewer?

16 Which Irish province has the greatest number of native Irish speakers?

17 Which Old Testament book contains both the shortest and longest chapters in the Bible?

18 Nicknamed 'The Bayonne Bleeder', which boxer claims to have inspired the film *Rocky*?

19 Which French alpine skier won the first two overall World Cup titles, in 1967 and 1968?

20 Name the pictured knife –

Answers to QUIZ 23 – Wildlife

1 Colobus monkey – they lack thumbs, unlike most primates

2 Douglas fir (*Pseudotsuga menziesii*) – named after David Douglas

3 Red kangaroo (*Macropus rufus*)

4 Goats

5 Grey Partridge

6 Bearded vulture

7 On bare rock or stone

8 Siberia

9 White Stork

10 Thylacine or Tasmanian tiger

11 Butterflies

12 Zebra & donkey

13 Ants

14 Horse

15 Rabbit

16 King penguin

17 Chinese giant salamander

18 Great Barrier Reef

19 Banana

20 Pine Marten (*Martes martes*)

1   The famous feline Tardar Sauce (b. 2012) is known by which internet name?

2   Which US actor (1919–93) was key in creating London's new Globe Theatre?

3   Who did Joyce describe as the "one-handled adulterer" in *Ulysses*?

4   Wootz, Damascus and Noric are renowned types of which alloy?

5   Sir Thomas Bertram owns which estate in an 1814 novel?

6   Which throwing device has a dingle arm, a lift arm and an elbow?

7   Who was assassinated as she walked to an interview with Peter Ustinov?

8   What is the nearest "yellow dwarf" to Earth?

9   The strangulation of Mrs. Boyle at the end of Act 1 is central to which play's plot?

10 The organ of Corti is found where in mammals?

11 Which motorcycle gang TV drama was set in the Californian town of Charming?

12 Which Japanese structure is the world's tallest tower?

13 "Discovered" in 1824 by the Scottish merchant Robert Hunter, Chang and Eng Bunker were the original what?

14 Roland Berrill and Dr. Lancelot Ware founded which high IQ society in 1946?

15 *Divers* (2015) is the fourth album by which harpist wife of US actor Andy Samberg?

16 Which king supposedly said: "Will no one rid me of this troublesome priest?"?

17 Giacomo Meyerbeer's last opera, *L'Africaine*, is about which Portuguese explorer?

18 Which country plays the All Blacks for rugby's Freedom Cup?

19 Which future Baroness became managing director of Birmingham City FC in 1993?

20 Name the South African-born entrepreneur in the picture –

Helga Esteb / Shutterstock.com

Answers to QUIZ 24 – General Knowledge

1	*Miss Saigon*	12	*Dragons' Den*
2	Keith Haring	13	*Howl*
3	Manuel Belgrano	14	Permafrost or cryotic soil
4	Timmy	15	Heineken International
5	The British Empire	16	Connacht or Connaught
6	Louis Pasteur's rabies vaccine	17	Psalms – Psalm 117 and Psalm 119
7	Computer-security software	18	Chuck Wepner
8	*It's Now or Never*	19	Jean-Claude Killy
9	A [single, five-pointed] star	20	Kukri – as used by Gurkha soldiers from Nepal
10	*Equus* by Peter Shaffer		
11	Miss World (in 1961)		

1   Zest from the Femminello St. Teresa or Sorrento lemon is traditionally used to make which liqueur?

2   Featuring stewed beef, which Cuban dish's name means 'old clothes'?

3   S. Daniel Abraham created which diet drink brand in 1977?

4   Which spirit derives its name from the Dutch for 'burnt wine'?

5   Which Swiss chocolatier invented the process of making milk chocolate?

6   What is the main ingredient of hummus?

7   Pat and Harry Olivieri supposedly invented which Philadelphia snack?

8   Sichel launched which kitsch German wine brand in 1923?

9   Miami cardiologist Arthur Agatston promotes which diet?

10 Rocamadour and Montrachet are varieties of what food?

11 What fruit is used in the dessert Tarte Tatin?

12 Associated with New Orleans, what type of snack is a beignet?

13 André Balazs opened which London restaurant and hotel in 2013?

14 Red Star is a popular brand of which Chinese 'white liquor'?

15 Which ThaiBev beer is named after the Thai for 'elephant'?

16 A food rich in vitamin C, what is *muktuk*?

17 Which single-issue consumer group produces the monthly newspaper *What's Brewing*?

18 Which South African national dish is curried meat baked with an egg-topping?

19 What is the single-largest day for food consumption in the USA?

20 Which type of cured ham is pictured?

Answers to QUIZ 25 – General Knowledge

1   "Grumpy Cat"
2   Sam Wanamaker
3   Lord Nelson
4   Steel
5   *Mansfield Park* by Jane Austen
6   Boomerang
7   Indira Gandhi
8   The Sun
9   *The Mousetrap* by Agatha Christie
10 Inner ear
11 *Sons of Anarchy*
12 Tokyo Skytree – which is 634m tall
13 Siamese twins
14 Mensa
15 Joanna Newsom
16 Henry II – referring to Thomas Becket
17 Vasco da Gama
18 South Africa
19 Karren Brady
20 Elon Musk

QUIZ 27 – General Knowledge

1   Reverend John Flynn founded which air ambulance service?

2   The Brockman family featured in which BBC One sitcom?

3   What type of delicacy are Isle of Man Queenies?

4   The Queen Alexandra's Birdwing is the world's largest what?

5   What invention was given the US Patent No. 174,465?

6   What type of vehicle is the purpose-built TX4?

7   *So You Win Again* (1977) was which group's sole UK no 1?

8   Peterman is slang for what type of specialist criminal?

9   Which shrub is named after the first US Ambassador to Mexico?

10   Which London venue is Europe's largest multi-arts centre?

11   Which actor suffered the first of many on-screen deaths, playing Ranuccio in the film *Caravaggio*?

12   Which Paco Rabanne fragrance shares its name with a poem by William Ernest Henley?

13   Which Victorian architect designed Westminster Cathedral in the Early Christian Byzantine style?

14   Which podcast re-investigated the 1999 murder of Hae Min Lee in Baltimore?

15   What was the only British fighter aircraft in continuous production throughout World War Two?

16   What is the Norfolk estate of the 7th Marquess of Cholmondeley?

17   In 1746, which painter married Margaret Burr, an illegitimate daughter of the Duke of Beaufort?

18   The Melbourne Ladies presented Ivo Bligh with which 11cm-high terracotta urn?

19 Prince Albert II of Monaco competed at the Winter Olympics in which sport?

20 Which machine is pictured?

Answers to QUIZ 26 – Food & Drink

1   Limoncello
2   Ropa vieja
3   *Slim-Fast*
4   Brandy
5   Daniel Peter
6   Chickpeas
7   The cheesesteak
8   Blue Nun
9   South Beach diet
10 Goat's cheese
11 Apple
12 A square doughnut with no hole
13 Chiltern Firehouse
14 Baijiu
15 Chang beer
16 Whale skin and blubber
17 CAMRA / Campaign for Real Ale
18 Bobotie
19 Thanksgiving Day (the second is Super Bowl Sunday)
20 Jamón Ibérico

QUIZ 28 – General Knowledge

1   First produced in 1981, what is Boeing's largest single-aisle passenger aircraft?

2   Which Australian city is named after the Governor of New South Wales (1821–25)?

3   Which Roman god of love is the son of Venus and husband of Psyche?

4   The Australian continent has how many time zones?

5   The Hamilton-Norwood scale measures the progression of which male problem?

6   What is the largest inhabited castle in the world?

7   Raf Ravenscroft played the sax solo on which big 1978 hit?

8   Bakery chain Greggs opened during the 1930s in which city?

9   Louis Mountbatten opened which theme park on May 24, 1979?

10 Wilson Carlile founded which religious organisation in 1882?

11 Ernst Lindemann was killed in 1941 as the captain of which battleship?

12 Now extinct, the huia was which country's largest species of wattlebird?

13 Robert Cornelius is credited with taking the first of which photos in 1839?

14 The internet abbreviation TL;DR stands for what?

15 Which Florentine museum houses Michelangelo's sculptures *Bacchus* and *Brutus*?

16 Aqua regia is a mixture of which two acids?

17 Commonly found in American football players, which disease is known as CTE?

18 The horse *Quiz* won which Classic race in 1801?

19 Peter Oborne's book *Wounded Tiger* is a history of cricket in which country?

20 Name the pictured star of musical theatre –

Featureflash Photo Agency / Shutterstock.com

Answers to QUIZ 27 – General Knowledge

1	Royal Flying Doctor Service of Australia	10	The Barbican
2	*Outnumbered*	11	Sean Bean
3	Queen Scallops	12	*Invictus*
4	Butterfly	13	John Francis Bentley
5	Alexander Graham Bell's telephone	14	*Serial*
6	London black cab taxi ("Hackney Carriage")	15	Supermarine Spitfire
		16	Houghton Hall
7	Hot Chocolate	17	Thomas Gainsborough
8	Safebreaker	18	The Ashes urn
9	Poinsettia (after Joel Roberts Poinsett)	19	Bobsleigh
		20	Van de Graaff generator

QUIZ 29 – Classical Music

1   Which symphony by Felix Mendelssohn celebrated the 300th anniversary of the Augsburg Confession?

2   Completed in 1962, *Montezuma* is which US composer's only full-length opera?

3   Sir Neville Marriner founded which chamber orchestra in 1958?

4   Which German composer's third symphony is known as the *Rhenish*?

5   Who composed *L'Amico Fritz* (1891) and *Guglielmo Ratcliff* (1895)?

6   Verdi and Rossini both wrote operas based on which Shakespeare tragedy?

7   Which Welsh lyric mezzo-soprano made her album debut with *Premiere* (2004)?

8   Which French composer wrote the rhapsodic piece *Tzigane* (1924)?

9   Which composer scored Laurence Olivier's films *Henry V* and *Hamlet*?

10 The composers Elgar, Holst and Delius all died in which year?

11 For which composer was the villa *Wahnfried* built in Bayreuth?

12 The dish *pasta alla Norma* took its name from an opera by which composer?

13 Which opera by Peter Maxwell Davies is about a 16th century English composer?

14 Which US minimalist composer wrote *Drumming* and *Music for 18 Musicians*?

15 Who is the title subject of the 2013 opera *Oscar* by composer Theodore Morrison?

16 Which younger brother of Joseph Haydn was also a highly regarded composer?

17 Peter Warlock was the byname of which English composer (1894–1930)?

18 Which composer is the first female Master of the Queen's Music?

19 The German composer Otto Nicolai founded which orchestra in 1842?

20 Who designed the pictured music venue –

DavidGraham86 / Shutterstock.com

Answers to QUIZ 28 – General Knowledge

1 Boeing 757
2 Brisbane – as in Sir Thomas Brisbane
3 Cupid
4 Three
5 Male pattern baldness or hair loss
6 Windsor Castle
7 *Baker Street* by Gerry Rafferty
8 Newcastle-upon-Tyne
9 Thorpe Park
10 Church Army
11 *Bismarck*
12 New Zealand
13 Self-portrait or 'selfie'
14 Too long; didn't read
15 The Bargello
16 Hydrochloric & nitric
17 Chronic traumatic encephalopathy
18 St. Leger Stakes
19 Pakistan
20 Elaine Paige

1   According to a classic tongue twister, what did Peter Piper pick?

2   What links the national anthems of Spain, Bosnia & Herzegovina, Kosovo and San Marino?

3   Austria's Bregenz Festival stages operas on the shores of which lake?

4   In South Africa, what type of social gathering is a *braai*?

5   *The Colour of Magic* (1983) was the first of which fantasy novels?

6   Which Italian ship collided with the SS *Stockholm* in 1956?

7   Which children's book creation had a heart "two sizes too small"?

8   Where was bandleader Wallace Hartley's last engagement?

9   What metal did Kipling call the "master of them all"?

10 Which video game heroine is the daughter of Lord Henshingly?

11 Which ancient Greek philosopher founded the Lyceum?

12 Mount Pilatus and its summits Tomlishorn and Esel overlook which Swiss city?

13 Which socialist British newspaper styles itself as "The People's Daily"?

14 The first space satellite orbited by the US, Explorer 1 discovered the innermost of which zones?

15 What is the Beatles' best-selling single in the UK?

16 Flying V, Firebird, Archtop, L7 and Super 400 are guitars made by which US company?

17 Known for its incredibly long legs, what is South America's largest canid?

18 Which Italian football team was wiped out in the 1949 Superga air diaster?

19 Whose one year, five day-reign as world chess champion is the briefest in history?

20 Name the pictured English actress –

Featureflash Photo Agency / Shutterstock.com

Answers to QUIZ 29 – Classical Music

1   *Reformation Symphony* or Symphony no.5
2   Roger Sessions
3   Academy of St Martin in the Fields
4   Robert Schumann
5   Pietro Mascagni
6   *Othello* (*Otello*)
7   Katherine Jenkins
8   Maurice Ravel
9   William Walton
10 1934
11 Richard Wagner
12 Vincenzo Bellini
13 *Taverner* – as in John Taverner
14 Steve Reich
15 Oscar Wilde
16 Michael Haydn or Johann Michael Haydn
17 Philip Heseltine
18 Judith Weir
19 Vienna Philharmonic or Wiener Philharmoniker
20 Norman Foster – it is the Sage Gateshead

1   Which entertainment company was founded by the former fire-eater Guy Laliberte in 1984?

2   Who composed the theme to the 1964 film *633 Squadron*?

3   How many syllables are there in a haiku?

4   Who opened his first fish 'n' chips restaurant in Bradford in 1926?

5   Heracles was the result of an affair Zeus had with which mortal?

6   Which Yorkshireman wrote the plays *Bouncers* and *Teechers*?

7   Who hosted infamous parties at 32 Ambleside Avenue, Streatham?

8   *Robin's Nest* and *George and Mildred* were spin-offs of what sitcom?

9   Which Englishman wrote *The Mathematical Analysis of Logic* (1847)?

10 Biman is the state-owned airline of which Asian country?

11 Musically, what links *Arabella, Daphne, Elektra* and *Salome*?

12 What did "Slasher Mary" Richardson attack with a meat cleaver on March 10, 1914?

13 In 1670, Louis XIV founded which Paris hospital for infirm soldiers?

14 Which clinical disorder's name, meaning 'to be seized by somnolence', was coined by Jean-Baptiste-Édouard Gélineau in 1880?

15 Co-founded by CEO James Park, which San Francisco-based company makes the Surge and Charge HR activity trackers?

16 In 1968, who was sacked from the Shadow Cabinet for his "Rivers of Blood" speech?

17 *St. Thomas, Oleo, Doxy* and *Airegin* are compositions by which US jazz saxophonist?

18 Set in 1992, which track world record is held by US athlete Kevin Young?

19 Who was killed at the Tamburello curve on May 1, 1994?

20 Which species of antelope is pictured?

Answers to QUIZ 30 – General Knowledge

1 "a peck of pickled peppers"
2 They have no official lyrics
3 Lake Constance or Bodensee
4 A barbecue
5 *Discworld* by Terry Pratchett
6 *Andrea Doria*
7 The Grinch in *How the Grinch Stole Christmas!*
8 *Titanic*
9 Iron
10 Lara Croft
11 Aristotle
12 Lucerne
13 *The Morning Star*
14 Van Allen radiation belts
15 *She Loves You*
16 Gibson
17 Maned wolf (*Chrysocyon brachyurus*)
18 Torino
19 Mikhail Tal – the 1960–61 champion lost his title rematch with Mikhail Botvinnik
20 Keeley Hawes

1   In 1922, which US swimmer broke the one-minute barrier in the 100m freestyle for the first time?

2   New Zealand's Crusaders rugby union team is based in which city?

3   Which Scottish golfer won the 1985 Open Championship and the 1988 Masters?

4   Which Wantage-born jockey became known as the 'Long Fellow'?

5   Ricardo Izecson dos Santos Leite is which Brazilian footballer's real name?

6   Which retired athlete became Tory MP for Falmouth and Camborne in 1992?

7   Where did Lewis Hamilton win his first F1 Grand Prix?

8   Which Glasgow team is Scotland's oldest football club?

9   Who upset Steve Davis to become world snooker champion in 1985?

10 Italy's Edoardo Mangiarotti won 13 Olympic medals (including six golds) in which sport?

11 Which American football coach said: "Winning isn't everything; it's the only thing"?

12 In 1930, which England player became the oldest man to play Test cricket?

13 In 1933, Ernie Schaaf died four days after he had been knocked out by which Italian heavyweight boxer?

14 Lyon (2008), Bordeaux (2009), Marseille (2010), Lille (2011) – what comes next?

15 Which British politician is the only person to have won an Olympic medal and a Nobel prize?

16 Riding Prince of Penzance, Michelle Payne has become the first female jockey to win which famous horse race?

17 Which golfer designed Augusta National with course architect Alister MacKenzie?

18 Founded by Steve Fairbairn and first contested in 1926, which rowing race runs from Mortlake to Putney?

19 *Los Charrúas* is a nickname of which South American national football team?

20 Who is the pictured Buenos Aires-born footballer?

Answers to QUIZ 31 – General Knowledge

1   Cirque du Soleil
2   Ron Goodwin
3   17
4   Harry Ramsden
5   Alcmene
6   John Godber
7   Cynthia Payne
8   *Man About the House*
9   George Boole
10 Bangladesh
11 They are the titles of Richard Strauss operas
12 *The Rokeby Venus* by Diego Velázquez
13 Les Invalides or Hôtel des Invalides
14 Narcolepsy
15 Fitbit
16 Enoch Powell
17 Sonny Rollins
18 400 metres hurdles
19 Ayrton Senna
20 Impala

1   Charles Dickens described which king as "a most intolerable ruffian"?

2   Kama, or Kamadeva, is the Hindu god of what?

3   Hipped, jerkin and monopitch are types of what universal structure?

4   Which Visigoth king led the sacking of Rome in 410AD?

5   Ventriloquist Peter Brough famously operated which puppet?

6   Paddington Bear lived with which family at 32 Windsor Gardens?

7   The *Almanach de Gotha* is a directory of what?

8   William Alexander Harvey designed which model village for the Cadburys?

9   Evangelista Torricelli invented which scientific instrument in 1643?

10 Which Channel 4 sitcom produced the catchphrase: "Yes, I can hear you, Clem Fandango"?

11 Named after a capital city, what is the last element in the lanthanide series?

12 Stars of their own 2015 film, who are Dave, Stuart, Jerry, Jorge, Tim, Mark, Phil, Kevin and Bob?

13 Which beef stew has been called "the most celebrated dish in France" by Raymond Blanc?

14 In 1901, the British engineer Hubert Cecil Booth invented the first powered what?

15 Which Moroccan city is home to the Koutoubia Mosque, La Mamounia hotel and El Badi Palace?

16 "We are running on line north and south" may have been the last radio transmission of which aviatrix?

17 Known for her albums *Traslocando* and *Carioca*, which Italian singer married the tennis star Björn Borg in 1989?

18 Which badminton trophy is named after a two-time British chess champion?

19 IOC president Thomas Bach won Olympic gold in which sport?

20 Name the pictured mushroom –

Answers to QUIZ 32 – Sport

1 Johnny Weissmuller – who set a world record of 58.6 seconds
2 Christchurch
3 Sandy Lyle
4 Lester Piggott
5 Kaka
6 Sebastian Coe
7 Montreal (Circuit Gilles Villeneuve)
8 Queen's Park (founded in 1867)
9 Dennis Taylor
10 Fencing
11 Vince Lombardi

12 Wilfred Rhodes – aged 52 years & 165 days
13 Primo Carnera
14 Montpellier, the French football club which won Ligue 1 in 2012
15 Philip Noel-Baker – a 1500m silver medallist in 1920, he won the Nobel Peace Prize in 1959
16 Melbourne Cup
17 Bobby Jones
18 The Head of the River Race
19 Uruguay
20 Alfredo di Stéfano

1 Luigi Boccherini composed *Night Music of the Streets of* which capital city?

2 Which December 1941 battle is sometimes called the "Alamo of the Pacific"?

3 The body of criminal Aris Kindt features in which 1632 painting?

4 Which UN secretary-general was killed in an air crash on the Zambian frontier?

5 A sambuca served *con mosca* ('with flies') has what added to it?

6 Which ancient Hindu text is the most famous work of Vatsyayana?

7 What did Cervantes call "short sentences drawn from long experience"?

8 Which Dutchman discovered Saturn's largest moon, Titan, in 1655?

9 What is Germany's biggest selling newspaper?

10 First explored in 1994, which French cave features the Megaloceros Gallery?

11 The Lyle's Golden Syrup trademark depicts which creatures?

12 What is the stage name of Hawaiian-born singer Peter Gene Hernandez?

13 Which US photojournalist was played by Candice Bergen in the film *Gandhi*?

14 Which volcano's eruption caused the 'Year Without Summer' of 1816?

15 Born in Geneva in 1936, Karim al-Husayn Shah has which hereditary title?

16 Edward Lear described which characters whose "heads are green, and their hands are blue"?

17 Dinosaurs first appeared during which geologic period, about 230 million years ago?

18 Who wrote about life as a county cricketer in *A Lot of Hard Yakka* (1998)?

19 Which race is known in the US as "The Fastest Two Minutes in Sports"?

20 Who is the pictured American fashion model?

Answers to QUIZ 33 – General Knowledge

1	Henry VIII	13	Pot-au-feu
2	Love	14	Vacuum cleaner
3	Roof	15	Marrakesh
4	Alaric I	16	Amelia Earhart
5	Archie Andrews	17	Loredana Berté
6	The Browns	18	Thomas Cup – which was donated by Sir George Thomas
7	Europe's nobility		
8	Bournville		
9	Barometer	19	Fencing – winning the team foil in 1976 with West Germany
10	*Toast of London*		
11	Lutetium – whose name is derived from the ancient Latin for Paris	20	Fly Agaric or fly amanita (*Amanita muscaria*)
12	Minions		

1   Dysnomia is the only moon of which dwarf planet?

2   Which zodiacal constellation lies in the southern sky between Libra and Sagittarius?

3   The constellation Cassiopeia is famous for having which distinctive letter shape?

4   What is the farthest planet in the Solar System from the Sun?

5   In 1959, the space probe Luna 3 took the first ever photographs of what?

6   Achernar (Arabic for 'end of the river') is the brightest star in which constellation?

7   Which galaxy, the largest of the Local Group, is expected to collide with the Milky Way in 3.75 billion years?

8   Who became the second Astronomer Royal on succeeding John Flamsteed in 1720?

9   William Herschel made which discovery on March 13, 1781?

10   Containing Barnard's Star, which constellation is the 'Snake-holder'?

11   The astronomy abbreviation CME refers to the Sun erupting with a what?

12   Despina, Larissa and Naiad are moons of which planet?

13   Which moon of Saturn is larger than the planet Mercury but is half of its mass?

14   Which astronaut served as an Ohio Democrat senator from 1974 to 1999?

15   Launched in 1973, what was America's first space station?

16   Launched in 1959, what was the first weather satellite?

17   Salyut I was the first ever type of which structure?

18 The impact basin Hellas is which planet's largest recognisable impact feature?

19 Which Apollo 13 astronaut said: "Okay, Houston, we've had a problem here"?

20 The image features which shield volcano on Mars?

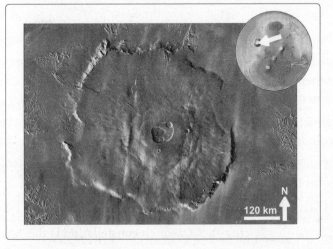

Answers to QUIZ 34 – General Knowledge

1   Madrid
2   Battle of Wake Island
3   *The Anatomy Lesson of Dr Nicolaes Tulp* by Rembrandt
4   Dag Hammarskjöld
5   Three coffee beans floating in the glass
6   The *Kama Sutra*
7   Proverbs
8   Christiaan Huygens
9   *Bild*
10 Chauvet Cave
11 A dead lion and a swarm of bees
12 Bruno Mars
13 Margaret Bourke-White
14 Mount Tambora – on the Indonesian island of Sumbawa
15 The Aga Khan [IV]
16 The Jumblies
17 Triassic period
18 Simon Hughes
19 Kentucky Derby
20 Karlie Kloss

1   Dipsomania refers to an uncontrollable craving for what?

2   The Isabella Stewart Gardner Museum is in which US city?

3   The Gran Teatre del Liceu opera house is in which Spanish city?

4   Larry David plays Larry David in which HBO comedy?

5   Meaning 'instruction', what is the Hebrew term for the Pentateuch?

6   Arthur Conan Doyle's 1929 novel *The Maracot Deep* centres on which legend?

7   Abraham Ortelius's *Theatrum Orbis Terrarum* (1570) was the first modern what?

8   Martin Luther was declared an outlaw at which 1521 'Diet'?

9   The Fourcault Process manufactures what inorganic material?

10   The 1939 film *Ninotchka* carried which famous two-word tagline?

11   Who was shot by Boston Corbett on April 26, 1865?

12   Which poem by Rainer Maria Rilke concludes: "You must change your life"?

13   Which dark nebula in Orion is also known as Barnard 33 or B33?

14   Which flap at the base of the tongue keeps food from going into the windpipe?

15   Traditionally made of silver, a bombilla is used as both a straw and a sieve when drinking which infusion?

16   Captain Louis Nolan was the first man killed in which 1854 action?

17   Possibly Cuba's most popular living author, which writer created the Havana cop Mario Conde?

18 Which chess-playing IBM computer beat Garry Kasparov in 1997?

19 Which race is held on the first Sunday of March between the village of Sälen and town of Mora?

20 Name the pictured English motorcycle racer –

Answers to QUIZ 35 – Astronomy

1   Eris
2   Scorpius
3   The letter M or W
4   Neptune
5   The far side of the Moon
6   Eridanus
7   Andromeda Galaxy
8   Edmond Halley
9   The planet Uranus
10 Ophiuchus
11 Coronal Mass Ejection
12 Neptune
13 Titan
14 John Glenn
15 Skylab
16 Vanguard 2
17 Space station
18 Mars (measuring c4400 miles across and 5 miles deep)
19 Jack Swigert
20 Olympus Mons

1 About 4,000 crocus stigmas are needed to yield one ounce of what?

2 *Juditha Triumphans* (1716) is which Italian composer's only surviving oratorio?

3 Which cathedral is home to the Hedda Stone and Catherine of Aragon's tomb?

4 What was the seventh commandment in the so-called 'Wicked Bible' of 1631?

5 Which bird can be Pink, Rock, Speckled, Nicobar or Domestic?

6 Which Pacific republic is the first country to enter the New Year?

7 What type of traditional Andean musical instrument is the *Siku*?

8 Thomas Lawrence's 1794 portrait of Sarah Barrett Moulton has what colourful nickname?

9 Alfred Eisenstaedt took a famous photograph of a couple kissing where on VJ Day 1945?

10 Roustam Raza was the faithful Mamluk bodyguard of which Frenchman?

11 Santa Cruz is the most populated of which Pacific islands?

12 The Icelandic dish harkal features what kind of rotted meat?

13 What did Anton van Leeuwenhoek first observe in 1674?

14 On February 9, 1976, who took up command of the minehunter HMS *Bronington*?

15 In which 1972 film does Tang Lung (Bruce Lee) fight Colt (Chuck Norris) at Rome's Colosseum?

16 In 1957, which drug was first sold in West Germany under the brand name Contergan?

17 Opening in 1971, which snooker-related venue was designed by Tanya Moiseiwitsch?

18 Which Turner Prize-nominee designed Partick Thistle's terrifying mascot Kingsley?

19 In 1968, who became the first Kenyan to win the Olympic 3000m steeplechase title?

20 Which famous musical instrument is pictured?

Answers to QUIZ 36 – General Knowledge

1	Alcohol	13	Horsehead Nebula
2	Boston	14	Epiglottis
3	Barcelona	15	Mate or *yerba mate*
4	*Curb Your Enthusiasm*	16	The Charge of the Light Brigade
5	*Torah*		
6	Atlantis	17	Leonardo Padura
7	Atlas	18	Deep Blue
8	Diet of Worms	19	The Vasaloppet – Sweden's 56 mile-long cross-country ski race
9	Glass		
10	"Garbo Laughs"		
11	John Wilkes Booth	20	Guy Martin
12	*Archaic Torso of Apollo*		

QUIZ 38 – Religion

1   Which UFO-based religion was founded by Claude Vorilhon in 1974?

2   One of the 5 Ks in Sikhism, what symbol of faith is a kirpan?

3   Also known as *semazen*, which Sufi Muslims perform the Mevlevi ritual dance or *Sema*?

4   Where did the Byzantine emperor Justinian build the present Church of the Nativity in 565 AD?

5   The Quorum of the Twelve Apostles is a governing body in which church?

6   Which Jewish holiday is also called the Feast of Tabernacles?

7   Founded by Apostles Bartholomew and Thaddeus, what is the world's oldest national church?

8   Venerated in Mexico, which female folk saint is known by a Spanish name meaning 'Holy Death'?

9   According to Genesis, Bera and Birsha were the respective kings of which cities?

10 Which Bible translator served as Bishop of Exeter from 1551 to 1553?

11 Born Vincenzo Pecci, who was the oldest pope, as he reigned until the age of 93?

12 Who is the patron saint of the Order of the Garter?

13 Who saw 18 visions of the Virgin Mary in the Grotte de Massabielle?

14 Which religion postulates that every person is a Thetan – an immortal spiritual being?

15 Which Hindu god also comes in the form of Nataraja, the Lord of Dance?

16 In Jewish dietary law, which word describes forbidden or non-kosher food?

17 Orongo was the ceremonial centre of which Easter Island cult?

18 Which Viennese cathedral is famed for its huge *Pummerin* bell?

19 Which mountain in Henan, China, is home to the Shaolin Temple?

20 Which English cathedral is pictured?

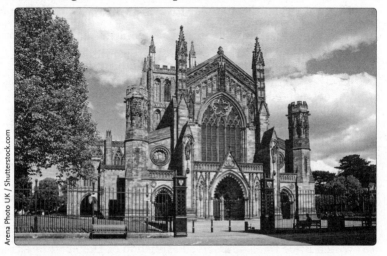

Answers to QUIZ 37 – General Knowledge

1	Saffron	12	Shark
2	Antonio Vivaldi	13	Bacteria
3	Peterborough Cathedral	14	Charles, Prince of Wales
4	"Thou shalt commit adultery"	15	*Way of the Dragon*
5	Pigeon	16	Thalidomide – developed by Chemie Grünenthal
6	Kiribati	17	The Crucible Theatre, Sheffield
7	Panpipe		
8	*Pinkie*	18	David Shrigley
9	Times Square, New York	19	Amos Biwott
10	Napoleon Bonaparte	20	Drake's Drum
11	Galapagos Islands		

1 Which Austrian Empress was assassinated by anarchist Luigi Lucheni in 1898?

2 Released in 1988, what was U2's first UK number one single?

3 Toblerone chocolate's shape is said to be inspired by which mountain?

4 Which 1945 J.B. Priestley play is set in the Birling family home?

5 Donald Shepherd introduced which relocatable buildings in 1961?

6 Located in Northumberland, what is England's largest forest?

7 Hired in 1886, Mrs P.F.E. Albee of Winchester, New Hampshire, was the first ever what?

8 Which Austrian physicist wrote the popular science book *What is Life?* (1944)?

9 Plitvice Lakes National Park is the largest in which country?

10 What is the name of the community college in the US TV comedy *Community*?

11 Which ancient Greek historian called Egypt the "gift of the Nile"?

12 Which R&B singer featured on the rapper Nelly's 2002 no.1 *Dilemma*?

13 Named from the Sanskrit for 'divine town script', which alphabet is used for Hindi?

14 In 1733, who succeeded Daniel Bernoulli to the chair of mathematics at the St. Petersburg Academy of Sciences?

15 Which black raspberry liqueur is named after the largest château in the Loire Valley?

16 Which city on the river Pegnitz is home to Germany's largest museum of cultural history?

17 Which traditional Japanese string instrument is the only one played with a bow?

18 Pencak Silat is a general term for martial arts created in which country?

19 Juha Kankkunen was a four-time world champion in which event?

20 Name the ancient sculpture in the Vatican Museums –

Answers to QUIZ 38 – Religion

1 Raëlism

2 Ceremonial sword or dagger

3 Whirling Dervishes or Mevlevi dervishes

4 Bethlehem

5 The Church of Jesus Christ of Latter-Day Saints or Mormons

6 Sukkot (Hebrew for 'Huts' or 'Booths')

7 Armenian Apostolic Church or *Hay Aṙak'elakan Yekeghetsi*

8 Santa Muerte – full name: Nuestra Señora de la Santa Muerte

9 Sodom and Gomorrah

10 Miles Coverdale

11 Leo XIII – whose papacy lasted from 1878 to 1903

12 St. George

13 Bernadette Soubirous aka St. Bernadette

14 Scientology

15 Shiva

16 *Tref*

17 Birdman cult

18 St Stephen's Cathedral or Stephansdom

19 Mount Song

20 Hereford Cathedral

QUIZ 40 – General Knowledge

1   Auguste Deter (1850–1906) was the first diagnosis of which disease?

2   Which soft drink was created in 1885 by Charles Alderton of Waco, Texas?

3   Nectanebo II was the last native ruler of which ancient country?

4   The Morosini explosion of 1687 greatly damaged which temple?

5   Which species of fly has the Latin name *Calliphora vomitoria*?

6   Which Frenchman said: "England has 42 religions and only two sauces"?

7   *Mojo* (1995) and *Jerusalem* (2009) are plays by which English dramatist?

8   "Building Better Worlds", Weyland-Yutani Corp features in which sci-fi film series?

9   Who is heir apparent to the Japanese throne?

10 Which Caribbean country's flag features an open Bible?

11 Salvador Dali called which French city's train station "the centre of the world"?

12 Richard Assmann and Léon Teisserenc de Bort discovered which layer of the atmosphere in 1902?

13 The acronym STEM refers to which four academic fields?

14 Launched in 1885, what was the world's first packaged and branded soap?

15 The Edinburgh ornithologist George Waterston bought which remote island in 1948?

16 Josh Meyers, Reggie Brown and Bobby Murphy developed which photo messaging app?

17 Who might use a quickdraw, carabiner, cam and crampons?

18 The *tienta* is an aggression test for animals used in which spectacle?

19 Which international women's rugby union team are known as the Nomads?

20 Which Edinburgh-born inventor is pictured?

Answers to QUIZ 39 – General Knowledge

1 Elisabeth ("Sisi") of Bavaria
2 *Desire*
3 The Matterhorn
4 *An Inspector Calls*
5 Portakabins
6 Kielder Forest
7 Avon Lady
8 Erwin Schrödinger
9 Croatia
10 Greendale Community College
11 Herodotus
12 Kelly Rowland
13 Devanagari script
14 Leonhard Euler
15 Chambord
16 Nuremberg – home to the Germanisches Nationalmuseum
17 Kokyū
18 Indonesia
19 World Rally Championship
20 *Laocoön and His Sons* or the *Laocoön Group*

QUIZ 41 – Fashion

1   Since 1992, Patrick Demarchelier has worked with which US fashion magazine, becoming its premier photographer?

2   Founded by Ulrich Dausien, which German outdoor wear brand uses a paw print logo?

3   Which tennis player founded the fashion label Aneres?

4   Worn by Hindu men, what item of clothing is a dhoti?

5   Which English model married the US actor Giovanni Ribisi in June 2012?

6   Which Italian fashion designer (1890–1973) created the 'Cocteau' Evening Jacket?

7   The billionaire brothers Alain and Gerard Wertheimer own which fashion company?

8   In 1995, trichologist Mark Constantine and beauty therapist Liz Weir founded which "Fresh Hand-Made Cosmetics" company?

9   Which woman designed the dress for Princess Anne's engagement photo in 1973?

10   Arguably the world's first supermodel, Lisa Fonssagrives married which US photographer in 1950?

11   Which US fashion designer's daughter owns the sweet shop chain Dylan's Candy Bar?

12   Elizabeth and James and The Row are fashion labels by which twin sisters?

13   Sara Blakely founded which undergarment company in 2000?

14   *Notebook on Cities and Clothes* is a 1989 documentary about which Japanese fashion designer?

15   Which French fashion house makes the Antigona and Pandora bags?

16   Bamboo, Guilty and Rush are perfumes by which Italian fashion house?

17 Which supermarket sells the F&F clothing collection?

18 Which canid is the logo of the Leicester-based clothing brand Wolsey?

19 Napoleon III's wife Empress Eugénie charged which malletier with "packing the most beautiful clothes in an exquisite way"?

20 Name the designer of the dress in the picture –

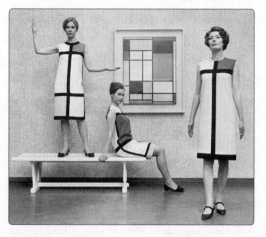

Answers to QUIZ 40 – General Knowledge

1 Alzheimer's disease
2 Dr Pepper
3 Egypt – he ruled from 360 to 342 BC
4 The Parthenon, Athens
5 Blue bottle fly
6 Voltaire
7 Jez Butterworth
8 *Alien*
9 Crown Prince Naruhito
10 Dominican Republic
11 Perpignan – more specifically, he used the phrase *"El centre del mon"*
12 Stratosphere
13 Science, technology, engineering, mathematics
14 Sunlight Soap – launched by Unilever founder William Hesketh Lever
15 Fair Isle
16 Snapchat
17 Mountaineer or climber
18 Bullfighting
19 Kazakhstan
20 Alexander Graham Bell

1   Leucopenia is an abnormal reduction in the number of what?

2   Which psychotherapeutic approach is abbreviated CBT?

3   Which US jazz bassist wrote *The Black Saint and the Sinner Lady* (1963)?

4   Kingscote, Horsted Keynes and Sheffield Park are stops on which line?

5   Founded in 1868, which Scottish company makes Royal Game Soup?

6   Which radio comedy centred on the frigate HMS *Troutbridge*?

7   Which device gives a Punch puppet his trademark voice?

8   In a 1915 novel, who is accused of the Portland Place murder?

9   Who married Samantha Gwendoline Sheffield in 1996?

10 Which Roman goddess was the personification of luck?

11 The Finnish drink Lappish Hag's Love Potion is made from which fruit?

12 Tskhinvali is the capital of which breakaway Georgian region?

13 Which 1985 Kate Bush song is about the Austrian psychoanalyst Wilhelm Reich?

14 In Shakespeare's *Julius Caesar*, who is described as "the noblest Roman of them all"?

15 Which halogen is the only liquid non-metallic element?

16 Which 1989 Andrew Lloyd Webber musical is based on a 1955 novel by David Garnett?

17 Alexander MacRae founded which Australian swimwear brand in 1914?

18 In 1986, the Ukrainian-born athlete Yuriy Sedykh set the world record in which field event?

19 A Gaelic football team features how many players?

20 Name the stock character of French pantomime in the picture –

Answers to QUIZ 41 – Fashion

1   *Harper's Bazaar*
2   Jack Wolfskin
3   Serena Williams
4   Loincloth
5   Agyness Deyn
6   Elsa Schiaparelli
7   Chanel
8   Lush
9   Zandra Rhodes
10 Irving Penn
11 Ralph Lauren
12 Ashley Olsen and Mary-Kate Olsen
13 SPANX
14 Yohji Yamamoto
15 Givenchy
16 Gucci
17 Tesco
18 Fox
19 Louis Vuitton
20 Yves Saint Laurent – it is his 'Mondrian' cocktail dress

QUIZ 43 – General Knowledge

1   D'Anjou, Williams, Bosc and Concorde are varieties of which fruit?

2   Lager Sylt was a Nazi concentration camp on which Channel island?

3   From 1516 to 1519, which artist lived in the Château de Cloux, now Clos Lucé?

4   Baroness Marie-Christine von Reibnitz married which prince in 1978?

5   Which cathedral has the longest nave in England?

6   Which Italian composed the 1892 opera *La Wally*?

7   What is the smallest bone in the human body?

8   What is the most abundant metal in the Earth's crust?

9   Seen on *Top Gear* being driven inside BBC Television Centre by Jeremy Clarkson, which Peel model is the smallest production car ever?

10 Starring Tom Cruise, which 2014 film is based on Hiroshi Sakurazaka's novel *All You Need is Kill*?

11 Thousands of which birds come together in a spectacle known as a 'murmuration'?

12 Flight Lieutenant Herbert Carmichael Irwin was captain of which airship when it crashed?

13 Werner Co. is the world's leading manufacturer and distributor of which equipment?

14 Which French landscape architect (1613–1700) created the gardens at the Palace of Versailles?

15 Topping lists of the world's most violent cities, San Pedro Sula is in which country?

16 Founded by Steve Huffman and Alexis Ohanian, which website calls itself "the front page of the internet"?

17 Which Swiss company has kept time at the Olympics since 1932?

18 Often taken to cricket matches in Australia, what is an Esky?

19 Which Jersey-born golfer won a record six Open Championships and was played by Stephen Dillane in the 2005 film *The Greatest Game Ever Played*?

20 Name the Canadian dish in the picture –

Answers to QUIZ 42 – General Knowledge

1 White blood cells found in the blood
2 Cognitive behavioural therapy
3 Charles Mingus
4 Bluebell Railway in Sussex
5 Baxters
6 *The Navy Lark*
7 A swazzle
8 Richard Hannay in *The Thirty-Nine Steps* by John Buchan
9 David Cameron
10 Fortuna
11 Blueberries
12 South Ossetia
13 *Cloudbusting*
14 Brutus
15 Bromine
16 *Aspects of Love*
17 Speedo
18 Men's hammer throw
19 15
20 Pierrot

QUIZ 44 – Transport

1   Adopted in 1876, which pattern of lines marks the limit to which a ship may be loaded?

2   Which French aviator was the first person to cross the Mediterranean Sea by air?

3   Which type of sailing vessel derives its name from the Tamil for 'tied-wood'?

4   The Dutch company Batavus manufactures which items?

5   The *Bucentaur* was the highly decorated galley of which city's doges?

6   Which Scottish engineer (1757–1834) designed the Caledonian Canal?

7   Margaret Rule led the project that raised which Tudor warship in 1982?

8   The 1941 sinking of the SS *Politician* inspired which Compton Mackenzie novel?

9   Which British motorcycle company launched its original Thunderbird in 1949?

10 Which 1965 book set out Ralph Nader's views on defective car design?

11 The largest in the Southern Hemisphere, TAM Airlines is based in which country?

12 The Soviet Mil V-12 is the largest example of which craft to have been built?

13 Which Irish-born explorer led his first Antarctic expedition on the ship *Nimrod*?

14 Founded in 1909, what was the first British aircraft manufacturing company?

15 Which Italian carmaker's logo features a serpent eating a man?

16 Which Moroccan city is served by Ibn Battouta Airport?

17 The airline Conviasa is the flag carrier of which South American country?

18 Which Asian automaker produces the cee'd compact car?

19 Which Ontario canal becomes the world's largest naturally frozen skating rink in winter?

20 Name the luxury SUV in the picture –

Kosarev Alexander / Shutterstock.com

Answers to QUIZ 43 – General Knowledge

1	Pear	11	Starlings
2	Alderney	12	R101
3	Leonardo da Vinci	13	Ladders and climbing equipment
4	Prince Michael of Kent		
5	St Albans Cathedral	14	André Le Nôtre
6	Alfredo Catalani	15	Honduras
7	Stapes or stirrup	16	Reddit
8	Aluminium	17	Omega watches
9	Peel P50	18	Cooler or ice box
10	*Edge of Tomorrow* or *Live Die Repeat*	19	Harry Vardon
		20	Poutine

QUIZ 45 – General Knowledge

1   Which Japanese corporation is the world's largest maker of musical instruments?

2   Launched in 2013, *Azzam* is the world's largest what?

3   Located in Canterbury, what is England's oldest working parish church?

4   Which landlocked Italian region does not border a foreign country?

5   Which conductor set up the West-Eastern Divan Orchestra with Edward Said?

6   Sarnath in India is the deer park where which man first taught the *Dharma*?

7   Which Irish travel author wrote *Full Tilt: Ireland to India with a Bicycle* (1965)?

8   The Scottish physician Neil Arnott invented a form of which bed in the 1800s?

9   Which aromatic resin is tapped from trees of the genus *Boswellia*?

10 Nathan Fillion played which titular mystery novelist, with the first name Richard, in a US TV drama?

11 The Galleria Sabauda is an art collection in which Italian city?

12 The Ten Commandments feature in Exodus and which other Old Testament book?

13 Inspired by a kitchen pasta maker, Adolf Ehinger created which office device in 1936?

14 Who was shot by Fanny Kaplan on August 30, 1918?

15 Telegonus was the youngest son of Circe and which mythical hero?

16 Which traditional Thai greeting gesture is similar to the Indian *namaste*?

17 The national fruit of Bangladesh, what is the world's largest tree-borne fruit?

18 Who was the first African American winner of a Grand Slam tennis title?

19 What was the last football club outside of the Old Firm to win a Scottish league title?

20 Name the British band –

Mat Hayward / Shutterstock.com

Answers to QUIZ 44 – Transport

1	Plimsoll line	**11**	Brazil
2	Roland Garros – in 1913	**12**	Helicopter
3	Catamaran	**13**	Ernest Shackleton
4	Bicycles and mopeds	**14**	Handley Page Ltd
5	Venice	**15**	Alfa Romeo
6	Thomas Telford	**16**	Tangier
7	*Mary Rose*	**17**	Venezuela
8	*Whisky Galore!*	**18**	Kia
9	Triumph	**19**	Rideau Canal
10	*Unsafe at Any Speed*	**20**	Cadillac Escalade

QUIZ 46 – General Knowledge

1   Which eye infection is also known as granular conjunctivitis and Egyptian ophthalmia?

2   Directed by Ana Lily Amirpour, which 2014 film has been called "the first Iranian vampire Western"?

3   Which Jane Austen heroine is introduced as "handsome, clever, and rich"?

4   Which astronomer coined the term "Big Bang" on BBC radio in 1949?

5   Which US band originally released the single *Dancing in the Moonlight* in 1972?

6   Bob Slattery composed which fragrance for Calvin Klein in 1985?

7   Cordwainer is an archaic term for which job?

8   Which Anglo-Saxon king succeeded Hardicanute in 1042?

9   Which German mathematician illustrated the problems of treating infinity as a number with his "Infinite Hotel"?

10 The lantern that Guy Fawkes carried on his arrest is in which museum?

11 The Senyera is the flag of which Autonomous Community?

12 Who performed the song *Get Happy* in her last MGM film, *Summer Stock* (1950)?

13 What is the SI unit of mass?

14 The holder of which American political office resides at Gracie Mansion?

15 Shirley Conran said "Life is too short to... " do what?

16 Who was the only actor to appear in all 295 episodes of *Last of the Summer Wine*?

17 What has been discovered to be the only known truly warm-blooded fish?

18 Graham Hill is the only driver to have completed which triple crown of motor sport?

19 Shotokan is the most widely practiced style of which martial art?

20 Name the pictured great ape –

Answers to QUIZ 45 – General Knowledge

1. Yamaha
2. Private motor yacht or superyacht
3. Church of St Martin
4. Umbria
5. Daniel Barenboim
6. The Buddha
7. Dervla Murphy
8. Waterbed
9. Frankincense
10. Richard Castle in *Castle*
11. Turin
12. Deuteronomy
13. The first commercially produced paper shredder
14. Lenin
15. Odysseus
16. The *wai*
17. Jackfruit (*Artocarpus heterophyllus*)
18. Althea Gibson – who won the 1956 French Open
19. Aberdeen FC – in the 1984–85 season
20. Mumford & Sons

1   Which longest-serving prime minister of Australia founded the Liberal Party?

2   Why didn't the Queen open the 1959 and 1963 sessions of Parliament?

3   Which Labour politician entered Parliament in 1945 as MP for Ormskirk?

4   After losing his seat in 1918, which future prime minister returned to the Commons as MP for Aberavon in 1922?

5   Labour Party leader Dom Mintoff was a two-time Prime Minister of which country?

6   Until Margaret Thatcher, who was the 20th century's longest continuously serving prime minister?

7   In 1945, which MP for Jarrow was appointed the first female Minister for Education?

8   Located in rue de Varenne in Paris, what is the official residence of France's prime minister?

9   Which Tory foreign secretary was MP for Witney from 1983 until 1997?

10 Winner of the 1934 Nobel Peace Prize, who was Britain's first Labour cabinet minister?

11 Jessica Gunning played which future MP for Swansea East in the 2014 film *Pride*?

12 In 1916, who was reelected US president on the slogan: "He kept us out of the war"?

13 Which city is home to Chile's bicameral parliament, the National Congress?

14 Assassinated in 1975, Sheikh Mujibur Rahman was which country's founding leader?

15 The holder of which political office resides at 24 Sussex Drive?

16 Which president was described by Gore Vidal as "a triumph of the embalmer's art"?

17 Which prime minister wrote in *The Times* under the pseudonym Runnymede?

18 Who did US President Franklin Roosevelt tell: "We need muscles like yours to beat Germany"?

19 Which 1976 110m hurdles Olympic champion became France's Minister of Youth and Sport in 1995?

20 Name the pictured Labour Chancellor –

Answers to QUIZ 46 – General Knowledge

1 Trachoma

2 *A Girl Walks Home Alone at Night*

3 Emma Woodhouse from *Emma*

4 Fred Hoyle

5 King Harvest

6 Obsession

7 Shoemaker

8 Edward the Confessor

9 David Hilbert

10 Ashmolean Museum, Oxford

11 Catalonia

12 Judy Garland

13 Kilogram

14 Mayor of New York

15 "Stuff a mushroom"

16 Peter Sallis – as Norman "Cleggy" Clegg

17 Opah or moonfish (*Lampris guttatus*)

18 Winning the Indianapolis 500, 24 Hours of Le Mans and Monaco Grand Prix (or Formula One championship)

19 Karate

20 Bonobo or pygmy chimpanzee (*Pan paniscus*)

QUIZ 48 – General Knowledge

1 The actress Valerie Hobson was married to which disgraced Tory politician?

2 The song *Zip-a-Dee-Doo-Dah* features in which controversial 1946 Disney film?

3 Which unit of length is named from the Latin for 'elbow'?

4 Jean Prouvost founded which weekly news-driven French magazine in 1949?

5 Opened in 2003, what is Britain's largest national park?

6 In China, which animal is known as *Xiongmao* meaning 'Giant Cat Bear'?

7 In 1980, Brian Souter founded which Perth-based transport group with his sister Ann Gloag and her former husband Robin?

8 Born in Amaseia, Pontus (modern-day Amasya, Turkey) in 64 or 63 BC, which Greek wrote the 17-book encyclopedia *Geographica*?

9 Farringford House on the Isle of Wight was the home of which Poet Laureate?

10 Rose, smoky and milky are common varieties of which mineral?

11 Which brand of apple juice is pressed on Boxford Farm in Suffolk?

12 The defence of Pavlov's House was a key event in which 1942–43 battle?

13 Which British illustrator created the *Where's Wally?* aka *Where's Waldo?* books?

14 *La virgen de los sicarios* or *Our Lady of the Assassins* (1994) is which Colombian writer's best known novel?

15 Which Thelonius Monk song is the most recorded jazz standard composed by a jazz musician?

16 The Washington DC-based Brookings Institution is often ranked the world's most influential what?

17 The lack of correlation between body size and cancer risk is known as whose paradox?

18 In 1990, which 45-year-old golfer became the oldest ever US Open champion?

19 Which Belfast-born F1 driver won the 1983 US GP West after starting 22nd on the grid?

20 Name the famous precious stone in the picture –

Answers to QUIZ 47 – Politics

1   Robert Menzies
2   She was pregnant with Prince Andrew and then Prince Edward
3   Harold Wilson
4   Ramsay MacDonald
5   Malta
6   H.H. Asquith or Herbert Henry Asquith, 1st Earl of Oxford and Asquith
7   Ellen Wilkinson
8   Hôtel Matignon
9   Douglas Hurd
10 Arthur Henderson
11 Siân James
12 Woodrow Wilson
13 Valparaiso
14 Bangladesh
15 Prime Minister of Canada – in Ottawa
16 Ronald Reagan
17 Benjamin Disraeli
18 Joe Louis – before his 1938 fight with Max Schmeling
19 Guy Drut
20 Stafford Cripps

QUIZ 49 – General Knowledge

1   Played on film by Eric Bana, the Australian criminal Mark Read had what nickname?

2   Who links Kirk Douglas, Tony Curran, Andy Serkis and Jacques Dutronc?

3   Which Holy Roman Emperor was Philip the Handsome and Joanna the Mad's eldest son?

4   Often described as the "world's worst airline", Air Koryo is which country's national carrier?

5   *The Strange Case of Peter the Lett* (1931) introduced which detective?

6   Béarnaise sauce becomes sauce Choron with the addition of which purée?

7   *De Ira* by Seneca the Younger is a philosophical treatise on which emotion?

8   Which Harold Pinter play is set at Petey and Meg Boles' seaside boarding house?

9   Low-density lipoprotein is the so-called "bad" form of which substance?

10 Which US designer launched her knitted jersey wrap dress in 1973?

11 Philematology is the science of which physical act?

12 In a 1984 novel by John Updike, who are the Rhode Island natives, Alexandra Spofford, Jane Smart and Sukie Rougemont?

13 The Dutch architect Rem Koolhaas designed the Casa da Música in which city?

14 Which John Adams opera centres on the hijack of the *Achille Lauro* cruise ship?

15 Which French company developed the AGV (Automotrice à grande vitesse) train?

16 H.R. Giger created the cover for which 1973 Emerson, Lake & Palmer album?

17 Which Italian building is adorned with 3,159 statues?

18 Aged 15, which Chelmsford-born swimmer won Olympic silver and bronze in 1984?

19 Which American race is the world's oldest annual marathon?

20 Name the fruit –

Answers to QUIZ 48 – General Knowledge

1 John Profumo	13 Martin Handford
2 *Song of the South*	14 Fernando Vallejo
3 Cubit (as in cubitum)	15 *'Round Midnight*
4 *Paris Match*	16 Think tank
5 Cairngorms National Park	17 Peto's paradox – named after
6 Giant Panda (*Ailuropoda melanoleuca*)	epidemiologist Richard Peto (animals with a 1,000 times
7 Stagecoach Group	more cells than humans do
8 Strabo	not exhibit an increased
9 Alfred Lord Tennyson	cancer risk)
10 Quartz	18 Hale Irwin
11 Copella	19 John Watson
12 Stalingrad	20 Hope Diamond

1 Queen Victoria saw which Irish playwright's drama *The Colleen Bawn* three times?

2 Dr. Thomas Stockmann is the main character in which Henrik Ibsen play?

3 Who is told he will only be defeated when Birnam wood comes to Dunsinane?

4 Which "Irish Chekhov" wrote the plays *Philadelphia, Here I Come!*, *Faith Healer* and *Translations*?

5 *Lady, Be Good* (1924) was which brothers' first Broadway musical?

6 Which British-based dramatist wrote the 1988 play *Our Country's Good*?

7 Which musical features the numbers *Don't Rain on My Parade*, *People* and *You Are Woman*?

8 *Hamletmachine* (1977) is a postmodernist drama by which German playwright?

9 In 1995, who became the first actor to win a Tony Award for playing Hamlet?

10 Arguing over "the reckyninge" (bill), Ingram Frizer stabbed which man to death in the Deptford home or victualling house of the widow Eleanor Bull?

11 Which playwright used the music critic pseudonym Corno di Bassetto?

12 Which English theatre director married the actress Leslie Caron in 1956?

13 Who wrote the 1970s plays *Sleuth*, *Murderer* and *Whodunnit*?

14 Which dramatist wrote the 1603 Roman tragedy *Sejanus his Fall*?

15 Whose play, *The Cyclops*, is the only extant satyr play?

16 In 1959, who did Kenneth Tynan call "the finest actor on earth from the neck up"?

17 In a Stephen Sondheim musical, Benjamin Barker becomes which title character?

18 Who composed the music for the 1927 musical *Show Boat*?

19 Harold Pinter based which play on his affair with Joan Bakewell?

20 Which "greatest stage actor of his generation" is pictured?

Answers to QUIZ 49 – General Knowledge

1 "Chopper"
2 Vincent van Gogh – they have all played the Dutch painter
3 Charles V / Charles I of Spain
4 North Korea
5 Inspector Jules Maigret
6 Tomato
7 Anger
8 *The Birthday Party*
9 Cholesterol
10 Diane von Furstenberg
11 Kissing
12 *The Witches of Eastwick*
13 Porto
14 *The Death of Klinghoffer*
15 Alstom
16 *Brain Salad Surgery*
17 Milan Cathedral or Duomo di Milano – it has more statues than any another building in existence
18 Sarah Hardcastle – in the 400m freestyle and 800m freestyle
19 Boston Marathon
20 Carambola or starfruit (*Averrhoa carambola*)

1   Whose lecture series, *The Chemical History of a Candle*, was printed as a book in 1861?

2   Also known as the nutria or river rat, what semi-aquatic mammal is the largest British rodent?

3   Which Keats poem begins: "A thing of beauty is a joy for ever"?

4   The world's tallest mosque, the Hassan II Mosque is in which city?

5   Which ballerina's last words were: "Get my swan costume ready!"?

6   The Acme Thunderer is a bestselling make of which woodwind instrument?

7   Benjamin Waugh founded which children's charity in 1889?

8   *Kane's Wrath* (2008) is an expansion pack for *Tiberium Wars*, the third installment in which real-time strategy video game series?

9   Which Bolton comedian's first volume of autobiography, *The Sound of Laughter*, sold 278,000 copies on its first day (including pre-orders)?

10   Which part of the brain derives its name from the Latin for 'almond'?

11   W.H. Smith opened its first railway bookstall at which London station in 1848?

12   What was the monstrous offspring of Pasiphaë and a snow-white bull?

13   Valhalla is the largest impact crater on which moon of Jupiter, the most heavily cratered object in the Solar System?

14   Whose coffin was assigned the last ever Factory Records catalogue number FAC-501?

15   In 1927, which actress was sentenced to 10 days in jail for obscenity for her play *Sex*?

16 Which radioactive isotope of carbon was discovered by Martin Kamen and Sam Ruben in 1940?

17 In 1968, the Missourian oil tycoon Robert P. McCulloch bought which five-arched structure?

18 Held in the Czech city of Ostrava, what type of event is the Golden Spike?

19 Which French pair are the first swimmer-siblings to both win Olympic gold medals?

20 Which early computer is pictured?

Answers to QUIZ 50 – Theatre

1	Dion Boucicault	12	(Sir) Peter Hall
2	*An Enemy of the People*	13	Anthony Shaffer
3	Shakespeare's Macbeth	14	Ben Jonson
4	Brian Friel	15	Euripides
5	George & Ira Gershwin	16	John Gielgud
6	Timberlake Wertenbaker	17	*Sweeney Todd: The Demon Barber of Fleet Street*
7	*Funny Girl*		
8	Heiner Müller	18	Jerome Kern – with a libretto by Oscar Hammerstein II
9	Ralph Fiennes		
10	Christopher Marlowe	19	*Betrayal*
11	George Bernard Shaw	20	Simon Russell Beale

1 Formed in 1570, which foundry is Britain's oldest manufacturing company?

2 Abbi Jacobson and Ilana Glazer both created and star in which Comedy Central sitcom, premiered in 2014?

3 Which mammal is named from a Malay word meaning 'something that rolls up'?

4 Which architect's Marseille *unité d'habitation*, an 18-floor vertical community, was completed in 1952?

5 Which book opens: "I come from Des Moines. Someone had to"?

6 The Hatfields fought which family in an infamous 19th century American feud?

7 "Mendips", aka 251 Menlove Avenue, was the childhood home of which Beatle?

8 Which Serbian-American inventor discovered the rotating magnetic field (1882)?

9 First flown in 1935, the Junkers Ju87 dive-bomber had which nickname?

10 "Big Suze" in the sitcom *Peep Show*, the actress Sophie Winkleman married which Lord in 2009?

11 In yoga, the body has how many chakras (major energy centres)?

12 Nahum Tate gave which Shakespeare tragedy a happy ending in 1681?

13 Which man's oldest surviving creation is Pierre the French Rat?

14 Which object was known in Gondorian lore as "Isildur's Bane"?

15 419 scams are named for a clause in which country's criminal code?

16 Georges Lemaître's 'hypothesis of the primeval atom' is known by what modern name?

17 Whose 1,093rd patent was for a 'Holder for Article to be Electroplated' (1931)?

18 Fondly remembered for playing the Man U-crazed games teacher Mr. Sugden in the film *Kes*, which late actor wrestled as "Leon Arras, the Man from Paris"?

19 Who won the first ever *Sports Illustrated* "Sportsman of the Year" title in 1954?

20 Which city is home to the pictured Nanpu Bridge?

Answers to QUIZ 51 – General Knowledge

1 Michael Faraday

2 Coypu (*Myocastor coypus*)

3 *Endymion*

4 Casablanca

5 Anna Pavlova

6 Whistle

7 NSPCC (National Society for the Prevention of Cruelty to Children)

8 *Command & Conquer*

9 Peter Kay

10 Amygdala

11 Euston

12 The Minotaur

13 Callisto

14 Tony Wilson

15 Mae West, written under the pen name Jane Mast

16 Carbon-14

17 London Bridge

18 Annual athletics meeting

19 Laure and Florent Manaudou – the former, a 400m freestyle champion in 2004; the latter, the 2012 50m freestyle champion

20 The Antikythera Mechanism – recovered in 1901, in 82 fragments, from a ship that sank off the southern coast of Greece in around 80 BC

1   Which French painter's first major work was *The Barque of Dante* (1822)?

2   Which theatre director was the first wife of musician Ewan MacColl?

3   The drug, rapamycin, was first discovered in which island's soil?

4   Leonard Bernstein's first symphony is named after which Biblical prophet?

5   Commissioned in 1963, what was Britain's first nuclear-powered submarine?

6   Deposed in 1969, Idris was which country's first and only king?

7   An ARP detachment leader, Thomas Alderson was the first recipient of which medal?

8   Bridget Bishop was the first woman to be tried and convicted at which 1692 trials?

9   What was first demonstrated at Merstham Quarry, Surrey, on July 14, 1867?

10 Which hotel hosted John Lennon and Yoko Ono's first 1969 'Bed-In' for peace?

11 In a Royal Family context, who were Dookie and Jane?

12 *Not a Penny More, Not Penny Less* (1976) was whose first novel?

13 Which German was the first photographer to win the Turner Prize?

14 In 1976, who became Spain's first democratically elected prime minister since the Second Spanish Republic?

15 The Canadian engineer, Sandford Fleming, was the first to propose which worldwide system?

16 In 1977, the user interface architect Bill Fernandez became which company's first employee?

17 Which country hosted the first World Sauna Championships in 1999?

18 Who became the first officially licensed female British boxer in 1998?

19 Which Zimbabwean-born batsman was first branded "a flat-track bully" by John Bracewell?

20 Which first American woman to win the Nobel prize in literature is pictured?

Answers to QUIZ 52 – General Knowledge

1   Whitechapel Bell Foundry
2   *Broad City*
3   Pangolin
4   Le Corbusier
5   *The Lost Continent* by Bill Bryson
6   The McCoys
7   John Lennon
8   Nikola Tesla
9   The *Stuka* – from *Sturzkampfflugzeug*, meaning 'dive-bomber'
10 Frederick Windsor
11 Seven
12 *King Lear*
13 Puppeteer Jim Henson
14 The One Ring in *The Lord of the Rings*
15 Nigeria
16 Big Bang theory of the origin of the universe
17 Thomas Edison
18 Brian Glover
19 Roger Bannister – he remains the only British winner of the title
20 Shanghai

1   Which dashing hero first appeared in Johnston McCulley's 1919 story *The Curse of Capistrano*?

2   The poet Saunders Lewis played a key role in founding which political party?

3   Which group had a hit in 1988 with *John Kettley is a Weatherman*?

4   What was demonstrated by the original Foucault pendulum in 1851?

5   The serial killer Red John was the family-murdering nemesis of which TV character?

6   A Salmanazar is equivalent to how many champagne bottles?

7   Jim Connell wrote which socialist anthem in 1889?

8   What is the actual first name of Indiana Jones?

9   King Edward VII popularised which felt hat after visiting Germany?

10 What is the largest private garden in London?

11 Daisuke Inoue invented which musical machine in 1971?

12 Which 1874 painting by Renoir in the National Museum Wales is often called 'The Blue Lady'?

13 Henry VIII described which teenage wife as his "rose without a thorn"?

14 Which assistant to Robert Koch invented a transparent dish for the culture of microorganisms?

15 Under a licence from László Bíró, which company launched the Cristal ballpoint pen in 1950?

16 Which 2014 play by Mike Bartlett imagines the Prince of Wales becoming king?

17 Which German chainsaw manufacturer sponsors the Timbersports World Championship?

18 Kays of Scotland manufactures which stones for the Olympics?

19 Driving for Peugeot, which Finn was World Rally Champion in 2000 and 2002?

20 The residential building in the picture is located in which city?

Answers to QUIZ 53 – First

1 Eugène Delacroix
2 Joan Littlewood
3 Easter Island
4 Jeremiah
5 HMS *Dreadnought*
6 Libya
7 George Cross
8 Salem Witch Trials
9 Dynamite – by Alfred Nobel
10 Amsterdam Hilton Hotel – Montreal hosted the second
11 The first royal corgis

12 Jeffrey Archer
13 Wolfgang Tillmans (in 2000)
14 Adolfo Suarez
15 Standard time zones or a standard or mean time and hourly variations from that according to established time zones
16 Apple
17 Finland
18 Jane Couch
19 Graeme Hick
20 Pearl S. Buck

1   Named after Mithridates VI of Pontus, Mithridatism is which practice?

2   Founded in 1926, America's oldest contemporary dance company is named after which woman?

3   Which Tire & Rubber Company is named after the inventor of vulcanised rubber?

4   Which late Polish journalist claimed to have witnessed 27 coups and revolutions?

5   Which "disease of kings" is caused by elevated uric acid levels in the blood?

6   The USS *Arizona* Memorial is located where?

7   What is the tallest skyscraper in the Western Hemisphere?

8   Which chef ran the London restaurant Harveys between 1987 and 1993?

9   The London bookshop Stanfords specialises in which field?

10 Who starred as Father James Lavelle in the 2014 film *Calvary*?

11 Which French artist (1930–2002) was famous for colourful figures called 'Nanas'?

12 Which German philosopher stated that "to write poetry after Auschwitz is barbaric"?

13 What sort of dolphin was TV's Flipper?

14 Alfama is the oldest district of which European capital?

15 Wolfram von Richthofen planned which April 26, 1937 bombing raid?

16 Which child film star always wore exactly 56 curls in her hair?

17 Which Frenchman wrote the plays *L'Alouette* (1952) and *Becket* (1959)?

18 Tabac, Massenet and Piscine are corners on which street circuit?

19 Founded in 1860, Forgan is the oldest maker of which sporting items?

20 Name the pictured footwear –

Answers to QUIZ 54 – General Knowledge

1   Zorro
2   Plaid Cymru The Party of Wales
3   A Tribe of Toffs
4   The rotation of the Earth on its axis
5   *The Mentalist*, aka Patrick Jane
6   12
7   *The Red Flag*
8   Henry
9   The homburg
10 Buckingham Palace Garden
11 Karaoke machine
12 *La Parisienne* or *The Parisian Girl*
13 Catherine Howard
14 Julius Richard Petri – as in the Petri dish
15 Bic
16 *King Charles III*
17 Stihl
18 Curling stones
19 Marcus Grönholm
20 Vienna – it is the Hundertwasser House

1   Who was both the mother and wife of Oedipus?

2   What is Múspellsheimr the realm of in Norse mythology?

3   Originally patron god of the city of Eridu, the Sumerian god
     Enki later became known by what name in Akkadian and
     Babylonian mythology?

4   Which Titan is the father of the Greek god Zeus?

5   Which watchman of the Norse gods guarded the rainbow
     bridge Bifrost?

6   Atlas and Prometheus are the sons of Clymene and which
     Titan in Greek myth?

7   Which Egyptian god of the earth is the father of Osiris, Isis,
     Set and Nephthys?

8   The Stymphalian birds killed by Heracles were pets of which
     Greek god?

9   The Cypriot city of Paphos was the primary place of worship
     for which Greek goddess?

10   Identified with Zeus, which chief Etruscan god was ruler of
     the skies, husband of Uni and father of Hercle?

11   Which son of the Egyptian god Osiris avenged his murder by
     Seth and became the new king of Egypt?

12   Járngreipr are the iron gloves of which Norse god?

13   Which *aulos*-playing satyr was flayed alive after losing a
     musical duel with Apollo?

14   Kū, Kanaloa, Kāne and Lono are the four great gods (*akua*) in
     which mythology?

15   Which Greek god of the cold north wind is also the bringer
     of winter?

16   Which Inca god of death ruled *Ukhu Pacha*, the land of the
     dead?

17 Which metallic element is named after the old Norse name for the Scandinavian goddess Freyja?

18 The successor to the Zonda, which Pagani supercar is named after the Incan god of wind?

19 Taken from a mythical horse, *Chollima* is which national football side's nickname?

20 The image depicts which Arthurian story?

Answers to QUIZ 55 – General Knowledge

1 Producing immunity against the action of poison by taking the poison in gradually increased doses

2 Martha Graham

3 Goodyear – named after Charles Goodyear

4 Ryszard Kapuściński

5 Gout

6 Pearl Harbor in Honolulu, Hawaii

7 One World Trade Center or 1 WTC, New York City

8 Marco Pierre White

9 Travel

10 Brendan Gleeson

11 Niki de Saint Phalle

12 Theodor W. Adorno

13 Bottlenose dolphin

14 Lisbon

15 Bombing of Guernica aka Operation Rügen

16 Shirley Temple

17 Jean Anouilh

18 Circuit de Monaco

19 Golf clubs

20 Espadrilles

1   What six-letter name is given to is the back-to-front slang spoken by raucous French youths in the banlieues?

2   Which title character in a novel in verse by Alexander Pushkin kills the young poet Vladimir Lensky?

3   Edward, the Black Prince won his spurs at which August 26, 1346 battle?

4   Meaning 'those who face death', what name is given to Kurdish freedom fighters?

5   In 1997, which Italian fashion house introduced the Baguette bag, an "enduring style icon" that has been produced in over 1,000 versions?

6   What 1982 song was Madness's only number one single?

7   The chemist S.P.L Sørensen introduced the concept of which scale in 1909?

8   Which Roman poet (c.84–54 BC) dedicated dozens of his poems to Lesbia, a possible false name for his married lover Clodia?

9   The Palaeozoic Era ended with which extinction event, the largest mass extinction in Earth's history?

10 Which 1935 musical comedy film features the Irving Berlin songs *Top Hat, White Tie and Tails* and *Cheek to Cheek*?

11 The disease beriberi is caused by a deficiency of which vitamin?

12 Which compact stars are the densest and smallest stars known to exist in the universe?

13 The author of the 2015 cookbook *Deliciously Ella* is the daughter of which former MP for St. Helens South?

14 Serving from 1949 until his death in 1976, who was the first Premier of the People's Republic of China?

15 What did D.H. Lawrence describe as "hard, isolate, stoic, and a killer"?

16 Which military decoration was instituted on March 17, 1813 by Frederick William III of Prussia?

17 Designed by Dirk Henn, which 2003 tile-based board game features the building of an Arabian palace in 13th century Granada?

18 Who was Yorkshire county cricket club's first overseas signing?

19 Russia's Fedor Emelianenko has been called which sport's greatest heavyweight fighter?

20 Name the pictured TV car –

Erin Cadigan / Shutterstock.com

Answers to QUIZ 56 – Mythology

1	Jocasta	12	Thor
2	Fire	13	Marsyas
3	Ea	14	Hawaiian
4	Cronus	15	Boreas
5	Heimdall	16	Supay
6	Iapetus	17	Vanadium – from Vanadis
7	Geb	18	Pagani Huayra
8	Ares	19	North Korea or Korea DPR
9	Aphrodite	20	*Sir Gawain and the Green Knight*
10	Tinia or Tina		
11	Horus		

QUIZ 58 – General Knowledge

1   In a 1963 film, what links the fates of the characters Danny Velinski, Willie Dickes and Louis Sedgwick?

2   The kingdom of Hyrule features in which video game series that debuted in 1986?

3   Which naming custom originated with the Australian meteorologist Clement Wragge (1852–1922)?

4   What is the fastest land animal on Earth?

5   A person described as an 'onychophagist' engages in which habit?

6   Created a baron in 1720, John Blunt was a director of which infamous company?

7   International Office 39 is a shadowy government organisation of which Asian country?

8   Which TV drama stars Keri Russell and Matthew Rhys as KGB spies Elizabeth and Philip Jennings?

9   Which group won the 1974 Eurovision Song Contest at the Brighton Dome?

10 Nathan Blecharczyk, Brian Chesky and Joe Gebbia founded which accommodation website in 2008?

11 What is the most abundant protein in the human body?

12 In 1875, which Impressionist painted *Les raboteurs de parquet* (*The Floor Planers*)?

13 Taken by Rosalind Franklin in 1952, "Photo 51" is an image of which molecule?

14 Which architect built the Queen Mary's Dolls' House (1924)?

15 The Kilchoman Distillery produces whisky on which of the Inner Hebrides?

16 Ahimsa is the Hindu and Buddhist doctrine of refraining from what?

17 The China Petroleum & Chemical Corp. is known by which one-word name?

18 Umberto Granaglia (1931–2008) won 13 World titles in which ball game?

19 Which Spaniard was quoted as saying 'Grass is just for cows" then went on to win the Wimbledon men's singles title in 1966?

20 Name the big cat from the image –

Answers to QUIZ 57 – General Knowledge

1   Verlan
2   Eugene Onegin
3   Crêcy
4   Peshmerga
5   Fendi
6   *House of Fun*
7   pH scale for measuring acidity and basicity – pH stands for potential hydrogen
8   Catullus or Gaius Valerius Catullus
9   Permian-Triassic extinction event aka the Great Dying or Great Permian Extinction
10 Irving Berlin
11 Thiamine or Vitamin B1
12 Neutron stars
13 Shaun Woodward
14 Zhou Enlai
15 "The essential American soul"
16 Iron Cross or *Eisernes Kreuz*
17 *Alhambra*
18 Sachin Tendulkar
19 Mixed Martial Arts (MMA)
20 The General Lee – the Dodge Charger from the TV show *The Dukes of Hazzard*

1 What was the first comet whose return was predicted?

2 Which mosquito-borne tropical disease is also known as breakbone fever?

3 The Wong-Baker FACES Scale is used to help children communicate what?

4 The Vermilion border defines which part of the face?

5 Which unit of time is one quintillionth of a second?

6 Hypokalaemia is a deficiency of which alkali metal in the blood?

7 Also known as occupational asthenopia, what is CVS?

8 Sapphire is a variety of which aluminium oxide mineral?

9 Used in demonstrations of tabletop "volcanoes", which compound is sometimes called "Vesuvian Fire"?

10 In 1957, the "Traitorous Eight" quit the Semiconductor Laboratory named after which Nobel laureate?

11 The spiral of Theodorus or Einstein spiral is composed of contiguous what?

12 Which flavour of quark is the heaviest subatomic particle ever observed?

13 Which allotrope of oxygen is measured in Dobson units?

14 Putting clocks on commercial jet flights, the 1971 Hafele-Keating experiment tested which theory in physics?

15 Which Swedish chemist is credited with identifying selenium, thorium and cerium?

16 David Hilbert said of which German mathematician: "No one shall expel us from the Paradise that [he] has created"?

17 In 1838, what did Theodor Schwann and Matthias Schleiden propose as the basic functional unit of all living things?

18 What does haptic technology recreate?

19 Which American futurist is the author of *Physics of the Impossible* (2008) and *Physics of the Future* (2011)?

20 Name the double Nobel Prize-winner in the image –

Answers to QUIZ 58 – General Knowledge

1	They are the only escapees in *The Great Escape* to make it to safety	10	Airbnb
		11	Collagen
2	*The Legend of Zelda*	12	Gustave Caillebotte
3	Assigning names to hurricanes and weather systems	13	DNA
		14	Edwin Lutyens
		15	Islay
4	Cheetah	16	Harming any living being – the term means 'not to injure' and 'compassion'
5	Biting their fingernails		
6	South Sea Company		
7	North Korea	17	Sinopec
8	*The Americans*	18	Bocce
9	ABBA – with *Waterloo*	19	Manuel Santana
		20	Jaguar (*Panthera onca*)

QUIZ 60 – General Knowledge

1   In 1974, which shoe designer became the first man to appear on the cover of British *Vogue*?

2   Which Bollywood film, about a radio exec (played by Shah Rukh Khan) falling in love with a suicide bomber, features the A.R. Rahman song *Chaiyya Chaiyya*?

3   Which German-born French composer wrote the 1867 operetta *Robinson Crusoé*?

4   Which car manufacturer's business was founded as the Swallow Sidecar Company in 1922?

5   Dr. James Sheppard commits the eponymous crime in which Agatha Christie novel?

6   In 2002, *Whenever, Wherever* became which Colombian singer's first UK hit?

7   Trepanging, a term derived from Indonesian, is the harvesting of which sea creatures?

8   In 1977, which German invented the "Plastination" method for preserving anatomical specimens?

9   Ratiocination is the process of what?

10 Which French writer (1913–2005) created the retired British officer Major W. Marmaduke Thompson?

11 Michael Ramsey was the 100th man appointed to which office?

12 Which infamous MP became the last ever Postmaster General in 1968?

13 Which TV detective was bossed around by "Horn-rimmed Harry" aka Superintendent Norman Mullett?

14 The word "Pinoy" is used to describe people from which Asian country?

15 The Copley Medal is given every year for "outstanding achievements in research in any branch of science" by which body?

16 Known by the Latin name *Falco rusticolus*, what is the world's largest falcon?

17 New Zealand's Nigel Richards is regarded as which board game's greatest player?

18 Which rugby union position is called *Losskakel* in Afrikaans?

19 The 1976 men's decathlon Olympic champion is now known by what name?

20 Name the former church in the picture –

Answers to QUIZ 59 – Sciences

1 Halley's Comet

2 Dengue fever

3 The amount of pain they are feeling

4 Lips

5 Attosecond

6 Potassium

7 Computer Vision Syndrome

8 Corundum

9 Ammonium dichromate

10 William Shockley – they left to form Fairchild Semiconductor

11 Right triangles

12 Top quark

13 Ozone

14 Theory of relativity

15 Jöns Jacob Berzelius

16 Georg Cantor

17 The cell – giving rise to cell theory

18 The sense of touch by applying forces, vibrations or motions to the user

19 Michio Kaku

20 Linus Pauling – winner of the 1954 Nobel Prize in Chemistry and 1962 Nobel Peace Prize

QUIZ 61 – General Knowledge

1   Will Kane is the marshal of Hadleyville forced to stand alone against Frank Miller and his gang in which Western?

2   Which US band released the 1982 song *Bad to the Bone*?

3   Which infectious disease is also known as "infantile paralysis"?

4   Eric Fenby became the amanuensis of which blind composer in 1928?

5   Which Biblical king was "a mighty hunter before the Lord"?

6   Which ancient Greek city-state lay on the right bank of the Eurotas River?

7   Which SI derived unit of work or energy is named after an English physicist?

8   Which regulatory protein is so named because it is present in almost all tissues of eukaryotic organisms?

9   The French liqueur St-Germain is made from which blossoms?

10 Founded in 1946, which Swiss film festival awards the Golden Leopard?

11 Which healing technique derives its name from the Japanese for 'universal life energy'?

12 Constantine XI Palaiologos (1404–53) was the last ruler of which empire?

13 Apophis or Apep was the demon of chaos in which mythology?

14 Matthew Holness won the Perrier Award for playing which spoof horror author?

15 In 1792, which European country became the first to ban the slave trade?

16 Which US artist began his *Onement* series of "zip" paintings in 1948?

17 Which digital pet gets its name from the Japanese for 'egg-watch'?

18 Zombies, Spider Jockeys and Creepers are hostile 'mobs' in which video game?

19 Which South Korean boxer died after his 1982 bout with Ray "Boom Boom" Mancini?

20 Name the king of the Hindu gods in the picture –

Answers to QUIZ 60 – General Knowledge

1 Manolo Blahnik
2 *Dil Se..* ('From the Heart')
3 Jacques Offenbach
4 Jaguar Cars
5 *The Murder of Roger Ackroyd*
6 Shakira [Isabel Mebarak Ripoli]
7 Sea cucumbers – known in Indonesian as *trepang*
8 Gunther von Hagens
9 Reasoning or exact thinking
10 Pierre Daninos
11 Archbishop of Canterbury
12 John Stonehouse
13 DI "Jack" Frost or Detective Inspector William Edward Frost – created by R.D. Wingfield
14 Philippines
15 Royal Society – first awarded 1731, it is perhaps the oldest surviving scientific award in the world
16 Gyrfalcon
17 Scrabble
18 Fly-half (meaning 'loose-link')
19 Caitlyn Jenner, formerly Bruce Jenner
20 Hagia Sophia or Ayasofya or *Sancta Sophia*, Istanbul

1 Who was Chairman and CEO of General Electric from 1981 to 2001?

2 Which German company was the originator and first marketer of aspirin (patented in 1899)?

3 Named after a Belgian-born designer, what was the first company founded by a woman to make the Fortune 500?

4 Which Panamanian law firm's files have been leaked as the Panama Papers?

5 Which bank took its name from the son-in-law of co-founder John Freame?

6 Which author bought the company Glidrose to hold the rights to his writing?

7 Founded by Ezra Cornell, which company introduced both the stock ticker and money transfer?

8 The Danish company Novo Nordisk manufactures which products?

9 Which furniture company opened its first store in Älmhult in 1958?

10 Noah Dietrich was chief aide to which US tycoon for more than 30 years?

11 Which footwear brand was founded in 1856 as the North British Rubber Company?

12 Which UK-based company is Europe's biggest defence contractor?

13 Which US investor wrote the 2000 personal finance book *Rich Dad, Poor Dad*?

14 Founded at a coffee house on Tower Street in 1688, which insurance market has the motto *Fidentia* (Latin for 'confidence')?

15 The world's biggest home appliance maker, which Chinese company was founded in 1984 as Qingdao Refrigerator Co.?

16 Which financial services company was founded in Berlin in 1890 by Carl von Thieme and Wilhelm von Finck?

17 Which Reliance Industries chairman owns the Mumbai home, Antilia – the world's most expensive private residential property?

18 The title of the Michael Moore documentary *Roger & Me* refers to which CEO?

19 Which NBA team is owned by the *Shark Tank* TV star and businessman Mark Cuban?

20 The pictured banknote comes from which county?

Answers to QUIZ 61 – General Knowledge

1 *High Noon*
2 George Thorogood & the Destroyers
3 Polio
4 Frederick Delius
5 Nimrod
6 Sparta
7 Joule – named after James Prescott Joule
8 Ubiquitin
9 Elderflower blossoms
10 Locarno Film Festival
11 Reiki
12 Byzantine Empire or Eastern Roman Empire
13 Ancient Egyptian religion
14 Garth Marenghi
15 Denmark
16 Barnett Newman
17 Tamagotchi
18 *Minecraft*
19 Kim Duk-Koo
20 Indra

1   Whose first true Pop Art painting featured Donald Duck and Mickey Mouse fishing?

2   A certified pilot and nurse, Ellen Church was also the world's first what?

3   Who rode horses named Intendant, Le Vizir, Tauris and the white mare Désirée?

4   Built by Domenico Montagnana in 1733, "Petunia" is played by which Chinese cellist?

5   In March 2012, Leanne Wood was elected which party's first female leader?

6   Which art is demonstrated by the diagrams of the Yoshizawa-Randlett system?

7   Read using smartphones, what does the QR in QR Code stand for?

8   Which ligament of the knee is the MCL?

9   The mayor of Munich opens which fair with the cry "*O'zapft is!*" ('It is tapped')?

10 Lugnaquilla is the highest peak of which Irish mountain range?

11 In Roman mythology, Tarpeia betrayed Rome to which tribe?

12 The Aral Sea disaster was caused by Soviet efforts to produce which crop?

13 Named after the Greek for 'unstable', what is the rarest natural element in the world?

14 The Younger Memnon is a colossal granite head in the British Museum depicting which pharaoh?

15 Which Dominican dictator (1891–1961) is the subject of Rita Dove's poem *Parsley*?

16 According to the RSPB, what is the commonest and most widespread UK bird of prey?

17 Which sport was described by the poet Walt Whitman as "America's game"?

18 Charlene, Princess of Monaco, was an Olympic swimmer for which country?

19 Which Swedish side is the only Nordic football club to have reached a European Cup final?

20 The pictured Donatello sculpture depicts which New Testament character?

Answers to QUIZ 62 – Business

1 Jack Welch
2 Bayer
3 Liz Claiborne Inc – founded in 1976
4 Mossack Fonseca
5 Barclays – James Barclay
6 Ian Fleming
7 Western Union
8 Pharmaceuticals, in particular, diabetes drugs
9 IKEA
10 Howard Hughes
11 Hunter Boot Ltd – founded in Scotland by the US entrepreneur Henry Lee Norris
12 BAE Systems
13 Robert Kiyosaki
14 Lloyd's of London
15 Haier Group
16 Allianz
17 Mukesh Ambani
18 Then General Motors CEO Roger Smith
19 Dallas Mavericks
20 Thailand

1 Which two countries' security forces perform the daily Wagah border ceremony?

2 In 1993, who divorced Allegra Mostyn-Owen and married Marina Wheeler?

3 In which Franz Lehar operetta is Danilo obsessed with the Paris restaurant Maxim's?

4 Who finished his Parma Cathedral dome fresco, the *Assumption of the Virgin*, in 1530?

5 Which song by Julia Ward Howe begins: "Mine eyes have seen the glory of the coming of the Lord"?

6 Which US financial journalist wrote the 2014 non-fiction book *Flash Boys*?

7 Which term describes the prominent parts of a catfish that resemble a cat's whiskers?

8 Salvatore Quasimodo wrote a poem describing which place "far from the Vistula" as "that pit of ashes"?

9 In Mexican cuisine, what is a chipotle?

10 In 2012, I.M. Pei's Green Building was transformed by MIT students into a playable form of which video game?

11 Which venue has hosted more annual Royal Variety Performances than any other theatre?

12 In which country was the Pentecostal megachurch Hillsong founded in 1983?

13 Named after an Indonesian island, what is the smallest living subspecies of tiger?

14 Who is the drummer in Dr. Teeth and The Electric Mayhem?

15 Which animal hospital is based at Haddenham, Buckinghamshire?

16 Which high school student used the aliases Calvin Klein, Darth Vader and Clint Eastwood?

17 The simplest alkane, which greenhouse gas has the formula CH4?

18 Which Soviet athlete won the 5,000m and 10,000m at the 1956 Olympics?

19 Which racetrack was nicknamed "The Green Hell" by Jackie Stewart?

20 Where is the pictured casino?

Answers to QUIZ 63 – General Knowledge

1 Roy Lichtenstein – *Look Mickey* (1961)
2 Airline stewardess
3 Napoleon Bonaparte
4 Yo-Yo Ma
5 Plaid Cymru
6 Origami
7 Quick Response
8 Medial Collateral Ligament
9 Oktoberfest
10 Wicklow Mountains
11 Sabines
12 Cotton
13 Astatine
14 Rameses II or Ramses the Great
15 Rafael Trujillo
16 Buzzard (*Buteo buteo*)
17 Baseball
18 South Africa
19 Malmö FF – defeated 1–0 by Nottingham Forest in the 1979 final
20 Mary Magdalene (*Penitent Magdalene*)

1   The elite army, the Sardaukar, features in which sci-fi universe?

2   One of the major Modernists, which Austrian novelist wrote *The Sleepwalkers: a Trilogy* (1931–32) and *The Death of Virgil* (1945)?

3   Which poem begins: "If I should die, think only this of me"?

4   Which Philip Larkin poem ends: "What will survive of us is love"?

5   Which Zambian-born author's debut novel was *When The Lion Feeds* (1964)?

6   Which journalist wrote *The English Constitution* in 1867?

7   *Shark* is Will Self's 2014 sequel to which Booker-shortlisted novel?

8   Which Dutch-born novelist wrote *Under the Skin* and *The Crimson Petal and the White*?

9   Published in 1928, what was A.A. Milne's second book of Winnie-the-Pooh stories?

10   Which author reimagined the Napoleonic Wars with dragons in her series *Temeraire*?

11   Which Canadian author wrote the 2014 sci-fi novel *Station Eleven*?

12   Which 1896 work includes *To an Athlete Dying Young, Loveliest of Trees, the Cherry Now* and *When I was One-and-Twenty*?

13   Which 1987 novel is about the writer Paul Sheldon and his crazed fan Annie Wilkes?

14   The Nome King is a major villain in which series of books?

15   Who is the British author of a series of five novels about Patrick Melrose that began with *Never Mind* and concluded with *At Last*?

16   *The Killings at Badger's Drift* (1987) was the first mystery novel in which series?

17   Which Vietnam vet and Oxford graduate published the memoir *This Boy's Life* in 1989?

18 *Grantchester Grind* is a sequel to which 1974 novel by Tom Sharpe?

19 Alexandre Dumas, *père,* wrote: "The difference between treason and patriotism is only a matter of..." what?

20 Which London-born novelist is pictured?

Answers to QUIZ 64 – General Knowledge

1 Pakistan and India
2 Boris Johnson
3 *The Merry Widow*
4 Correggio or Antonio Allegri
5 *The Battle Hymn of the Republic*
6 Michael Lewis
7 Barbels
8 Auschwitz
9 A ripe jalapeño pepper that has been dried and smoked for use in cooking
10 *Tetris*
11 The London Palladium
12 Australia – founded in Sydney
13 Sumatran tiger
14 Animal the Muppet
15 Tiggywinkles Wildlife Hospital
16 Marty McFly in the *Back to the Future* film series
17 Methane
18 Vladimir Kuts
19 The Nürburgring [NordschleifeI]
20 Monaco – it is the Casino de Monte-Carlo or Monte Carlo Casino

QUIZ 66 – General Knowledge

1   The Swedish chemist Georg Brandt discovered which metal as a dark blue pigment in copper ore?

2   Which marsupial is the only known animal that produces cube-shaped droppings?

3   *The Jewish Cemetery* is a seminal work by which Mennonite Dutch landscape painter (c.1628–82)?

4   Which fungus was called "the diamond of the kitchen" by Brillat-Savarin?

5   Which princess "nearly married" the future Canadian prime minister John Turner?

6   In which city, the second largest in the Arab world, was OPEC founded in 1960?

7   Walter Potter became known for his eccentric Victorian collection of what?

8   Which planet is named after the Roman god of agriculture?

9   Which US guitarist sued Coldplay over similarities between *Viva La Vida* and his song *If I Could Fly*?

10 Badwater Basin, the lowest point in North America, is in which valley?

11 The Qurikancha or Inti Wasi ('sun house') was the most important temple of which empire?

12 Bathsheba Everdene is the heroine of which novel by Thomas Hardy?

13 Which sitcom title character ended up marrying Harry Kennedy (played by Richard Armitage)?

14 Which US professor of cognitive science wrote the 1979 book *Gödel, Escher, Bach: an Eternal Golden Braid*?

15 Chiromancy is divination by what means?

16 Frank Bowden founded which bicycle company in 1887?

17 Rich Uncle Moneybags is associated with which board game?

18 Which Syrian woman became Olympic heptathlon champion in 1996?

19 Which Russian center for Pittsburgh Penguins won the 2006–2007 Calder Memorial Trophy as the NHL's best rookie?

20 On which Yemeni island does the pictured tree grow?

Answers to QUIZ 65 – Literature

1   Frank Herbert's *Dune* universe
2   Hermann Broch
3   *The Soldier* by Rupert Brooke
4   *An Arundel Tomb*
5   Wilbur Smith
6   Walter Bagehot
7   *Umbrella*
8   Michel Faber
9   *The House at Pooh Corner*
10 Naomi Novik
11 Emily St. John Mandel
12 The poetry collection *A Shropshire Lad* by A.E. Housman
13 *Misery* by Stephen King
14 The *Oz* books by L. Frank Baum
15 Edward St. Aubyn
16 Chief Inspector Barnaby series by Caroline Graham, aka the *Midsomer Murder* books
17 Tobias Wolff
18 *Porterhouse Blue*
19 Dates – in *The Count of Monte Cristo*
20 Zadie Smith

1   Hans Riegel Sr. formed which German confectionery maker in 1920?

2   Who became the Berliner Philharmoniker's chief conductor in 1954?

3   Which Chicago blues legend recorded *Smokestack Lightning* in 1956?

4   The Bottle Inn in Marshwood, Dorset, hosts which "world famous" world eating championship?

5   Possessed by the Norse god Odin, what is Draupnir?

6   Charlotte Amalie is the capital of which Caribbean island group?

7   In which 1981 film does a hike across the North York Moors end up in The Slaughtered Lamb pub?

8   Which St John restaurant founder and chef wrote the 1999 book *Nose to Tail Eating: A Kind of British Eating*?

9   The first director of the Royal College of Music is best remembered in the name of which reference work?

10 What is the oldest remaining British overseas territory?

11 The Hexamilion Wall is thought to be the largest archaeological structure in which country?

12 In 1905, which Liberal began the longest continuous term of any foreign secretary?

13 Who coined the term "gamma ray" in 1903 following early studies of the emissions of radioactive nuclei?

14 The highest in the world, Tanggula Railway Station is located where?

15 Psychiatrists Thomas Holmes and Richard Rahe developed a scale for quantifying what?

16 Charles Napier never actually sent which punning dispatch when he conquered Sindh in 1843?

17 Which German-born fur trader (1763–1848) was America's first multimillionaire?

18 Which javelin thrower is the first Kenyan to win a world championship gold in a field event?

19 Which national rugby union team performs the Siva Tau war dance?

20 Which Chvrches lead vocalist is pictured?

Christian Bertrand / Shutterstock.com

Answers to QUIZ 66 – General Knowledge

1 Cobalt
2 Wombat
3 Jacob van Ruisdael
4 The truffle
5 Princess Margaret
6 Baghdad – Cairo is the largest
7 Stuffed animals or anthropomorphic dioramas – including the museum centrepiece "The Death & Burial of Cock Robin", with its 98 species of British birds
8 Saturn
9 Joe Satriani
10 Death Valley
11 Inca Empire
12 *Far from the Madding Crowd*
13 Geraldine Granger – in *The Vicar of Dibley*
14 Douglas Hofstadter
15 Palm reading
16 Raleigh
17 *Monopoly*
18 Ghada Shouaa
19 Evgeni Malkin
20 Socotra – it is a Socotra dragon tree or dragon's blood tree (*Dracaena cinnabari*)

QUIZ 68 – Film

1 In 2000, John Irving won an Oscar for adapting which of his own novels?

2 In 1963, which Austrian-born actress married Tony Curtis after meeting on the set of *Taras Bulba*?

3 The first ever film sequel, *The Fall of a Nation* is a 1916 follow-up to which movie?

4 Which Terry Gilliam film was inspired by the Chris Marker short *La Jetée*?

5 Which French composer won an Oscar for scoring *A Passage to India*?

6 Which Frenchman directed the cinéma du look films *Diva* (1981) and *Betty Blue* (1986)?

7 *The Cocoanuts* (1929) was which comedy team's first feature-length film?

8 The 2014 New Zealand film *The Dark Horse* is about Genesis Potini, a player of which game?

9 Which German actress dressed up in a gorilla suit for the 1932 film *Blonde Venus*?

10 Which Cameron Crowe film features John Cusack holding up a boombox playing *In Your Eyes* by Peter Gabriel?

11 Which Puerto Rican was the first Hispanic actor to win an Oscar?

12 Which 1986 film featured the Colonial Marines, Vasquez, Hicks, Hudson and Apone?

13 In which 1957 film did famed Broadway singing coach Kay Thompson sing the number *Think Pink*?

14 "Long live the new flesh" is the last line spoken by James Woods in which film?

15 Which Oscar-winning animated film features the inflatable healthcare robot Baymax?

16 Playing the villain Mister Midnight, Christopher Lee performed the song *Name Your Poison* in which 1983 film?

17 Who died on October 10, 1985 – the same day as his *Battle of Neretva* co-star Orson Welles?

18 Which 1968 Western features the struggle for a piece of land called Sweetwater?

19 Michael C. Gross designed and artist Brent Boates drew up which logo, as seen on the car *Ecto-1*?

20 Name the pictured French actress –

Jaguar PS / Shutterstock.com

Answers to QUIZ 67 – General Knowledge

1 Haribo
2 Herbert von Karajan
3 Howlin' Wolf aka Chester Arthur Burnett
4 World Stinging Nettle Eating Championship
5 A magic gold ring
6 US Virgin Islands
7 *An American Werewolf in London*
8 Fergus Henderson
9 *Grove's Dictionary of Music and Musicians* – named after Sir George Grove
10 Bermuda
11 Greece
12 Edward Grey, 1st Viscount Grey of Fallodon – his tenure ended in 1916
13 Ernest Rutherford
14 Tibet
15 The amount of stress in your life – the Holmes and Rahe stress scale identifies 43 stressful life events, each one awarded a Life Change Unit
16 *Peccavi* – Latin for "I have sinned"
17 John Jacob Astor
18 Julius Yego – who won the 2015 world title
19 Samoa
20 Lauren Mayberry

1   Which TV title character has a lazy manservant named Jud (played by Phil Davis)?

2   Maris Peer, Estima, Charlotte and Marfona are common varieties of what?

3   *Catch a Fire* (1973) was which band's first album on Island Records?

4   Amethyst and citrine are varieties of which mineral?

5   Which English actor wrote the verse play *East* (1975) and the one-man show *Shakespeare's Villains* (1998)?

6   Using Ukrainian folk melodies, which composer's Symphony no. 2 is nicknamed the *Little Russian*?

7   The German painter Franz Marc was killed at which 1916 battle?

8   The Martin-Schultz scale is used to establish the colour of what?

9   Which appetisers are the Basque equivalent of Spanish tapas?

10 Which comic book detectives are known in French as *Dupont et Dupond*?

11 Held in Park City, Utah, what is the largest independent cinema festival in the US?

12 Which scientist published her classic *Treatise on Radioactivity* in 1910?

13 Which US President first proposed the Strategic Defense Initiative (SDI), aka "Star Wars"?

14 The piano virtuoso Claudio Arrau (1903–91) was born in which country?

15 Which "Glamour Cat" sings the ballad *Memory* in the musical *Cats*?

16 In 1917, who wrote *The Times* obituary for Ian Fleming's MP father Valentine?

17 Which Andy Warhol artwork repeats an image from the 1960 film *Flaming Star* three times?

18 Ring announcer Michael Buffer famously uses which trademarked phrase?

19 In 1934, what became the only horse to win both the Cheltenham Gold Cup and Grand National in the same year?

20 Which bridge over the River Tarn is pictured?

Migel / Shutterstock.com

Answers to QUIZ 68 – Film

1 *The Cider House Rules*
2 Christine Kaufmann
3 *The Birth of a Nation*
4 *12 Monkeys*
5 Maurice Jarre
6 Jean-Jacques Beineix
7 Marx Brothers
8 Chess or speed chess
9 Marlene Dietrich
10 *Say Anything...*
11 José Ferrer – in 1950, for *Cyrano de Bergerac*
12 *Aliens*
13 *Funny Face*
14 *Videodrome*
15 *Big Hero 6*
16 *The Return of Captain Invincible*
17 Yul Brynner
18 *Once Upon a Time in the West*
19 Ghostbusters 'no ghost' logo
20 Emmanuelle Béart

1   Which US filmmaker directed the TV pilot episodes of *Boardwalk Empire* and *Vinyl*?

2   What type of elite service is Gray & Farrar?

3   In France, the term 'un nègre' is used to describe which literary role?

4   Which disaster site's clean-up operation involved around 830,000 "liquidators"?

5   Dibatag, gerenuk, chinkara, puku and lechwe are species of what?

6   What is the most abundant mineral in Earth's continental crust?

7   In 1826, which elite infantry corps was forcibly disbanded by Sultan Mahmud II in the Auspicious Incident?

8   Jim Backus voiced which nearsighted cartoon character with the first name Quincy?

9   Gifts made of what material are given on a 15th wedding anniversary?

10 Which author took off in a P38 plane from Corsica on July 31, 1944, and vanished?

11 Which British heavy metal band released the 1980 single *Breaking the Law*?

12 In 1994, Tom Ford became creative director of which Italian fashion group?

13 Which element, the final member of the actinide series, is named after the inventor of the cyclotron?

14 Who painted *The Shrimp Girl* (c.1740–45) and *David Garrick as Richard III* (1745)?

15 In 1916, Berlin, Ontario was renamed after which British Army officer?

16 In which US state is the historic site Cahokia Mounds?

17 Which Uddingston, Lanarkshire-based biscuit maker is famed for its Teacakes and Caramel Wafer?

18 In which type of fencing is the entire body a valid target?

19 Which Great Britain competitor won 2014 Winter Olympic gold in the women's skeleton bob?

20 Name the pictured NASA rover –

Answers to QUIZ 69 – General Knowledge

1   Ross Poldark – played by Aidan Turner in *Poldark*
2   Potato
3   Bob Marley and the Wailers
4   Quartz
5   Steven Berkoff
6   Pyotr llyich Tchaikovsky
7   Battle of Verdun
8   A person's eye colour
9   Pintxos
10 The *Tintin* characters Thomson and Thompson
11 Sundance Film Festival
12 Marie Curie
13 Ronald Reagan
14 Chile
15 Grizabella
16 Winston Churchill
17 *Triple Elvis (Ferus Type)*
18 "Let's get ready to rumble!"
19 Golden Miller
20 Millau Viaduct

1   Jack Cade led a 1450 uprising against which king's government?

2   Which King of Italy was assassinated by the anarchist Gaetano Bresci in 1900?

3   Pope Alexander II gave his blessing to which man's invasion of England?

4   Simon Vouet was court painter to which French king?

5   The Marconi scandal rocked the government of which Liberal Prime Minister?

6   The Battle of Chamdo took place during which 1950 invasion?

7   Built in 1382 by Emir Djaharks el-Khalili, what is the Khan el-Khalili?

8   A stateless Albert Einstein became a citizen of which country in 1901?

9   Who led the Welsh rebels to victory at the 1402 Battle of Bryn Glas?

10   Which English king died of "camp fever' at the Château de Vincennes in 1422?

11   Which Chinese imperial dynasty succeeded the Qin Dynasty in 206 BC?

12   Which Gallic leader defeated Caesar at the Battle of Gergovia (52 BC)?

13   The Battle of Sheriffmuir was the key clash of which rebellion?

14   The ancient city of Apollonia in Illyria is in which modern-day country?

15   Anna Anderson (1896–1984) claimed to be which Romanov dynasty princess?

16   Herod the Great was the Roman-appointed king of which province?

17   Which Vietnamese leader was born Nguyen Sinh Cung in 1890?

18 The Babington Plot led to the execution of which queen?

19 In 1782, King Rama I established the Chakri dynasty in which country?

20 Name the pictured Tory prime minister –

Answers to QUIZ 70 – General Knowledge

1 Martin Scorsese
2 Matchmaking service
3 Ghost-writer
4 Chernobyl
5 Antelope
6 Feldspar
7 Janissaries or Janissary corps
8 Mr. Magoo
9 Crystal
10 Antoine de Saint-Exupéry
11 Judas Priest
12 Gucci
13 Lawrencium (atomic no. 103, it is named after Ernest Lawrence)
14 William Hogarth
15 Herbert Kitchener, 1st Earl Kitchener or Lord Kitchener of Khartoum – the city is now called Kitchener
16 Illinois
17 Tunnock's
18 Épée fencing
19 Lizzy Yarnold
20 Mars rover *Curiosity*

1 Which Roman governor is associated with the ancient Scottish tree, the Fortingall Yew?

2 Who was King of England during the 1381 Peasants' Revolt?

3 The Dublin criminal Martin Cahill (1949–94) is the subject of which John Boorman film?

4 Torta Setteveli is a seven-layered Italian cake named after which dance?

5 What is the most populous city in the USA?

6 Which German dramatist wrote the play *The Resistible Rise of Arturo Ui*?

7 The Spanish coastal town of Muxia has a monument to which 2002 oil spill?

8 What is the fruit of the rose plant called?

9 Which brothers created the illuminated manuscript, the Trés Riches Heures du Duc de Berry?

10 The world's tallest statue of a woman, *The Motherland Calls*, overlooks which Russian city?

11 The title of which song, traditionally sung at Jewish celebrations, means 'Let us rejoice'?

12 Which Russian composer is the subject of the 2016 Julian Barnes novel *The Noise of Time*?

13 Who once slept in the Cupboard Under the Stairs at 4 Privet Drive in Little Whinging, Surrey?

14 Which Manfred Mann singer wrote the much-covered song *Handbags and Gladrags*?

15 What is Britain's largest protected wetland?

16 Ronald Binge's musical piece *Sailing By* is played before which radio broadcast?

17 Which Stephen Sondheim musical is set in Japan in the year 1853?

18 Which belt was named after the "Yellow Earl" Hugh Cecil Lowther (1857–1944)?

19 Phillip Island is a Grand Prix Circuit in which country?

20 Identify the Inca city site –

Answers to QUIZ 71 – History

1	Henry VI	11	Han Dynasty
2	Umberto I	12	Vercingetorix
3	William the Conqueror	13	The Jacobite Rising of 1715
4	Louis XIII	14	Albania
5	H.H. Asquith	15	Grand Duchess Anastasia of Russia
6	China's invasion of Tibet		
7	A giant *souk* or market in Cairo	16	Judaea (37 – 4 BC)
8	Switzerland	17	Ho Ch Minh (meaning 'he who enlightens')
9	Owain Glyn Dwr or Owen Glendower	18	Mary, Queen of Scots
10	Henry V	19	Thailand
		20	Stanley Baldwin

QUIZ 73 – General Knowledge

1 Who based his drawings of Winnie-the-Pooh on Growler, his son Graham's teddy bear?

2 Maidenhead railway bridge features in which 1844 painting by J.M.W. Turner?

3 Which Austrian family moved into 20 Maresfield Gardens, Hampstead, in 1938?

4 119 copies of which book by John James Audubon are known to survive?

5 Which children's TV duo spoke the language Oddle Poddle?

6 Who married Giovanni Sforza, Alfonso of Aragon and, finally, Alfonso d'Este?

7 Thomas Gibson Bowles founded which women's weekly magazine in 1885?

8 Which Austrian-born biographer (1921–2012) wrote *The Case of Mary Bell: A Portrait of a Child Who Murdered* and *Albert Speer: His Battle with Truth*?

9 Berlioz composed an 1838 opera about which Florentine sculptor and goldsmith?

10 Which French composer wrote the music for the 1964 film *The Umbrellas of Cherbourg*?

11 Werner Heisenberg won the 1932 Nobel Prize in Physics "for the creation of" what?

12 Which Bush frontman is the father of fashion model Daisy Lowe?

13 Quarried in Dorset, which limestone was used to build the Cenotaph in Whitehall?

14 Jane Goodall is considered the world's foremost expert on which animals?

15 *Revelations* (1960) is regarded as the modern dance masterpiece of which American choreographer?

16 Who invented the bouncing bomb used by the RAF in the 1943 "Dambusters" raid?

17 Cavity Sam is the patient in which board game?

18 "Fast Eddie" Parker (1931–2001) was a legendary American player of which sport?

19 British swimmer James Guy won which individual title at the 2015 World Aquatics Championships?

20 What is the pictured rodent?

Answers to QUIZ 72 – General Knowledge

1 Pontius Pilate
2 Richard II
3 *The General*
4 Salome's Dance of the Seven Veils
5 New York City
6 Bertolt Brecht
7 *Prestige* oil tanker spill
8 Rose hip (aka rose haw or rose hep)
9 The Limbourg brothers (Herman, Paul and Johan)
10 Volgograd, formerly Stalingrad
11 *Hava Nagila*
12 Dmitri Shostakovich
13 Harry Potter
14 Mike d'Abo
15 The Broads or Norfolk and Suffolk Broads
16 Radio 4's late-night Shipping Forecast
17 *Pacific Overtures*
18 British boxing's Lonsdale Belt (he was the 5th Earl of Lonsdale)
19 Australia
20 Machu Picchu

QUIZ 74 – Structures

1   Featuring buildings at Naiku and Geku and the Uji Bridge, which complex is Japan's most sacred Shinto shrine?

2   Which cantilever railway bridge was opened by the future Edward VII on March 4, 1890?

3   Arecibo Observatory, site of the world's largest single-unit radio telescope, is found where?

4   The Hotel Attraction (1908) is an unbuilt design by which Catalan architect?

5   Which chateau, c. 25 miles north of Paris, houses the Musée Condé?

6   The Delta Works, the world's largest flood protection project, is in which country?

7   In the city of York, the Lendal Bridge, Millennium Bridge and Skeldergate Bridge span which river?

8   The Hotel Negresco first opened in 1913 in which French resort city?

9   60 Andrassy Street was which country's much-feared secret police HQ?

10 Graham Sutherland's tapestry *Christ in Glory* is in which English cathedral?

11 Designed by I.M. Pei, which Hall of Fame sits on the shore of Lake Erie?

12 Which Birmingham Town Hall architect invented a two-wheeled cab in 1834?

13 Eel Marsh House is a haunted abode in which spine-chilling Susan Hill novel?

14 Princess Anne's home Gatcombe Park is in which county?

15 Which New York nightclub opened in 1977 at 254 West 54th Street?

16 Built in 1924, Los Angeles's Ennis House was designed by which architect?

17 Opened in 2002, City Hall, London, was designed by which British architect?

18 Which Spanish architect designed the tallest building in the Nordic countries, the Turning Torso in Malmö?

19 Carved into granite cliffs on the south Cornish coast, which open-air theatre was created by Rowena Cade?

20 Which twin tower skyscraper complex in Mississauga, Canada, is pictured?

Paul McKinnon / Shutterstock.com

Answers to QUIZ 73 – General Knowledge

1 E. H. Shepard
2 *Rain, Steam, and Speed – The Great Western Railway*
3 The Freuds
4 *The Birds of America*
5 Bill & Ben – The Flower Pot Men
6 Lucrezia Borgia
7 *The Lady*
8 Gitta Sereny
9 Benvenuto Cellini
10 Michel Legrand
11 Quantum mechanics
12 Gavin Rossdale
13 Portland stone – which is quarried on the Isle of Portland
14 Chimpanzees
15 Alvin Ailey
16 Barnes Wallis
17 *Operation*
18 Billiards or pool
19 200m freestyle
20 Naked mole-rat (*Heterocephalus glaber*) or sand puppy

QUIZ 75 – General Knowledge

1   Charles Darwin published which major work in 1871?

2   Who has been Labour MP for both Ormskirk and Knowsley North, UKIP MEP for the East Midlands and leader of Veritas?

3   Which *Coronation Street* character got *two* spin-offs: *Pardon the Expression* (1965–66) and *Turn Out the Lights* (1967)?

4   In which constellation are the Pleiades and Hyades star clusters?

5   The RICE procedure involves what steps?

6   Dandy Dan and Fat Sam are crime bosses in which musical?

7   The only member of the genus *Satan*, the widemouth blindcat is a type of what?

8   The German word, *backpfeifengesicht*, means "a face in need of..." what?

9   Hearing the Burt Bacharach song *The Look of Love* inspired Mike Myers to create which film character?

10 A *Chilango* is a resident of which capital city in Latin America?

11 The large bird-like creature Garuda is the mount (*vahana*) of which Hindu deity?

12 In 1748, which Swiss mathematician developed the concept of function in his *Introductio in analysin infinitorum*?

13 Philip Roth first used which alter-ego as a narrator in his 1979 novel *The Ghost Writer*?

14 Financed by Sun Myung Moon, which 1981 Korean War film was called "the worst movie ever made" by *Newsweek*?

15 Describing it as "bright, cleansing, and revealing", which colour was called the "great clarifier" by Diana Vreeland?

16 Who was the only child of Mary, Princess Royal, the daughter of Charles I?

17 What is the largest national park in the Canadian Rockies?

18 Which tennis player won his only ATP Masters singles title at the 2003 Paris Masters?

19 Which Sussex and England fast bowler wrote the 1976 autobiography *Cricket Rebel*?

20 Who is the pictured celebrity chef?

Answers to QUIZ 74 – Structures

1   Ise Grand Shrine or Ise Jingu
2   Forth Bridge
3   Puerto Rico – or 10 miles south of the town of Arecibo in Puerto Rico
4   Antoni Gaudi
5   Château de Chantilly
6   Netherlands
7   River Ouse
8   Nice
9   Hungary – in Budapest
10 Coventry Cathedral
11 Rock and Roll Hall of Fame in Cleveland, Ohio
12 Joseph Aloysius Hansom
13 *The Woman in Black*
14 Gloucestershire
15 Studio 54
16 Frank Lloyd Wright
17 Norman Foster
18 Santiago Calatrava
19 Minack Theatre
20 Absolute World aka the Marilyn Monroe Towers

1   Which French president was unseated by François Mitterrand in 1981?

2   *Flush* by Virginia Woolf is a biography of which poet's pet cocker spaniel?

3   The subject of a 2014 book, Choupette is which fashion designer's pet cat?

4   Which practice involves giving a tenth of one's income to the church?

5   In 1967, which band had its first top 10 hit single with *See Emily Play*?

6   John Ruskin's wife Effie left him for which Pre-Raphaelite Brotherhood member?

7   In Norse myth, Huginn and Muninn are a pair of which birds?

8   Aged 17, Felix Mendelssohn wrote a concert overture for which Shakespeare comedy?

9   Also known as Cenni di Pepo, who painted the *Santa Trinità Maestà* (c.1290–1300)?

10 Why was 26-year-old Gerda Taro's death in the Spanish Civil War significant?

11 Paul Coia's voice was the very first heard on which TV channel?

12 The extraction of which metal uses the Kroll process or the Hunter process?

13 In 1935, the entomologist Reginald Mungomery imported 102 of which creatures into Queensland?

14 The Kiswah is a black cloth used to cover which holy structure?

15 What is the largest prehistoric man-made mound in Europe?

16 Which music venue is situated on Bennelong Point?

17 The leader in the field of off-road competition, which Austrian firm is Europe's largest motorcycle manufacturer?

18 Who scored the winner in the 1986 FIFA World Cup final?

19 The cyclist Hugh Porter married which former Olympic 200m breaststroke champion in 1965?

20 Which fairy tale castle is pictured?

Answers to QUIZ 75 – General Knowledge

1	*The Descent of Man*	11	Lord Vishnu
2	Robert Kilroy-Silk	12	Leonhard Euler
3	Leonard Swindley – played by Arthur Lowe	13	Nathan Zuckerman
4	Taurus	14	*Inchon*
5	Rest, Ice, Compress, Elevate	15	Red
6	*Bugsy Malone*	16	William III
7	Freshwater catfish	17	Jasper National Park
8	"... a fist"	18	Tim Henman
9	Austin Powers	19	John Snow
10	Mexico City	20	Tom Kerridge

QUIZ 77 – Geography

1   What is the world's longest man-made waterway?

2   Where are the UK Sovereign Base Areas of Akrotiri and Dhekelia?

3   Which city-state is 0.44 square kilometres in area?

4   The Gettysburg Battlefield is in which US state?

5   Which country comes first in an alphabetical list of the Commonwealth nations?

6   Which Pakistani city was known as Lyallpur until 1979?

7   North Ronaldsay is the northernmost inhabited island in which group?

8   Which country has the largest proven oil reserves in Africa?

9   Which lake has the largest volume of freshwater in Great Britain?

10 The Ilz and the Inn enter which river at the Bavarian city of Passau?

11 Famously photographed by Ansel Adams, Half Dome is perhaps the most recognised landmark of which national park?

12 Located on the River Alun, what is Britain's smallest city by size and population?

13 Which mountain's north wall has the German nickname *Mordwand* ('murder wall')?

14 The USA's only military base in Africa, Camp Lemonnier, is in which country?

15 What is the most populous US city to have been founded in the 20th century?

16 Which Caribbean nation is the poorest country in the Western Hemisphere?

17 The largest earthquake recorded in the 20th century hit which country in May 1960?

18 The world's largest flower market is in which Dutch town?

19 Which prison island was named by Juan Manuel de Ayala after the pelicans that roosted there?

20 Name the pictured French mountain –

Answers to QUIZ 76 – General Knowledge

1 Valéry Giscard d'Estaing
2 Elizabeth Barrett Browning
3 Karl Lagerfeld – the book is titled *Choupette: The Private Life of a High-Flying Fashion Cat*
4 Tithe or tithing
5 Pink Floyd
6 John Everett Millais
7 Ravens
8 *A Midsummer Night's Dream*
9 Cimabue
10 She was the first female war photographer to die in in her line of work
11 Channel 4
12 Titanium
13 Cane toad or *Rhinella marina* (formerly *Bufo marinus*)
14 The Kaaba in Mecca
15 Silbury Hill in Wiltshire
16 Sydney Opera House
17 KTM
18 Jorge Burruchaga – whose goal made it Argentina 3–2 West Germany
19 Anita Lonsbrough
20 Neuschwanstein Castle

1   Slaked lime is the traditional name of which inorganic compound?

2   The 2013 film *The Look of Love* told the story of which "King of Soho"?

3   In 1906, which Fauve painted *Charing Cross Bridge, London* and *The Pool of London*?

4   Which *Doctor Who* character was born Melody Pond?

5   Which philosopher gives his name to the paradox that states "All Cretans are liars"?

6   Bob Jackson took a picture of the moment when which assassin was assassinated?

7   Who was Margaret Thatcher's longest-serving Cabinet minister?

8   Which company makes the Trent family of aircraft engines?

9   Which late rock musician is the subject of the 2015 documentary *Montage of Heck*?

10 Which girl group was founded by choreographer Robin Antin as a burlesque troupe in 1995?

11 Which King of England was murdered in Corfe Castle, Dorset, in 978?

12 The self-confessed "chauvinist" Sir Tim Hunt won which Nobel prize in 2001?

13 Popular in Central Asia, Chal or Shubat is a beverage of what fermented milk?

14 In which animated TV series is Princess Bubblegum monarch of the Candy Kingdom?

15 Which subject is studied by the title character in Willy Russell's play *Educating Rita*?

16 Malia and Sitia are resorts on which Mediterranean island?

17 Which playing card is nicknamed the "Curse of Scotland"?

18 What is the world's oldest endurance sports car race?

19 Who scored twice in Great Britain's 1988 Olympic men's hockey 3–1 final defeat of West Germany?

20 Name the pictured Philadelphia building?

Answers to QUIZ 77 – Geography

1 Grand Canal of China or Beijing-Hangzhou Canal
2 Cyprus
3 Vatican City (The Holy See)
4 Pennsylvania
5 Antigua and Barbuda
6 Faisalabad
7 Orkney Islands
8 Libya
9 Loch Ness
10 Danube
11 Yosemite National Park
12 St. Davids
13 The Eiger
14 Djibouti
15 Las Vegas
16 Haiti
17 Chile
18 Aalsmeer
19 Alcatraz Island in San Francisco Bay – from "La Isla de los Alcatraces"
20 Mont Ventoux

1   The confection *Lokum* is known by what name in the West?

2   Which Hans Christian Andersen title character slept in a walnut shell?

3   Rising to 3415m, Emi Koussi is the highest summit in which desert?

4   Which "very friendly lion" featured in the children's TV show *The Herbs*?

5   Cyril Kenneth Bird (1887–1965) was the real name of which *Punch* cartoonist, the only one to become the magazine's editor?

6   Friedrich Fröbel pioneered what concept in the preschool education?

7   Who modelled Beatrice Portinari in the c.1864–70 painting *Beata Beatrix* after his late wife, Elizabeth Siddal?

8   *Victoria amazonica* is the largest species in the Nymphaeaceae family of which flowering plants?

9   What does the Latin saying "homo homini lupus" mean?

10 What were deciphered by Jean-François Champollion in the early 19th century?

11 King George II was the last monarch to reside at which palace?

12 Potiphar's wife attempted to seduce which Old Testament prophet?

13 What are Hungarian, Pencil, Fu Manchu and Walrus types of?

14 Which wife of Michael Frayn has written biographies of Jane Austen, Samuel Pepys and Thomas Hardy?

15 In 1937, the mosquito-borne West Nile virus was first isolated in the West Nile district of which country?

16 In 1947, Maurice Wilks tested a prototype for which off-road utility vehicle in fields at Red Wharf Bay on Anglesey?

17 Founded in 1804, what claims to be "the world's largest gardening charity"?

18 The great racing greyhound Mick The Miller was born in which country?

19 Nicknamed 'The Fighting Marine', which US heavyweight boxer starred in the 1926 film *The Fighting Marine*?

20 Who is this British inventor?

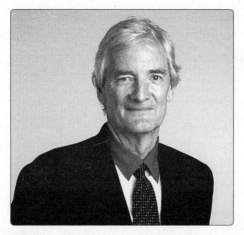

Answers to QUIZ 78 – General Knowledge

1   Calcium hydroxide
2   Paul Raymond
3   André Derain
4   River Song
5   Epimenides, who was a Cretan
6   When Lee Harvey Oswald was shot by Jack Ruby
7   Geoffrey Howe
8   Rolls-Royce
9   Kurt Cobain
10 The Pussycat Dolls
11 Edward the Martyr
12 Nobel Prize in Physiology or Medicine
13 Camel's milk
14 *Adventure Time*
15 English literature
16 Crete
17 Nine of diamonds
18 24 Hours of Le Mans
19 Imran Sherwani
20 Independence Hall

QUIZ 80 – USA

1 Which "Gateway to the West" is the largest city in the state of Nebraska?

2 Which company released the motion picture film format, Super 8, in 1965?

3 Robert De Niro learned to play the saxophone for which 1977 film?

4 The last US president born as a British subject, who was the first president to die in office?

5 John Schnatter is the eponymous founder of which delivery pizza chain?

6 Which US songwriter had his right leg amputated in 1958, a consequence of a 1937 riding accident?

7 Which US psychologist proposed a hierarchy of needs in his 1943 paper *A Theory of Human Motivation*?

8 Who is the US composer of a 1933 overture to *The School for Scandal* and the 1958 opera *Vanessa*?

9 Christopher Nicholas Sarantakos is the real name of which American magician and illusionist (b.1967)?

10 Who has hosted the TV series *Inside the Actors Studio* since its debut in 1994?

11 The Shure 55H Series II is known as 'The legendary "Elvis-..."' what?

12 Calling itself the "Geographical Center of North America", Rugby is a town in which state?

13 The Gibbs-Coolidge paintings are the only surviving complete set of which portraits?

14 Which TV miniseries centred on the Marines, Robert Leckie, Eugene Sledge and John Basilone?

15 The dry goods store A. Schwab is the only original business remaining on which Memphis street?

16 Using the stereolithography process, Chuck Hull of 3D Systems designed the first working what?

17 Which American (1908–91) is the only two-time winner of the Nobel Prize in Physics?

18 Which NFL franchise is the only not-for-profit, community-owned major league professional sports team in the US?

19 Nicknamed "The Thumper", which Boston Red Sox legend had a career batting average of .344?

20 Which US ballet dancer is pictured?

Debby Wong / Shutterstock.com

Answers to QUIZ 79 – General Knowledge

1	Turkish delight	11	Hampton Court Palace
2	Thumbelina	12	Joseph
3	Sahara Desert	13	Moustache
4	Parsley the Lion	14	Claire Tomalin
5	Fougasse	15	Uganda
6	Kindergarten	16	Land Rover
7	Dante Gabriel Rossetti	17	Royal Horticultural Society (RHS)
8	Water lilies – it is also known as Queen Victoria's water lily	18	Ireland – in Killeigh, County Offaly in 1926
9	"Man is a wolf to man"	19	Gene Tunney
10	Egyptian hieroglyphs (thanks to his translating parts of the Rosetta Stone)	20	James Dyson

QUIZ 81 – General Knowledge

1 The oldest of the group, which Impressionist painted *The Avenue, Sydenham* (1871) and *Bath Road, Chiswick* (1897)?

2 Founded by Lei Jun, which low-cost smartphone maker is named after the Chinese word for millet?

3 The French singer and actor Claude Moine (b.1942) is known by what stage name?

4 *My Brilliant Friend* (2011) is the first of four "Neapolitan Novels" by which Italian author?

5 Who wrote *On Floating Bodies*, the first known work on hydrostatics?

6 The triangular Nishan Sahib flag marks which places of worship?

7 Who opened his first restaurant, The Soup Kitchen, with Ivan Storey, in 1953?

8 Who dedicated the *Simple Symphony* (1934) to his childhood viola teacher Audrey Alston?

9 P.T. Barnum paid $10,000 to the Royal Zoological Society for which elephant?

10 Which musical features the songs *When I Grow Up*, *Naughty* and *Revolting Children*?

11 What is the simplest, lightest and most common chemical element?

12 On July 28, 1945, William F. Smith Jr. crashed his B-25 Mitchell bomber where?

13 Painter's colic is intense intestinal pain caused by which metal poisoning?

14 Legend has it that which drink was named in honour of the priest Marco d'Aviano's order?

15 The Olympic Australis is the largest example of which gemstone ever found?

16 "All those moments will be lost in time, like tears in rain. Time to die" is a quote from which film?

17 The first photographer to receive a Guggenheim Fellowship, who took the 1927 photo *Nautilus*?

18 Kawarau Gorge Suspension Bridge was the first permanent commercial site for which activity?

19 Which Australian was the first woman swimmer to win gold at three consecutive Olympic Games?

20 Who designed the chapel in the picture?

Mihai-Bogdan Lazar / Shutterstock.com

Answers to QUIZ 80 – USA

1	Omaha	11	Microphone
2	Eastman Kodak	12	North Dakokta
2	*New York, New York*	13	Portraits by Gilbert Stuart depicting the first five US presidents
4	William Henry Harrison – who died in 1841 on his 32nd day in office		
		14	*The Pacific*
5	Papa John's	15	Beale Street
6	Cole Porter	16	3D printer
7	Abraham Maslow	17	John Bardeen – in 1956 & 1972
8	Samuel Barber	18	Green Bay Packers
9	Criss Angel	19	Ted Williams
10	James Lipton	20	Misty Copeland

1   Who played Father Dougal in the sitcom *Father Ted*?

2   From 1987 to 2010, who served as MP for Banff & Buchan?

3   What is the largest animal ever known to have lived on Earth?

4   In Saudi Arabia, what would a man do with a *thawb*?

5   Which composer wrote the *Children's Corner* piano suite (1908) for his daughter, nicknamed "Chouchou"?

6   Born Claire Elise Boucher, which Canadian musician released her fourth studio album, *Art Angels*, in 2015?

7   Cannabis' psychoactive constituent THC is known by what full name?

8   Which German won the 1920 Nobel Prize in chemistry for his statement of the third law of thermodynamics?

9   Which explorer dictated *Il milione* to his cellmate Rustichello da Pisa?

10 In 1991, the Munich currency printer Giesecke & Devrient produced the first of which cards?

11 Which US TV drama centres on the crisis management firm Olivia Pope & Associates?

12 Blanche is the actual name of the white cat in which David Hockney painting?

13 Mistress Overdone, Pompey, Elbow and Abhorson the executioner are characters in which Shakespeare play?

14 HMS *Vanguard* was which rear admiral's flagship at the 1798 Battle of the Nile?

15 Launched in 1988, Buran was the first and only Soviet what?

16 Built by CERN, what is the world's largest and most powerful particle accelerator?

17 The lightest halogen, which pale yellow gas is the most reactive chemical element?

18 Nicknamed 'Kid Poker', which Canadian is the highest earning live tournament poker player of all time?

19 Which world title was won by East Germany's Detlef Michel and the Finns, Seppo Räty and Kimmo Kinnunen?

20 Which Aztec god of music and dance is pictured?

Answers to QUIZ 81 – General Knowledge

1	Camille Pissarro	13	Lead poisoning
2	Xiaomi	14	Cappuccino – named by the Viennese from the Capuchin order
3	Eddy Mitchell		
4	Elena Ferrante		
5	Archimedes	15	Opal
6	Gurdwaras or Sikh places of worship	16	*Blade Runner*
		17	Edward Weston
7	Terence Conran	18	Bungee jumping – the Kawarau Bridge Bungy is in New Zealand
8	Benjamin Britten		
9	Jumbo		
10	*Matilda*	19	Dawn Fraser (1956, 1960, 1964)
11	Hydrogen	20	Le Corbusier – it is the chapel of Notre Dame du Haut, Ronchamp
12	Into the Empire State Building		

QUIZ 83 – Popular Music

1   *Master of Reality* (1971) was which English rock band's first top 10 album in the US?

2   Which member of The Slits wrote the memoir *Clothes, Clothes, Clothes. Music, Music, Music. Boys, Boys, Boys.*?

3   Which English band released the 2015 debut album *My Love is Cool*?

4   Which US singer had a no.2 hit with her single *Heartbreaker* in 1982?

5   Formed in 1981 by Nicolas Sirkis and Dominique Nicolas, which French band's 2002 album *Paradize* included the chart-topper *J'ai demandé à la lune*?

6   Which group's debut album features the songs *VCR*, *Crystalised* and *Islands*?

7   Whose albums include *Blue*, *The Hissing of Summer Lawns* and *Hejira*?

8   In a 1968 no.1 single, which "saviour of the human race ... invented medicinal compound"?

9   Which song begins: "When Britain first, at Heaven's command, / Arose from out the azure main"?

10 Who had his second no.1 with *Poor Me* in 1960?

11 Which 17-year-old Canadian singer-songwriter had a 2016 no.1 with *Stitches*?

12 The family business D'Addario is best known for making which musical equipment?

13 Which US band released the "rural hippie anthem" *Going Up the Country* (1968)?

14 In a Beatles song, who "picks up the rice in a church where a wedding has been"?

15 *Girl in a Band* is a 2015 memoir by which former Sonic Youth member?

16 Which Bee Gees song's 103 beats per minute is the perfect rhythm for performing CPR?

17 Which British rock band had a US no.1 single with *Here I Go Again* in 1987?

18 Which former *Loose Women* panellist is the mother of The 1975 lead singer Matt Healy?

19 Which South African-born artist painted the 2011 Amy Winehouse portrait *Amy-Blue*?

20 Which Public Enemy member is pictured?

Answers to QUIZ 82 – General Knowledge

1 Ardal O'Hanlon
2 Alex Salmond
3 Blue Whale
4 Wear it – it is a traditional full-length Arabian garment for men
5 Claude Debussy
6 Grimes
7 Tetrahydrocannabinol
8 Walther Nernst
9 Marco Polo
10 SIM card (as in 'subscriber identity module')
11 *Scandal*
12 *Mr and Mrs Clark and Percy*
13 *Measure for Measure*
14 Sir Horatio Nelson
15 Space shuttle
16 Large Hadron Collider (LHC)
17 Fluorine
18 Daniel Negreanu – with over $29m in prize money
19 Men's javelin – in 1983, 1987, 1991
20 Xochipilli

1   Sable is the heraldic term for which colour?

2   Thomas Young's double-slit experiment disproved which scientist's corpuscular theory of light?

3   Which Egyptian was the first Muslim Nobel laureate?

4   Which comedy legend wrote the 1963 comic novel *Puckoon*?

5   Chopin referred to which work, dedicated to the Countess Delfina Potocka, as *The Little Dog Waltz*?

6   The Austrian, Erwin Perzy I, invented which type of transparent sphere by accident in 1900?

7   Which TV family lives at 742 Evergreen Terrace?

8   Which southern province of Spain is Europe's driest region?

9   Also known for his 1920 opera *Die tote Stadt*, which Brno-born composer won an Oscar for his score to *The Adventures of Robin Hood* (1938)?

10 The world's largest book stands upright, set in stone, in the grounds of the Kuthodaw Pagoda in which Burmese city?

11 By what grisly name is titan arum (*Amorphophallus titanum*), the flowering plant with the largest unbranched inflorescence in the world, also known?

12 The photographer Rankin and Jefferson Hack founded which style magazine in 1991?

13 What is the longest motorway in the UK?

14 The Pythian Games were held in honour of which Greek god?

15 Chicago's Rydell High School is the setting for which musical?

16 *Dangerous Lady* (1992) was which crime writer's first published novel?

17 "The relentless building block video puzzle" was a slogan used for which game?

18 Copse is the first corner on which racing circuit?

19 Launched in 1997, the perfume Bolero was endorsed by which Argentine tennis star?

20 Name the city from the pictured skyline?

Answers to QUIZ 83 – Popular Music

1	Black Sabbath	**12**	Strings, primarily for guitars
2	Viv Albertine		
3	Wolf Alice	**13**	Canned Heat
4	Dionne Warwick	**14**	Eleanor Rigby
5	Indochine	**15**	Kim Gordon
6	The xx (from the album *XX*)	**16**	*Stayin' Alive*
7	Joni Mitchell	**17**	Whitesnake
8	*Lily the Pink* (by The Scaffold)	**18**	Denise Welch
9	*Rule, Britannia!*	**19**	Marlene Dumas
10	Adam Faith	**20**	Flavor Flav (born William Jonathan Drayton Jr.)
11	Shawn Mendes		

1   The city of Swakopmund is a beach resort in which African country?

2   Which English jazz musician released the 1986 debut album *Journey to the Urge Within*?

3   Introduced in 1965, which geometric drawing toy was invented by the engineer Denys Fisher?

4   Horace Walpole's tortoiseshell tabby Selima inspired which 1748 Thomas Gray poem?

5   The Khan Shatyr in Astana, Kazakhstan has been billed as the world's biggest type of what structure?

6   Who wrote, directed and starred in the sci-fi films *Primer* and *Upstream Color*?

7   Which energy drink was originally manufactured in 1927 by Newcastle chemist William Owen?

8   The 311 and 353 or Knight were models made by which East German carmaker?

9   Appearing in numerous TV shows, Finder-Spyder is a fictional brand of what?

10 Which 1884 Tchaikovsky opera was inspired by Alexander Pushkin's poem *Poltava*?

11 Which 1964 novel by Gore Vidal is about a Roman emperor and nephew of Constantine I?

12 Which grilled marinated beef dish derives its name from the Korean for 'fire meat'?

13 Which US state was named in honour of Charles I's queen consort?

14 Who duetted with George Michael on the 1987 no.1 *I Knew You Were Waiting (for Me)*?

15 Which country's national oil company is popularly known as Aramco?

16 Sharing his name with a planet, which Greek god was the father of the Titans?

17 Which London Zoo gorilla (1946–78) inspired an Ian Botham nickname?

18 Which duo won their first Ice Dancing world title in 1981?

19 Which US golfer gives his name to a lemonade-iced tea beverage?

20 Which Chicago sculpture is pictured?

Francesca Moscatelli / Shutterstock.com

Answers to QUIZ 84 – General Knowledge

1 Black

2 Isaac Newton

3 Anwar al-Sadat – who won the 1978 peace prize

4 Spike Milligan

5 *Minute Waltz* or *Waltz in D-flat major*

6 Snow globe

7 The Simpsons

8 Almería

9 Erich Wolfgang Korngold

10 Mandalay

11 Corpse flower or corpse plant – because it smells like a rotting animal

12 *Dazed & Confused*, now known as *Dazed*

13 M6

14 Apollo

15 *Grease*

16 Martina Cole

17 *Tetris*

18 Silverstone

19 Gabriela Sabatini

20 Hong Kong

1 Which rodent is by far the most commonly genetically altered mammal in scientific research?

2 *Turritopsis dohrnii* is a species of biologically immortal what?

3 Which American ornithologist wrote *Birds of the West Indies* (1936)?

4 What is the largest toothed animal in the world?

5 Found on the islands of Rinca, Flores, Gili, Motang and Padar, what is the largest living species of lizard?

6 Which animal features on Greenland's coat of arms?

7 The longest venomous snake indigenous to the African continent, what is the fastest land snake?

8 What is the largest living species of reptile?

9 Which type of bird features on the national flag of Zambia?

10 Up to 100 Garra Rufa or doctor fish are used in which spa treatment?

11 The Amur, Malayan and South China are living subspecies of which big cat?

12 Which creatures have the largest eyes documented in the animal kingdom?

13 Which Tasmanian novelist wrote *Gould's Book of Fish* (2001)?

14 A Dorkie is a cross between a dachshund and which other dog breed?

15 Which bird has the Latin name *Hirundo rustica*?

16 The coat of arms of the Bahamas features a flamingo and which silvery blue fish?

17 The Baldwin is a rare and hairless breed of which pet rodent?

18 Which bird features on the head badge of Raleigh Bicycles?

19 Which reptile is the largest living chelonian?

20 Which small mammal with a toxic bite is pictured?

Answers to QUIZ 85 – General Knowledge

1 Namibia

2 Courtney Pine

3 Spirograph

4 *Ode on the Death of a Favourite Cat, Drowned in a Tub of Gold Fishes*

5 Tent

6 Shane Carruth

7 Lucozade – originally called Glucozade

8 Wartburg

9 Internet search engine, used in the same way as the fictitious 555 phone number

10 *Mazeppa*

11 *Julian* – about the Roman emperor Julian the Apostate

12 Bulgogi

13 Maryland – after Henrietta Maria of France

14 Aretha Franklin

15 Saudi Arabia

16 Uranus

17 Guy the Gorilla

18 Jayne Torvill & Christopher Dean

19 Arnold Palmer

20 *Cloud Gate* by Anish Kapoor

QUIZ 87 – General Knowledge

1   Which Converse trainer is the biggest selling basketball shoe of all time?

2   What is the most populous city in Oceania?

3   Which Azerbaijani singer (1942–2008) was dubbed the "King of Songs" and the "Soviet Sinatra"?

4   The GRU is which country's largest foreign intelligence agency?

5   Which species of bustard is the world's heaviest flying bird?

6   The tourist resort of Magaluf is on which island?

7   Which animal features in the logo of the drink Jägermeister?

8   The actress Lillie Langtry was the mistress of which king?

9   Luis A. Ferré is credited with saving which Frederic Leighton painting from oblivion?

10 Isla Nublar, a fictional island off Costa Rica's west coast, is the setting for which 1993 film?

11 Which 1937 self-help book by Napoleon Hill has sold over 70 million copies?

12 Which chemical compound is also known as caustic soda or lye?

13 Which company made the Panhead and the Shovelhead motorcycle engines?

14 Fronted by Dan Smith, which band had a 2013 hit single with *Pompeii*?

15 Jacques de Molay was the last Grand Master of which religious military order?

16 Which cosmetics brand, founded in 1834, uses the motto "Get the London Look"?

17 Which former England cricket captain published *The Art of Captaincy* (1985)?

18 *Tam Samson's Elegy* by Robert Burns is about a player of which winter sport?

19 Wide receiver Odell Beckham Jr. debuted for which NFL team in 2014?

20 Name the pictured dinosaur –

Answers to QUIZ 86 – Wildlife

1 House mouse (*Mus musculus*)
2 Jellyfish
3 James Bond
4 Sperm whale or cachalot (*Physeter macrocephalus*)
5 Komodo dragon or Komodo monitor (*Varanus komodoensis*)
6 Polar bear (*Ursus maritimus*)
7 Black mamba (*Dendroaspis polylepis*)
8 Saltwater crocodile or estuarine crocodile (*Crocodylus porosus*)
9 [An orange-coloured] Eagle

10 Fish pedicure – the fish eat the dead skin (or exfoliate) to leave the feet soft and refreshed
11 Tiger
12 Giant and Colossal squid
13 Richard Flanagan
14 Yorkshire terrier
15 Swallow or barn swallow
16 Marlin
17 Guinea pig or cavy
18 Heron
19 Leatherback sea turtle or lute turtle or leathery turtle (*Dermochelys coriacea*)
20 Slow loris (genus *Nycticebus*)

1   Which whale, the second largest on the planet, is known as the "greyhound of the sea"?

2   First banded in 1956 by Chandler Robbins, Wisdom is the world's oldest known wild bird. What albatross species is she?

3   Created by J.M. Barrie, who are Tootles, Nibs, Slightly, Curly and the Twins?

4   Royal jelly is a larval food secreted by which creatures?

5   Born Karl Anderson, Jr, which American became the first women's ready-to-wear designer for Céline in 1997?

6   The 1796 Battle of Montenotte was which man's first victory in command of an army?

7   Which Dutch violinist and conductor created the Johann Strauss Orchestra in 1987?

8   The former British soldier Jonathan Pine is the title character in which 1993 John le Carré novel?

9   Which early 1970s backing band featured Mick Ronson, Trevor Bolder and Mick Woodmansey?

10 The late comedy writer Harris Wittels coined which word for "The Art of False Modesty"?

11 Which English scientist discovered the principle of electromagnetic induction in 1831?

12 In 1816, Bussa led the largest slave revolt in which Caribbean island's history?

13 Which title star of the 2015 film *Cinderella* played Lady Rose Aldridge in *Downton Abbey*?

14 Recorded by Murray Head in 1984, the song *One Night in Bangkok* features in which musical?

15 Which US psychologist wrote the 2004 book *The Paradox of Choice: Why More is Less*?

16 Which acclaimed video game sequel of 2015 is subtitled *The Phantom Pain*?

17 Which retired cricketer hosted the pub games TV show *The Indoor League* (1973–78)?

18 Used in Sky Sports' darts coverage, *Chase the Sun* was a 2001 hit for which Italian dance act?

19 Which golfer won four of his six majors with the caddie Fanny Sunesson?

20 Name the "Stealth Fighter" in the picture –

Answers to QUIZ 87 – General Knowledge

1	Chuck Taylor All-Stars	12	Sodium hydroxide (NaOH)
2	Sydney, Australia	13	Harley-Davidson
3	Muslim Magomayev	14	Bastille
4	Russia	15	Knights Templar or Poor
5	Kori bustard		Knights of Christ and of the
6	Majorca		Temple of Solomon
7	Stag	16	Rimmel
8	Edward VII	17	Mike Brearley
9	*Flaming June*	18	Curling
10	*Jurassic Park*	19	New York Giants
11	*Think and Grow Rich*	20	Spinosaurus

QUIZ 89 – Food & Drink

1 The full name of which dip in Arabic means 'chickpeas with tahini'?

2 Which malted cereal grain is used to make malt whisky?

3 A *molinillo* is a Mexican whisk used to froth which common drink?

4 Sam Panopoulos claims to have invented which pizza at the Satellite Restaurant in Chatham, Ontario, in 1962?

5 The cheese spread, cervelle de canut, is a speciality of which French city?

6 Which US movie star began the company, Casamigos Tequila, with Rande Gerbe and Mike Meldman?

7 What does the French cookery term *omelette baveuse* mean in English?

8 The name of which espresso coffee drink with a dash of steamed milk is the Italian word for 'stained'?

9 Le Train Bleu is a famous restaurant located in which Paris station?

10 Which white rum, pineapple juice, grenadine and maraschino liqueur cocktail is named after a silent film star?

11 The rockstar-haired chef Michael O'Hare won a Michelin star for which highly original Leeds restaurant in its first year?

12 Made famous by chef Louis Paquet, which chicken pasta dish is named after an Italian coloratura soprano (1871–1940)?

13 Which champagne house – the world's largest – launched Dom Pérignon as a prestige cuvée in 1936?

14 *Gule ærter* is the Danish name for which soup?

15 Loose-leaf, iceberg, stem, oilseed and summer crisp are types of what?

16 A traditional brew of Tanzania's Chagga people, Mbege is beer made from which fruit?

17 Often linked with Chairman Mao, what is the Chinese meat dish, *hong shao rou*?

18 The Sicilian pastry tubes, cannoli, are usually filled with which cheese?

19 Eaten in many Asian countries, what type of dish is congee?

20 Which British pudding is pictured?

Answers to QUIZ 88 – General Knowledge

1   Fin whale or finback whale (*Balaenoptera physalus*)
2   Laysan albatross (*Phoebastria immutabilis*)
3   The Lost Boys
4   Worker honeybees
5   Michael Kors
6   Napoleon Bonaparte
7   André Rieu
8   *The Night Manager*
9   The Spiders from Mars – Ziggy Stardust aka David Bowie's backing band
10 Humblebrag
11 Michael Faraday
12 Barbados
13 Lily James
14 *Chess*
15 Barry Schwartz
16 *Metal Gear Solid* V
17 Fred Trueman
18 Planet Funk
19 Nick Faldo
20 F-117 Nighthawk

QUIZ 90 – General Knowledge

1   Pediophobia is the fear of which toys?

2   Which South African president ordered Nelson Mandela's release from prison?

3   Which Steven Spielberg film is based on the story of conman Frank Abagnale Jr.?

4   Which English dramatist (b.1968) wrote the plays *No Boys Cricket Club*, *Sing Yer Heart Out for the Lads* and *Sucker Punch*?

5   In 1987, Robert Brozin and Fernando Duarte founded which Mozambican-Portuguese-themed restaurant chain in the Johannesburg suburb Rosettenville?

6   Mark Billingham introduced which Detective Inspector, played on TV by David Morrissey, in the 2001 novel *Sleepyhead*?

7   Which Flemish artist painted the 24-picture *Marie de' Médici* cycle?

8   Which academic press is the world's oldest printer and publisher?

9   Trinidad Turn, Orchid Turn and Balboa Reach are points on which canal?

10   Vincenzo Bellini's final opera *I Puritani* is set during which war?

11   Pigeon drop, Pig in a poke and the Spanish Prisoner are types of what?

12   The "Venice of the Pacific", Nan Madol is a ruined city in which country?

13   Outperforming spider silk, what is the strongest biological material ever tested?

14   Which 1857 symphony by Franz Liszt was inspired by Goethe's namesake drama?

15   Corresponding to a medicine man, the *angakkuq* is a spiritual figure among which people?

16 Sir Henry Bessemer gave his name to a process for the manufacture of which alloy?

17 Which former NASA roboticist began the webcomic *xkcd* in 2005?

18 Which England bowler (1865–1901) holds the record for lowest strike rate in all Test history?

19 Who won the 1989 Tour de France by just eight seconds from Laurent Fignon?

20 Name the bombard gun in the picture –

Answers to QUIZ 89 – Food & Drink

1   Hummus – from *ḥummuṣ bi ṭaḥīna*
2   Barley
3   Hot chocolate
4   Hawaiian pizza (with ham and pineapple)
5   Lyon
6   George Clooney
7   Runny omelette
8   Macchiato
9   Gare de Lyon
10 Mary Pickford
11 The Man Behind the Curtain
12 Chicken Tetrazzini – named after Luisa Tetrazzini
13 Moët & Chandon
14 Split-pea soup
15 Lettuce
16 Banana
17 Braised pork belly or 'red-braised pork'
18 Ricotta
19 Rice porridge
20 Spotted dick

QUIZ 91 – General Knowledge

1 In the 1990s, the conman Alan Conway passed himself off as which film director?

2 Which 1983 Wham! music video was filmed at Pikes Hotel in Ibiza?

3 Ernest Hemingway wrote that "all modern American literature" comes from which book?

4 In 2013, who began playing Mick Carter in *EastEnders*?

5 Jeanne Hébuterne was the common-law wife of which Italian artist (1884–1920)?

6 In 1865, the first ascent of which mountain cost the lives of four alpinists?

7 Which Russian composed the piano fantasy *Islamey* and symphonic poem *Tamara*?

8 Which song was composed in 1893 as *Good Morning to All*?

9 Lope de Vega's epic poem *La Dragontea* is about which Elizabethan sailor?

10 What did an Ancient Greek woman do with a peplos and a himation?

11 Which industry in France was devastated by the pest, phylloxera, in the 1870s?

12 Invented by Bob Frankston and Dan Bricklin, VisiCalc was the first electronic what?

13 Which Russian-born US photographer published *A Vanished World* in 1983?

14 In 910, William I, Duke of Aquitaine, founded which Benedictine abbey in Burgundy?

15 Which US actor-comedian and star of *The Hangover* movies hosts the internet comedy series *Between Two Ferns*?

16 The 'Rice Portrait' is a disputed likeness of which author in her youth?

17 Sir Eric Drummond (1876–1951) was which organisation's first Secretary General?

18 Which horse won the Cheltenham Gold Cup in 1989?

19 Golfer Ian Poulter was given which nickname because he always delivers?

20 What is the pictured hat style?

Answers to QUIZ 90 – General Knowledge

1 Dolls
2 F. W. de Klerk
3 *Catch Me If You Can*
4 Roy Williams
5 Nando's
6 Tom Thorne
7 Sir Peter Paul Rubens
8 Cambridge University Press
9 Panama Canal
10 English Civil War
11 Confidence tricks
12 Federated States of Micronesia
13 Limpets' teeth
14 *Faust Symphony*
15 The Inuit – indigenous peoples of Greenland, Canada and Alaska
16 Steel
17 Randall Munroe
18 George Lohmann
19 Greg LeMond
20 Mons Meg – located at Edinburgh Castle

1   The PIDE was which European country's secret police force?

2   Which Chinese lager is the best-selling beer brand in the world?

3   Which "High Priest of Soul" released the 1962 album *Modern Sounds in Country and Western Music*?

4   What is the surname of the unruly Wolverhampton-based family in the sitcom *Raised by Wolves*?

5   Which small strait in the Norwegian municipality of Bodø has the world's strongest tidal current?

6   Who is the only monarch to be born and die at Buckingham Palace?

7   What is the oldest university in the English-speaking world?

8   Monica Ali's 2011 novel *Untold Story* imagines that which princess faked her own death?

9   Which dictator, who died in Saudi Arabia in 2003, said: "I don't like human flesh – it's too salty for me"?

10 The 5p coin is legal tender for amounts up to how many pounds?

11 Ludovic Kennedy married which Scottish ballet dancer in 1950?

12 PC George Dixon (played by Jack Warner) was shot by a young Dirk Bogarde (playing "hardened" criminal Tom Riley) in which 1950 film?

13 Charles Babbage, Anthony Trollope, Wilkie Collins, Isambard Kingdom Brunel and Harold Pinter are buried in which London cemetery?

14 Which Venetian painted *Laura*, *The Three Philosophers* and *The Tempest*?

15 What did James I call "a custome lothesome to the eye [and] hatefull to the Nose"?

16 Which elephant-headed Hindu god is the son of Shiva and Parvati?

17 Which Australian woman won a record 62 Grand Slam tennis titles?

18 "Ring Taw" is the version of which game played at its British and World Championship?

19 Contested every four years, what type of race is the Route du Rhum?

20 Which brutal dictator, who seized power in the Gambia in 1994, is pictured?

Answers to QUIZ 91 – General Knowledge

1 Stanley Kubrick
2 *Club Tropicana*
3 *Adventures of Huckleberry Finn* by Mark Twain
4 Danny Dyer
5 Amedeo Modigliani
6 The Matterhorn
7 Mily Balakirev
8 *Happy Birthday* – by sisters Patty Smith Hill and Mildred Hill
9 Sir Francis Drake
10 Wear them – they are a body length garment and a cloak
11 Wine industry
12 Spreadsheet (or spreadsheet computer program)
13 Roman Vishniac
14 Cluny Abbey
15 Zach Galifianakis
16 Jane Austen
17 League of Nations
18 Desert Orchid
19 "The Postman"
20 Homburg

1   Which "human-powered search engine" is named after the Hawaiian word for 'thank you'?

2   Pietro Torrigiano (1472–1528) famously broke which fellow artist's nose in a fight?

3   Timothy Treadwell is the tragic subject of which 2005 Werner Herzog documentary?

4   Matt Cardle's no.1 hit *When We Collide* adapted which Biffy Clyro song?

5   The Jericho Parlour, Islip Chapel and Jerusalem Chamber are found where?

6   Which 2007 video game casts bartender Desmond Miles as an Arabic fighter in 1191?

7   Illustrator Peggy Fortnum was the very first person to draw which bear?

8   The pygmy chimpanzee (*Pan paniscus*) is known by what common name?

9   The Tuol Sleng Genocide Museum, once used as the notorious Security Prison 21 (S-21), is in which country?

10 The Italian company Perugina is famed for which hazelnut-filled chocolate 'kisses'?

11 Bright's disease affects which of the organs in the human body?

12 Complete the Dorothy Parker quote: "The only 'ism' Hollywood believes in is..."?

13 A *bouchon* is a type of traditional bistro found in which French city?

14 Which French fashion house launched the perfume Arpège in 1927?

15 In physics, which letter represents the Boltzmann constant?

16 Which Shakespeare character says: "I am constant as the northern star"?

17 Which Tudor poet wrote the line: "These bloody days have broken my heart"?

18 Which 1983 world darts champion was nicknamed "The Milky Bar Kid"?

19 What is the Finnish sport of *eukonkanto*?

20 Which mythical couple is depicted in the picture?

Luxerendering / Shutterstock.com

Answers to QUIZ 92 – General Knowledge

1   Portugal
2   Snow beer
3   Ray Charles
4   Garry
5   Saltstraumen
6   Edward VII
7   University of Oxford
8   Princess Diana
9   Idi Amin
10 £5
11 Moira Shearer
12 *The Blue Lamp* – Warner's character was resurrected in

1955 for the TV series *Dixon of Dock Green*
13 Kensal Green Cemetery
14 Giorgione
15 Smoking
16 Ganesh
17 Margaret Court (maiden name Smith)
18 Marbles
19 Transatlantic single-handed yacht race
20 Yahya Jammeh

QUIZ 94 – Theatre

1   Hugh Whitemore's play *Breaking the Code* centres on which mathematician?

2   Which 1947 musical introduced the song *How Are Things in Glocca Morra?*?

3   Which dramatist wrote the screenplay *Up Against It* for The Beatles in 1967?

4   Who wrote the musicals *Fifty Million Frenchmen*, *Can-Can* and *Gay Divorce*?

5   Which Harold Pinter play centres on the enigmatic drifter Davies?

6   The US oilman Henry Clay Folger, Jr obsessively acquired 82 copies of what?

7   What did George Bernard Shaw call "a man who leaves no turn unstoned"?

8   Which theatre awards were known as the Urnies in their early years?

9   Which Kander & Ebb musical features the songs *Willkommen*, *Tomorrow Belongs To Me* and *Maybe This Time*?

10 *Zanni* is a stock servant character in which Italian theatre tradition?

11 The evil Mouse King features in which 1892 ballet, described by Tchaikovsky as "rather boring" and "infinitely worse than *Sleeping Beauty*"?

12 *Buried Child* won which playwright a 1979 Pulitzer Prize?

13 Mark Rylance became which London theatre's first Artistic Director in 1995?

14 In the play *The Tempest*, who sings 'Where the bees suck, there suck I'?

15 The Teatro degli Arcimboldi is a theatre and opera house in which city?

16 Who is Kevin Spacey's successor as artistic director of The Old Vic theatre?

17 King Claudius, Polonius and Ophelia are characters in which Tom Stoppard play?

18 Which German dramatist wrote the plays *The Deputy* (1963) and *Alan Turing* (1987)?

19 Who wrote the 1969 play *Christie in Love* about the serial killer John Christie?

20 Name the pictured British playwright –

Answers to QUIZ 93 – General Knowledge

1	Mahalo.com	**10**	*Baci*
2	Michelangelo	**11**	Kidneys
3	*Grizzly Man*	**12**	"plagiarism"
4	*Many of Horror*	**13**	Lyon
5	Westminster Abbey	**14**	Lanvin
6	*Assassin's Creed*	**15**	*k*
7	Paddington Bear	**16**	Julius Caesar
8	Mars	**17**	Sir Thomas Wyatt, the Elder
9	Cambodia – located in Phnom Penh, Tuol Seng means 'Hill of the Poisonous Trees' or 'Strychnine Hill'	**18**	Keith Deller
		19	Wife carrying
		20	Apollo and Daphne – in the sculpture by Gian Lorenzo Bernini

1   In 1865, the French wine merchant Daniel Nicols opened which Regent Street venue?

2   Beginning 66 million years ago, what is the current geological era?

3   The Houthi rebellion began in which country in 2004?

4   The fictional title setting of the film *Brokeback Mountain* is in which US state?

5   In 1975, copywriter Gary Dahl got the idea for which fad "pet"?

6   Who succeeded Leonid Brezhnev as leader of the USSR?

7   Which Australian rock band released the 1987 album *Diesel and Dust*?

8   What is the largest Baroque fountain in Rome?

9   Which region in South Australia includes the wineries Wolf Blass, Yalumba and Seppelt?

10 "We open governments" is the slogan of which non-profit organisation?

11 Which German artist built the *Black Room Cycle* installation (1958), the first artwork to integrate a TV set?

12 Nev Shulman and Max Joseph investigate dodgy online relationships in which MTV show?

13 Bangkok's Damnoen Saduak is said to be the most famous example of which market?

14 The London skyscraper at 20 Fenchurch Street is known by which nickname?

15 The R.F. Delderfield play *The Bull Boys* inspired which *Carry On* film?

16 Winkie, Gillikin, Munchkin and Quadling are the four countries that form which land?

17 Which national board game of India derives its name from the Hindi for 'twenty-five'?

18 Which cricketer wrote the 1967 children's novel *Bonaventure and the Flashing Blade*?

19 Which Canadian snooker player was dubbed "the Rhett Butler of the green baize"?

20 What desk toy is seen in the picture?

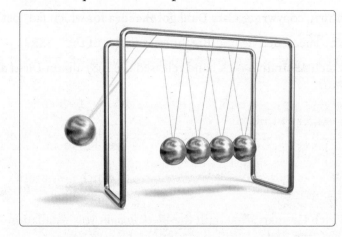

Answers to QUIZ 94 – Theatre

1	Alan Turing	11	*The Nutcracker*
2	*Finian's Rainbow*	12	Sam Shepard
3	Joe Orton	13	Shakespeare's Globe
4	Cole Porter	14	Ariel
5	*The Caretaker*	15	Milan
6	The 1623 Shakespeare *First Folio*	16	Matthew Warchus
7	A drama critic	17	*Rosencrantz and Guildenstern are Dead*
8	Laurence Olivier Awards	18	Rolf Hochhuth
9	*Cabaret*	19	Howard Brenton
10	Commedia dell'arte	20	John Osborne

1   Which Wilfred Owen poem features the line "I am the enemy you killed, my friend"?

2   Launched in 1797, which US heavy frigate is the world's oldest commissioned naval vessel afloat?

3   What is the world's largest independent conservation organisation?

4   What is the only country that borders the Gambia?

5   Which US pop rock band was formed in 1994 as Kara's Flowers?

6   The Egyptian god of creation Khnum was usually depicted with which animal's head?

7   John Cornell played Strop, the dim sidekick of which Australian comedian?

8   Using stones from his round, the postman Ferdinand Cheval spent 33 years creating which building?

9   Which British artist's 1993 work *Pop* is a waxwork of himself as Sid Vicious?

10   Who was the first Pope from a Slavic country?

11   Who is the subject of Joyce Carol Oates' historical novel *Blonde*?

12   Brian Acton and Jan Koum founded which instant messaging app for smartphones?

13   Which duck-billed dinosaurs derive their name from the Greek word for 'thick' or 'bulky'?

14   In the US TV show *House of Cards*, Frank Underwood was a congressman from which state?

15   Since 1889, the US company Lyon & Healy has produced which string instruments?

16   Who succeeded his father Genghis Khan as the Great Khan of the Mongol Empire?

17 Which 2012 film centres on the a cappella singing group, The Barden Bellas?

18 New Zealand's four-time Wimbledon singles champion, Anthony Wilding, died in which conflict?

19 What did Ashis Nandy say was an Indian game that was "accidentally discovered by the English"?

20 Located on the Columbia River, what is the pictured dam?

Answers to QUIZ 95 – General Knowledge

1 Café Royal
2 Cenozoic Era
3 Yemen
4 Wyoming
5 Pet Rock
6 Yuri Andropov
7 Midnight Oil
8 Trevi Fountain
9 Barossa Valley
10 WikiLeaks
11 Wolf Vostell
12 *Catfish: The TV Show*

13 Floating market
14 "The Walkie-Talkie"
15 *Carry On Sergeant*
16 Land of Oz – introduced in *The Wonderful Wizard of Oz* by L. Frank Baum
17 Pachisi – from *pachis*
18 Gary Sobers
19 Cliff Thorburn
20 Newton's cradle or Newton's balls

QUIZ 97 – Sciences

1 Baking soda is known by what other name?

2 Host of the 2014 TV series *Cosmos*, which US astrophysicist is director of the Hayden Planetarium?

3 What is the most abundant element in the Earth's crust?

4 What was the farthest of the planets known to ancient observers?

5 The extinct 3m-tall *Gigantopithecus blacki* was the largest ever type of which creature?

6 The Linnean Society of London awards the Darwin-Wallace Medal for work in which field?

7 Which SI derived unit of magnetic flux density is named after a Serbian-American inventor?

8 *How the Mind Works* and *The Stuff of Thought* are books by which Harvard psychologist?

9 Including DNA and RNA, which macromolecules are essential for all known forms of life?

10 *I Have Landed* (2002) was the 10th and final essay collection by which US palaeontologist?

11 The structure of which aromatic molecule came to August Kekulé in a dream?

12 Consisting of a mass of hyphae, what is the vegetative part of a fungus called?

13 The term 'jade' is applied to jadeite and which other metamorphic rock?

14 Which US mathematician shared the 2015 Abel Prize with Louis Nirenberg for work in the field of geometric analysis?

15 T cells mature within which organ of the immune system?

16 Pertussis is the medical name for which disease?

17 The biochemist Albert Szent-Györgyi (1893–1986) is credited with discovering which vitamin?

18 The Hall–Héroult process is used for smelting which metal?

19 Which antibiotic was first isolated by Albert Schatz on October 19, 1943?

20 Name the pictured Nobel prize-winning scientists –

Answers to QUIZ 96 – General Knowledge

1 *Strange Meeting*
2 USS *Constitution*
3 World Wide Fund for Nature or WWF
4 Senegal
5 Maroon 5
6 Ram
7 Paul Hogan
8 Le Palais idéal in Hauterives, France
9 Gavin Turk
10 Saint John Paul II
11 Marilyn Monroe
12 WhatsApp
13 Hadrosaurids or hadrosaurs
14 South Carolina
15 Harps
16 Ögedei Khan
17 *Pitch Perfect*
18 World War One
19 Cricket
20 Grand Coulee Dam

1 Which female giant panda died at London Zoo in July 1972?

2 The Riga-born inventor Walter Zapp created which 8x11mm spy camera?

3 The philosopher A.J. Ayer was the stepfather of which TV chef?

4 Former Major Roy Bates declared which fortress-island an independent state?

5 Reinhold Wolff and Walter Palmers founded which Bregenz-based luxury hosiery brand in 1950?

6 Danish prime minister Birgitte Nyborg was the heroine of which TV drama?

7 Mohammed V International Airport serves which African city?

8 Archdeacon Claude Frollo is the villain in which 1831 novel?

9 Yap, Chuuk, Pohnpei and Kosrae form the Federated States of where?

10 *Els Segadors* ("The Reapers") is the official anthem of which region?

11 Which Japanese fashion designer created the "Flying Saucer" dress (1994)?

12 *Some Voices* (1994) and *Blue/Orange* (2000) are plays by which English dramatist?

13 Who began his biography of Lyndon B. Johnson with *The Path to Power* (1982)?

14 Who founded the White Oak Dance Project with Mark Morris in 1990?

15 Said to be the world's steepest street, Baldwin Street is in which New Zealand city?

16 Named after a Peruvian physician, Monge's disease is also called CMS, which stands for what?

17 Brad Pitt played which Oakland A's general manager in the film *Moneyball*?

18 In winter sports, military officer Olaf Rye is known as the first what?

19 Which Hungarian striker top scored at the 1954 World Cup with 11 goals?

20 Name the pictured cat breed –

Answers to QUIZ 97 – Sciences

1 Sodium bicarbonate or sodium hydrogen carbonate
2 Neil deGrasse Tyson
3 Oxygen
4 Saturn
5 Ape
6 Evolutionary biology
7 Tesla – named after Nikola Tesla
8 Steven Pinker
9 Nucleic acids
10 Stephen Jay Gould
11 Benzene
12 Mycelium
13 Nephrite
14 John Forbes Nash, Jr – of *A Beautiful Mind* fame
15 Thymus
16 Whooping cough
17 Vitamin C
18 Aluminium
19 Streptomycin – the first antibiotic remedy for tuberculosis
20 James Watson and Francis Crick – the discoverers of the structure of DNA

QUIZ 99 – Classical Music

1 Which Spanish composer is best known for his 1923 zarzuela *Doña Francisquita*?

2 Chopin's Piano Sonata No.2 in B-flat minor is known by which popular name?

3 Which Polish composer wrote the 1969 opera *The Devils of Loudun*?

4 Which Italian composed the operas *Salvatore Giuliano* (1986) and *Charlotte Corday* (1989)?

5 Which Puccini opera centres on Magda, the mistress of the elderly Rambaldo?

6 Mozart's 31st Symphony is nicknamed after which capital city?

7 Started in 1822, only a scherzo and two movements survive of which Schubert symphony?

8 *Fisch-Ton-Kan*, *L'étoile* and *Gwendoline* are operas by which French composer?

9 *Clapping Music* (1972) and the *Mallet Quartet* (2009) are works by which US composer?

10 *Intolleranza 1960* and *Prometeo* are operas by which Italian composer (1924–90)?

11 Which Austrian composer (1885–1935) wrote the operas *Wozzeck* and *Lulu*?

12 Who composed the oratorios *Saul* (1739) and *Hercules* (1744)?

13 The Portuguese musician Guilhermina Suggia (1885–1950) was a noted soloist on which instrument?

14 The cellist Pablo Casals was discovered playing in a café trio by which Spanish composer of the opera *Henry Clifford*?

15 Berlioz based his opera *Les Troyens* on which Latin epic?

16 Who composed the 1912 tone poem *On Hearing the First Cuckoo in Spring*?

17 Terrence McNally's play *Master Class* centres on which legendary soprano?

18 Which opera star was born Claire Mary Teresa Rawstron in 1944?

19 Which 1900 Elgar oratorio is based on a poem by Cardinal Newman?

20 Name the pictured woodwind instrument –

Answers to QUIZ 98 – General Knowledge

1 Chi-Chi
2 Minox or Minox Riga Model
3 Nigella Lawson – via Ayer's marriage to Vanessa Salmon
4 The Principality of Sealand
5 Wolford
6 *Borgen* – she was played by Sidse Babett Knudsen
7 Casablanca
8 *The Hunchback of Notre-Dame* or *Notre-Dame de Paris* by Victor Hugo
9 Micronesia
10 Catalonia
11 Issey Miyake
12 Joe Penhall
13 Robert Caro
14 Mikhail Baryshnikov
15 Dunedin
16 Chronic mountain sickness
17 Billy Beane
18 Ski jumper
19 Sándor Kocsis
20 Tonkinese

QUIZ 100 – General Knowledge

1   The 2015 play *Fish in the Dark* was which comedian's Broadway debut as an actor and playwright?

2   New Zealand, California, Gibraltar and Egypt are hamlets in which county?

3   An important source of protein for southern Africans, what are mopane worms?

4   A Paris museum dedicated to which French symbolist painter is at 14 rue de la Rochefoucauld?

5   *The Dollar Princess* and *Madame Pompadour* are operettas by which Austrian composer (1873–1925)?

6   Dalmatian molly, rummy-nose tetra and cherry barb are types of what?

7   The process of haematopoiesis (blood cell formation) mostly takes place where?

8   In Shinto, which place is Yomi ('yellow springs')?

9   Ed Bruce sang *Mammas Don't Let Your Babies Grow Up To Be...* what?

10   Which Royal Family member married the former wife of Thomas Troubridge in 1978?

11   Alexander Blok dedicated *Verses About the Beautiful Lady* to Lyuba, the daughter of which chemist?

12   What is the USA's highest and oldest state capital?

13   Which sacred scripture opens with the *Mul Mantra* or *Mool Mantar*?

14   Jules Munshin played the third and oft-forgotten sailor in which musical film?

15   Scottish botanist Robert Fortune is best known for introducing which plants from China to India?

16   In 1941, Lev Landau published a theory that explains superfluidity in liquid what?

17 Billionaire software engineer Harold Finch created The Machine to predict crime in which TV drama?

18 Which recreational activity is central to Frederick Kohner's 1957 novel *Gidget*?

19 In September 1958, which golfer won the national championships of Italy, Spain and Portugal in three consecutive weeks?

20 Name the pictured Italian pastry –

Answers to QUIZ 99 – Classical Music

1 Amadeo Vives
2 The Funeral March
3 Krzysztof Penderecki
4 Lorenzo Ferrero
5 *La Rondine*
6 Paris
7 Unfinished Symphony or Symphony no.8 or Symphony in B Minor
8 Emmanuel Chabrier
9 Steve Reich
10 Luigi Nono
11 Alban Berg
12 George Frideric Handel
13 Cello
14 Isaac Albéniz
15 *The Aeneid* by Virgil
16 Frederick Delius
17 Maria Callas
18 Dame Kiri Te Kanawa
19 *The Dream of Gerontius*
20 Contrabassoon or double bassoon

QUIZ 101 – General Knowledge

1   Who composed the 1902 opera *Adriana Lecouvreur*?

2   The best-selling manga in history, which series follows Monkey D. Luffy and the Straw Hat Pirates?

3   Which German painter (1876–1907) depicted herself pregnant in *Self-Portrait on Her Sixth Wedding Anniversary*?

4   Chrysaor and Pegasus sprang from the blood of which Gorgon when her head was cut off?

5   Jeanne Baret (1740–1807) was the first woman to complete which voyage?

6   Which city features the Valens Aqueduct, Maiden's Tower and Gülhane Park?

7   Founded in Mandello del Lario in 1921, what is the oldest European manufacturer in continuous motorcycle production?

8   Who played the human rights lawyer Gareth Peirce in the 1993 film *In the Name of the Father*?

9   *Ian Fleming's Solo* was the original title of which spy TV show?

10 Which politician's best ever result was in Rotherham in May 1994 when he polled 1,114 votes?

11 Puck is the largest inner moon of which planet?

12 The Taegeuk symbol features in the centre of which national flag?

13 What is the biggest radio station in the UK, with 15.1m listeners every week?

14 The Whig statesman Charles James Fox (1749–1806) was the arch-rival of which prime minister?

15 Amazonas is the largest state by area in which country?

16 Located at St. Pancras, what is the largest public building constructed in the UK in the 20th century?

17 Launched by Toyota in 1997, what is the world's first mass-produced hybrid passenger car?

18 Which motorcycle racer died in 1981, aged 40, after his car collided with a lorry on the A435 in Warwickshire?

19 The first Italian woman to win Olympic gold, Ondina Valla won which athletics event in 1936?

20 Name the punk rock band, formed in Vancouver in 2006, in the image –

Answers to QUIZ 100 – General Knowledge

1 Larry David

2 Buckinghamshire

3 Edible caterpillars of the moth *Gonimbrasia belina*

4 Gustave Moreau

5 Leo Fall

6 Tropical or aquarium fish

7 In the bone marrow

8 The land of the dead or underworld

9 ... *Cowboys*

10 Prince Michael of Kent

11 Dmitri Mendeleev

12 Santa Fe, New Mexico

13 *Guru Granth Sahib* or *Adi Granth* – the scripture that Sikhs treat as a living Guru

14 *On the Town* – the other stars being Gene Kelly and Frank Sinatra

15 Tea plants

16 Helium

17 *Person of Interest*

18 Surfing

19 Peter Alliss

20 Cannoli or cannolo

1   The *Apocalypse* (1498), properly *Apocalypsis cum Figuris* ('Apocalypse with Pictures'), is a series of 15 woodcuts by which German artist?

2   Michelangelo sculpted the *Rebellious Slave*, the *Dying Slave* and *The Genius of Victory* for which pope's tomb?

3   *Double Standard* is a celebrated 1961 photograph of two Standard Oil signs seen through a car windshield. Which late US actor took it?

4   The painter Johannes Vermeer was baptised and buried in which Dutch city?

5   What are the Hen, Cockerel, Mauve, Pansy, Pelican, Rosebud, Swan, Standard Yacht and Steel Military?

6   Which West Point dropout included his anti-Ruskinian 1885 'Ten O'Clock Lecture' in his book *The Gentle Art of Making Enemies* (1890)?

7   Founded in 1811, what is the world's first purpose-built public art gallery?

8   Which 15th century mural is known in Italian as *Il Cenacolo Vinciano*?

9   Lucian Freud's first wife, Kitty Garman, was the daughter of which sculptor?

10 Located next to the Oslo Opera House, the sculpture *She Lies* by Monica Bonvicini is a 3D interpretation of which Caspar David Friedrich painting?

11 Which Italian painted *Still-Life with Partridge and Gauntlets* (1504), the first known example of *trompe-l'œil* since antiquity?

12 Which Futurist painted *Street Light* (1909) and *Dynamism of a Dog on a Leash* (1912), and created the sculpture *Boccioni's Fist* (1915)?

13 Who painted *Fur Traders Descending the Missouri* (1845) and *The Emigration of Daniel Boone* (1851)?

14 Which US artist began his 14-painting series, *The Stations of the Cross: Lema Sabachthani* (1958–66), shortly after he had recovered from a heart attack?

15 *Vision of the Sermon* (1888) by Gauguin references which story in Genesis?

16 In Claude's last painting, which future founder of Alba Longa is about to provoke war with Latium by *Shooting the Stag of Sylvia* (1682)?

17 Who created the photo-triptych *Dropping a Han Dynasty Urn* (1995)?

18 Featuring her in 27 portraits, who married Marie-Hortense Fiquet in 1886?

19 In 2000, Dennis Hwang became "official chief doodler" for which corporation?

20 Which Austrian sculptor's *Guardians of Time* project uses the pictured statues?

Answers to QUIZ 101 – General Knowledge

1 Francesco Cilea
2 *One Piece*
3 Paula Modersohn-Becker
4 Medusa
5 Circumnavigation of the Earth
6 Istanbul
7 Moto Guzzi
8 Emma Thompson
9 *The Man from U.N.C.L.E.*
10 Screaming Lord Sutch or David Edward Sutch or 3rd Earl of Harrow

11 Uranus
12 South Korea or Republic of Korea flag
13 BBC Radio 2
14 William Pitt the Younger
15 Brazil
16 British Library
17 Prius – name derived from the Latin for 'prior to'
18 Mike Hailwood
19 80m hurdles
20 White Lung

1   Which 2014 film is named after a 1973 piece by the jazz composer Hank Levy?

2   Launched in 1977, what is the farthest human-built object from Earth?

3   In 1709, who was discovered by Captain Woodes Rogers living on the island of Juan Fernandez?

4   Which historian wrote *The Great Terror: Stalin's Purges of the Thirties* (1968)?

5   Which Spanish designer created the Knossos scarf (1906) and Delphos gown (1907)?

6   In 1956, the Australian inventor David Warren built the prototype of which recording device?

7   The opening of *Saving Private Ryan* depicts the assault on which D-Day beach?

8   The 2009 album *21st Century Breakdown* is which US band's second rock opera?

9   The baked pasta dish Pastitsio comes from which country?

10 Who did Hamlet describe as "a fellow of infinite jest, of most excellent fancy"?

11 In 1957, Nudie Cohn made which singer's famous $10,000 gold lamé suit?

12 *Mother* (1926) and *Storm over Asia* (1928) are silent films by which Soviet director?

13 The clear sky and deep sea both appear blue because of which "scattering" optical effect?

14 Edward II was allegedly murdered at which castle in 1327?

15 Which cod icefish is sold under the trade names Chilean seabass (in the US) and *légine australe* (in France)?

16 Which British filmmaker directed the documentaries *Senna* and *Amy*?

17 Which Swede took the photo, seen in his book *Café Lehmitz*, that is the cover of Tom Waits' album *Rain Dogs*?

18 Which Austrian-American chess master lost the world championship to Emanuel Lasker in 1894?

19 Which driver won his first British Grand Prix at Aintree in 1955?

20 The leopard species of which lizard is pictured?

Answers to QUIZ 102 – Art

1	Albrecht Dürer	**11**	Jacopo de' Barbari or Jacob Walch
2	Pope Julius II (born Giuliano della Rovere)	**12**	Giacomo Balla
3	Dennis Hopper	**13**	George Caleb Bingham
4	Delft	**14**	Barnett Newman
5	Nine of the Imperial Easter Eggs made by Fabergé for the Russian Tsars	**15**	"Jacob Wrestling with the Angel"
6	James McNeill Whistler	**16**	Ascanius
7	Dulwich Picture Gallery	**17**	Ai Weiwei
8	*The Last Supper* by Leonardo da Vinci	**18**	Paul Cézanne
9	Jacob Epstein	**19**	Google – his drawings are the homepage 'Google Doodles'
10	*The Sea of Ice (Das Eismeer)* aka *The Wreck of Hope* (1823–24)	**20**	Manfred Kielnhofer aka "KILI"

1 Which Australian composed the TV themes for *Steptoe and Son*, *Doctor Who* and *The Prisoner*?

2 J.S. Bach's *Air on a G String* was used in TV adverts for which cigar?

3 The end-bulbs of Krause are receptors in the skin that sense what?

4 The Chinese-made DJI Phantom 3 is a best-selling model of which aerial device?

5 Featuring a tartan ribbon, the world's first colour photograph was made by which Scottish scientist in 1861?

6 Flores, Corvo, Pico, Graciosa and Santa Maria are islands in which archipelago?

7 Adapted into a 1933 film, which musical centres on the dictatorial Broadway director Julian Marsh?

8 The Italian firm Persol specialises in making which items?

9 Which actor's TV roles include Sejanus in *I, Claudius* (1976) and Karla in *Tinker Tailor Soldier Spy* (1979) and *Smiley's People* (1982)?

10 Forfar is famed for which Scottish meat-filled pastie?

11 *Arcadia 1* is a 2007 work by which Op Art pioneer?

12 What did the actor David Garrick call "a damned serious business"?

13 Which US company built the C-5 Galaxy military transport plane?

14 What is the "world's largest manufacturer of daylight fluorescent pigments"?

15 Who launched the "Rather Go Naked Than Wear Fur" campaign in 1991?

16 Which 2002 novel by Italian judge Giancarlo De Cataldo spawned a 2005 Michele Placido film and 2008–2010 TV series directed by Stefano Sollima?

17 Developed in 1902, the Verneuil process or flame fusion method is used to produce what?

18 24-year-old Seattle waiter Rob Angel created which board game?

19 Which baseball star gave the 1939 "luckiest man on the face of this earth" farewell speech?

20 Which pilgrimage site is pictured?

Answers to QUIZ 103 – General Knowledge

1	*Whiplash*	**11**	Elvis Presley
2	Voyager 1	**12**	Vsevolod Pudovkin
3	Alexander Selkirk, the Scottish sailor who inspired Robinson Crusoe	**13**	Rayleigh scattering
		14	Berkeley Castle
4	Robert Conquest	**15**	Patagonian toothfish (*Dissostichus eleginoides*) or Antarctic toothfish (*Dissostichus mawsoni*)
5	Mariano Fortuny		
6	Flight data recorder (FDR) or "black box"		
7	Omaha Beach	**16**	Asif Kapadia
8	Green Day	**17**	Anders Petersen
9	Greece	**18**	Wilhelm Steinitz
10	Yorick	**19**	Stirling Moss
		20	Gecko (*Eublepharis macularius*)

1   In 1962, jousting became the official sport of which Mid-Atlantic US state?

2   Which BBC broadcaster commentated on the Boat Race from 1931 to 1980?

3   Born in 1988, which Australian one-day cricket star is nicknamed "The Big Show"?

4   Which snooker player won the 1993 UK Championship at the age of 17 years, 358 days?

5   Which national rugby union team is nicknamed "Los Teros"?

6   Vladimir Parfenovich (USSR) won three golds in which sport at the 1980 Moscow Olympics?

7   What is the maximum number of touches a volleyball team can make to return the ball?

8   In 2014, the late driver Jules Bianchi scored which team's first points in Formula One?

9   Mary Rand won a silver medal in which athletics event at the 1964 Tokyo Olympics?

10 Which seven-time National Hunt champion jockey co-wrote the 1989 novel *Blood Stock*?

11 Which Soviet pairs skater won six world titles with Alexander Zaitsev, three as husband and wife?

12 Who was beaten for a second time by Muhammad Ali on May 25, 1965?

13 Which Scottish athlete won the men's 400m at the 1924 Paris Olympics?

14 The Willows is the home of which rugby league club?

15 Which South African golfer won the US Open in 2001 and 2004?

16 Who was the surprise winner of snooker's 1986 World Championship?

17 Which US athlete won the women's 100m and 200m at the Rome Olympics?

18 What was the first Dutch football club to win the European Cup?

19 Ben Ainslie won his first Olympic gold in which sailing class?

20 Which Chelsea midfielder is pictured?

Answers to QUIZ 104 – General Knowledge

1 Ron Grainer
2 Hamlet
3 Temperature – they are thermoreceptors
4 Drone or quadcopter or aerial photography system
5 James Clerk Maxwell
6 Azores
7 *42nd Street*
8 Sunglasses
9 Patrick Stewart
10 Bridie
11 Bridget Riley
12 "Comedy"
13 Lockheed (now Lockheed Martin)
14 DayGlo Color Corp.
15 PETA – People for the Ethical Treatment of Animals (helped by an ad featuring The Go-Go's)
16 *Romanzo Criminale*
17 Synthetic gemstones, e.g. rubies and sapphires
18 *Pictionary*
19 Lou Gehrig of the New York Yankees
20 Grotto of Massabielle, Lourdes – featuring the Statue of Our Lady of Lourdes

1   Which French designer (b.1967) is known for her Dicker suede ankle boots?

2   Which composer was called "our little Mozart of the Champs-Élysées" by Rossini?

3   Which "Soul Brother No.1" is the world's most sampled recording artist?

4   Nilsson's no.1 single *Without You* was a cover of a song by which Welsh band?

5   In 1982, Eli Lilly introduced Humulin, medication identical to which hormone produced by the body?

6   *The Sculptor* is a 2015 graphic novel by which *Understanding Comics* author?

7   Who won the 1944 Nobel Prize in Chemistry for "his discovery of the fission of heavy nuclei"?

8   A print of which Luxembourg-born photographer's *The Pond-Moonlight* sold at auction in 2006 for $2.9m?

9   May Maxwell is which fictional character's loyal and elderly Scottish housekeeper?

10 In 1963, Pedigree Toys launched which rival to Barbie as "the doll you love to dress"?

11 What is thought to be the last major land mass to be colonised by pre-industrial humans?

12 Which Nepalese mountain's 41 per cent fatality rate makes it the world's deadliest for climbers?

13 Which Cuban ballet star wrote the debut novel *Pig's Foot*?

14 Which Mauritanian filmmaker directed *Bamako* (2006) and *Timbuktu* (2014)?

15 The words alchemy, soda, sugar and zenith come from which language?

16 What is the most widely used alphabetic writing system in the world?

17 The nectarine is a smooth-skinned variety of which fruit?

18 In 2008, Dutchman Erik Akkersdijk took 7.08 seconds to set which world record?

19 The Ethiopian town of Bekoji has produced many notable what?

20 Who is the pictured Irish comedian?

Featureflash Photo Agency / Shutterstock.com

Answers to QUIZ 105 – Sport

1 Maryland
2 John Snagge
3 Glenn Maxwell
4 Ronnie O'Sullivan
5 Uruguay – the southern lapwing is the national bird of Uruguay, where it is called the tero
6 Canoeing or Men's canoe sprint – K-1 500m, K-2 500m, K-2 1000m
7 Three
8 Marussia – since renamed Manor
9 Pentathlon
10 John Francome (with James MacGregor)
11 Irina Rodnina
12 Sonny Liston
13 Eric Liddell
14 Salford City Reds
15 Retief Goosen
16 Joe Johnson
17 Wilma Rudolph
18 Feyenoord – in 1970
19 Laser – in 2000
20 N'golo Kanté

1   Which sitcom character inspired the name of the Swedish band I'm from Barcelona?

2   Where did Wellington crush Auguste de Marmont's French forces on July 22, 1812?

3   Often seen in Vietnam War films being worn by the Vietnamese, what is a *nón lá*?

4   In the title of a 2015 TV show, Bertie Carvel and Eddie Marsan were which magicians?

5   In May 1963, Richard Vaughan was the last man to be officially discharged from what?

6   Which bone at the back of the nasal cavity shares its name with a hill of Rome?

7   What is the world's largest military force in terms of personnel?

8   "The Bus Tapes" bootleg recordings provide evidence of which jazz drummer's notorious temper?

9   Which name links Argentina's second largest city and the currency of Nicaragua?

10 Which hard, bluish-white metal is the densest naturally occurring element?

11 The 1910 painting *The City Rises (La città che sale)* is a major Futurist work by which Italian artist?

12 Which Scottish engineer and inventor coined the term "horsepower"?

13 What is the most widely spoken non-Indo-European language in Europe?

14 Which gangster is the only real-life person depicted in *The Adventures of Tintin* series?

15 The Australian physician Barry Marshall deliberately infected himself with the *Helicobacter pylori* bacterium to do what?

16 What is the largest member of the dolphin family?

17 Which twin children of Leto slaughtered the children of Niobe?

18 Putting brine shrimp in hatching kits, Harold von Braunhut invented which "instant pets" in 1957?

19 Which boxer often jokes: "I fought Sugar Ray so many times, it's a wonder I don't have diabetes"?

20 What is the pictured European capital?

Answers to QUIZ 106 – General Knowledge

1   Isabel Marant
2   Jacques Offenbach
3   James Brown
4   Badfinger
5   Insulin
6   Scott McCloud
7   Otto Hahn
8   Edward Steichen
9   James Bond
10 Sindy
11 New Zealand – first settled around the end of the 13th century by canoe voyagers from tropical eastern Polynesia
12 Annapurna
13 Carlos Acosta
14 Abderrahmane Sissako
15 Arabic
16 Latin or Roman alphabet
17 Peach
18 Solving a standard 3x3x3 Rubik's Cube
19 Athletes or long distance runners such as the Bekele brothers, Dibaba sisters and Derartu Tulu
20 Ed Byrne

1   Who established the National Motor Museum at the Hampshire estate Beaulieu?

2   Which German automaker introduced the R8 supercar?

3   Waitemata Harbour is the main access by sea to which major city?

4   General Motors describes which Chevrolet model as the "world's longest-running, continuously produced passenger car"?

5   Originally designed by Robert Stephenson, the Britannia Bridge spans which strait?

6   Lester B. Pearson International Airport serves which Canadian city?

7   Vauxhall is the UK division of which German carmaker?

8   Her Majesty's Yacht *Britannia* is permanently berthed where?

9   Introduced on August 7, 1972, which design by Massimo Vignelli outraged many New Yorkers?

10 Which US aviator was the first woman to fly solo across the Atlantic?

11 What type of bomber was Bockscar, the plane that dropped the atomic bomb on Nagasaki?

12 What type of car is a CUV?

13 Which Porsche 4x4 car derives its name from the Indonesian word for tiger?

14 In 1989, the US oceanographer Robert Ballard located the wreck of which German battleship?

15 Which sister ship to the *Titanic* sank in the Aegean Sea on November 21, 1916?

16 With 26 victories, who was America's most successful fighter ace in the First World War?

17   Who designed the Fiat Nuova 500 that was launched in July 1957?

18   The Channel Tunnel links Folkestone with which village near Calais?

19   What term describes a car built between 1919 and 1930?

20   Which Italian carmaker's Urus SUV is pictured?

Answers to QUIZ 107 – General Knowledge

1	Manuel from *Fawlty Towers*	12	James Watt
2	[Battle of] Salamanca	13	Hungarian – which belongs to the Uralic language family
3	A type of conical hat ('leaf hat') that has become a symbol of Vietnam	14	Al Capone
4	*Jonathan Strange & Mr. Norrell*	15	To prove that *H. pylori* can cause gastric inflammation and peptic ulcers aka stomach ulcers
5	National Service		
6	Palatine bone	16	Orca or killer whale (*Orcinus orca*)
7	People's Liberation Army of China	17	Apollo & Artemis
8	Buddy Rich	18	Sea-Monkeys – also marketed as "Instant Life"
9	Córdoba		
10	Osmium	19	Jake LaMotta
11	Umberto Boccioni	20	Budapest

1 Which London museum is named after the last of the Victorian toy theatre printers?

2 The 'Ghostface' identity is adopted by the killers in which horror film series?

3 Who won a 2011 Pulitzer for her novel *A Visit from the Goon Squad*?

4 Taomasina is which island-country's largest port?

5 Henry Vandyke Carter drew the illustrations for which 1858 textbook?

6 Which comic strip Great Dane belongs to the Winslow family?

7 Which schoolboy's friends – Ginger, Henry and Douglas – formed The Outlaws?

8 Which group first had a hit with the 1982 single *Last Night a DJ Saved My Life*?

9 Pha That Luang is a gold-covered Buddhist stupa in which Asian capital city?

10 Who composed the 1691 semi-opera *King Arthur or, The British Worthy*?

11 Which creatures include Handy, Clumsy, Brainy, Jokey, Grouchy and Papa?

12 Who published his photographs of New Brighton in *The Last Resort* (1986)?

13 Which dynasty took over the Spanish throne in 1700 with Philip V?

14 The photographer Herb Ritts shot the cover of which 1986 Madonna album?

15 Which TV title character was an attorney with Cage, Fish & Associates?

16 Which Wing Commander led the 'Dambusters' raid of May 16-17, 1943?

17 What is the most common carpal bone to fracture?

18 Windsurfer Gal Fridman won which country's first ever Olympic gold in 2004?

19 Which Belarus-born gymnast won four Olympic golds on the same day in 1992?

20 Which Hampshire country house is pictured?

Answers to QUIZ 108 – Transport

1 Lord Montagu or Edward Douglas-Scott-Montagu, 3rd Baron Montagu of Beaulieu

2 Audi

3 Auckland, New Zealand

4 Chevrolet Corvette – which rolled off the assembly line on June 30, 1953

5 Menai Strait (between Anglesey and the Welsh mainland)

6 Toronto

7 Opel

8 Ocean Terminal, Leith, Edinburgh

9 His diagrammatic map of the New York subway system – the public preferred a geographical one

10 Amelia Earhart – in May 20-21, 1932

11 Boeing B-29 Superfortress

12 Crossover utility vehicle

13 Macan

14 *Bismarck*

15 HMHS *Britannic*

16 Eddie Rickenbacker

17 Dante Giacosa

18 Coquelles

19 "Vintage" car

20 Lamborghini

1   Which Soviet journalist wrote the epic World War Two novel *Life and Fate*?

2   Which British folk-rock band released the 1968 double LP *Sweet Child*?

3   The TV drama *Rizzoli & Isles* is based on a series by which US novelist?

4   Opened in 1923, Liseberg is an amusement park in which Swedish city?

5   Which subatomic particle derives its name from the Greek for 'bulky'?

6   Which physician wrote the 1635 book of reflections, *Religio Medici*?

7   Who did Alan Partridge call "the band the Beatles could have been"?

8   Which YBA created the sculpture *Two Fried Eggs and a Kebab* (1992)?

9   Voiced by Stephen Merchant, Wheatley helps Chell in which video game sequel?

10 A kyōgen is a comic interlude played during which form of Japanese drama?

11 La Chascona was the Santiago home of which Chilean "people's poet"?

12 Who is the husband of "Comrade Ri Sol-ju"?

13 Which US actor was National Rifle Association president from 1998 to 2003?

14 A prized game fish, the steelhead is a saltwater form of which trout?

15 "Androgenetic alopecia" has what common three-word name?

16 Founded at Basel in 1930, what is the world's oldest international financial institution?

17 Gregorio Allegri's *Miserere* was composed for performance in which chapel?

18 In 1931, which Indian scientist calculated that a black hole must have a radius of zero?

19 Which Argentine golfer's only Major win was the 1967 Open Championship?

20 Name the Italian bridge in the picture

Answers to QUIZ 109 – General Knowledge

1 Pollock's Toy Museum – named after Benjamin Pollock

2 *Scream*

3 Jennifer Egan

4 Madagascar

5 [Henry] *Gray's Anatomy*

6 Marmaduke

7 William Brown (in the *Just William* stories)

8 Indeep

9 Vientiane, Laos

10 Henry Purcell (with a libretto by John Dryden)

11 The Smurfs

12 Martin Parr

13 Bourbons

14 *True Blue*

15 Ally McBeal

16 Guy Gibson

17 Scaphoid bone

18 Israel

19 Vitaly Scherbo

20 Highclere Castle – as seen on *Downton Abbey*

QUIZ 111 – Business

1   What is the largest of the "Big Four" American banks?

2   Dailymotion co-founder Didier Rappaport is the CEO and founder of which dating app?

3   Scottish entrepreneur Michelle Mone founded which lingerie brand in 1996?

4   Based in Milford, Connecticut, what is the world's biggest restaurant chain by number of stores worldwide?

5   Formed in a 1930 merger, what type of business is McCann Erickson?

6   The world's most commercially exploited banana, the Cavendish, was named in whose honour?

7   Which Colombian "King of Cocaine" is regarded as the richest criminal in history?

8   In 1879, Benjamin Henry Blackwell opened a bookshop on Broad Street in which city?

9   Which hairdressing company was founded in London in 1963 by brothers Giuseppe and Gaetano Mascolo?

10 Habanos S.A. controls the promotion, distribution and export of which products worldwide?

11 Which English entrepreneur invented the Air Miles and Nectar Card schemes?

12 Which Bavarian handmade-paper mill produces the golden envelopes that are opened at the Oscars?

13 Lord [Karan] Bilimoria of Chelsea made his fortune by co-founding which Indian beer brand?

14 In 1966, the Urengoy gas field was discovered in which country?

15 Which late US architect's stainless steel whistling bird kettle (1985) is Alessi's best-selling product?

16 Joseph Malin is said to have opened the first example of what shop in London's Cleveland Street in 1860?

17 The All Ordinaries is the oldest index of shares in which country?

18 The financier William Waldorf Astor bought which Kent castle in 1903?

19 In 1565, Sir Thomas Gresham founded which centre for commerce?

20 Who is the father of the pictured businesswoman?

s_bukley / Shutterstock.com

Answers to QUIZ 110 – General Knowledge

1 Vasily Grossman

2 Pentangle

3 Tess Gerritsen

4 Gothenburg

5 Hadron

6 Sir Thomas Browne

7 Paul McCartney's band Wings

8 Sarah Lucas

9 *Portal 2*

10 Noh

11 Pablo Neruda

12 North Korean leader Kim Jong-un

13 Charlton Heston

14 Rainbow trout

15 Male pattern baldness

16 Bank for International Settlements (BIS)

17 Sistine Chapel

18 Subrahmanyan Chandrasekhar

19 Roberto De Vicenzo

20 Ponte Vecchio, Florence

QUIZ 112 – General Knowledge

1   Michael J. Fox replaced Eric Stoltz five weeks into the filming of which 1985 movie?

2   Which German composer (1653-1706) is best known for his *Canon in D* and *Chaconne in F minor*?

3   Linking the Baltic and North Seas, what is the world's busiest artificial waterway?

4   Sir John Charnley pioneered a technique that became the gold standard for which surgical procedure?

5   The Egyptian god Horus was usually depicted in the form of which bird?

6   Xenophon's *Apology* recounts which man's self-defence at his trial and execution?

7   Creator of the cubist sculpture *Horse*, which brother of Marcel Duchamp died of typhoid fever in 1918?

8   In 1872, which physician founded the New Hospital for Women in London?

9   Covered in what looks like silky white fur, the crustacean *Kiwa hirsuta* has which nickname?

10 Known for his bubble dresses, which French designer opened a women's boutique called Eve in 1954?

11 Which sister of the actress Catherine Deneuve died in a 1967 car crash?

12 Which South African trumpeter had a 1968 US no.1 with *Grazing in the Grass*?

13 The Malakhov was a vital defensive position during which Crimean War siege?

14 Which US president held Patent No. 6469 for a device to lift boats over shoals?

15 In US politics, what does the acronym PAC, as in "Super PAC", stand for?

16 Great Bear Lake is the largest lake entirely within which country?

17 Azonto is a dance craze from which West African country?

18 Magnus Wislander (Sweden) was voted which sport's "Player of the [20th] Century"?

19 Which Canadian cyclist won the 2012 Giro d'Italia?

20 Which Welsh bass-baritone features in the image?

Answers to QUIZ 111 – Business

1	JPMorgan Chase	**11**	Sir Keith Mills
2	Happn	**12**	Gmund
3	Ultimo	**13**	Cobra Beer
4	Subway	**14**	Russia
5	Advertising agency	**15**	Michael Graves – its proper
6	William Cavendish, 6th		name is the 9093
	Duke of Devonshire	**16**	Fish and chip shop
7	Pablo Escobar	**17**	Australia
8	Oxford – the shop was	**18**	Hever Castle
	called B.H. Blackwell's	**19**	The Royal Exchange
9	Toni & Guy	**20**	Donald Trump – his
10	Cuban cigars and related		daughter Ivanka is pictured
	tobacco products		

1   Which US jeweller created its first mail order catalogue, the *Blue Book*, in 1845?

2   Which Irish poet was paid £3,000 for his Oriental romance *Lalla Rookh* (1817)?

3   Located on the island of Hawaii, what is the world's largest volcano?

4   Which 1924 Sigmund Romberg operetta features the *Drinking Song*?

5   The high school film *Easy A* was loosely based on which Nathaniel Hawthorne novel?

6   What did the playwright George S. Kaufman say "is what closes on Saturday night"?

7   Which Russian composed the *Ebony Concerto* for clarinettist Woody Herman?

8   *Avenging Angel* is a 2011 album by which US jazz keyboardist?

9   Which national bird of Trinidad gets its colour from eating red crustaceans?

10 Which Russian writer created the historical detective Erast Fandorin?

11 Which ridiculous hairstyle is known in Germany as "Vokuhila"?

12 Marc Okrand first published the dictionary for which fictional language in 1985?

13 Samuel Hahnemann founded which method of treating disease by drugs?

14 Home to the Copper Canyon, what is Mexico's largest state?

15 The Via Francigena is the ancient pilgrim route from Canterbury to which city?

16 Sterling Malory are the first names of which American TV cartoon spy?

17 Which US artist (1922-93) painted the *Ocean Park* series?

18 Which animals fight in a Swiss tradition known as *Combats de Reines*?

19 Which horse won the 2012 Royal Ascot Queen Anne Stakes by 11 lengths?

20 Which video game adventuress is pictured?

Answers to QUIZ 112 – General Knowledge

1	*Back to the Future*	12	Hugh Masekela
2	Johann Pachelbel	13	Siege of Sevastopol (October 1854 – September 1855)
3	Kiel Canal or Nord-Ostsee-Kanal		
4	Hip replacement or total hip arthroplasty (THA)	14	Abraham Lincoln – granted in 1849, making him the only president to hold a patent
5	Falcon		
6	Socrates	15	Political Action Committee
7	Raymond Duchamp-Villon	16	Canada
8	Elizabeth Garrett Anderson	17	Ghana
9	Yeti crab or yeti lobster	18	Handball
10	Pierre Cardin	19	Ryder Hesjedal
11	Françoise Dorléac	20	Bryn Terfel

QUIZ 114 – France

1 Who painted *Oath of the Horatii* (1784) and *Madame Récamier* (1800)?

2 Who played the title role in the 1986 film *Jean de Florette*?

3 The French group Rexel is a global leader in which industry?

4 Which TV show was called *La maison de Toutou* in its native France?

5 Which French luggage maker uses the slogan "Malletier Depuis 1853"?

6 Which French automaker introduced the *DS* 19 car in 1955?

7 Which Count of Paris became King of France in 987?

8 The musical film *Gigi* was based on a book by which French writer?

9 What is the four-letter abbreviation for France's foreign intelligence service?

10 Which French novelist wrote *Michael Strogoff: The Courier of the Czar* (1876)?

11 A Béchamel sauce becomes a Mornay sauce with the addition of what?

12 Which French hotel group owns the Ibis, Mercure and Sofitel hotel chains?

13 Which 1867 Gounod opera features the waltz song *Je veux vivre* for the soprano?

14 Which volume of poetry includes *A Voyage to Cythera, The Bad Monk, The Sick Muse* and *The Vampire*?

15 Which French composer's *Roma Symphony* was first performed in 1869?

16 Which American movie awards inspired France's Gérard du cinéma prizes?

17 What tragic accident claimed the life of the French king Henry II in 1559?

18 Which French explorer (1491-1557) is credited with naming Canada?

19 Which French chef opened his Moulin de Mougins restaurant in 1969 with his wife Denise?

20 Who is the pictured French composer?

Answers to QUIZ 113 – General Knowledge

1	Tiffany & Co.	12	Klingon
2	Thomas Moore	13	Homeopathy
3	Mauna Loa	14	Chihuahua
4	*The Student Prince*	15	Rome
5	*The Scarlet Letter*	16	*Archer*
6	Satire	17	Richard Diebenkorn
7	Igor Stravinsky	18	Cows
8	Craig Taborn	19	Frankel
9	Scarlet Ibis	20	Lara Croft
10	Boris Akunin		
11	Mullet – it is an abbreviation for 'short in front, long in back'		

1   Billy Childish and Charles Thomson founded which pro-figurative painting movement?

2   Which John Grogan book is subtitled *Life and Love with the World's Worst Dog*?

3   *The Embarrassment of Riches* by Simon Schama is about which country's Golden Age?

4   Which 1974 film featured the subway hijackers Mr. Blue, Mr. Grey, Mr. Green and Mr. Brown?

5   Meaning 'empty quarter', what is the world's largest continuous sand area?

6   Sometimes called *carta da musica*, what is Sardinia's best-known bread?

7   Which philologist constructed the languages Quenya and Sindarin?

8   Which haemorrhagic fever virus is named after a city in Hessen, Germany?

9   Claiming the world's tallest minaret, the Hassan II Mosque is in which city?

10 Which Pakistani physicist was the first Muslim scientist to win a Nobel Prize?

11 Mademoiselle La Fontaine was the first professional performer of which type?

12 Philippa of Hainault was the wife of which King of England?

13 The Melek Taus, or Peacock Angel, is a central figure of which people's faith?

14 Which Italian company introduced the Ape three-wheeled vehicle in 1948?

15 Axwell, Steve Angello and Sebastian Ingrosso formed which DJ supergroup?

16 *Gargantua* was Honoré Daumier's notorious caricature of which French king?

17 Awarded Grade II listed status, what is the Rom in Hornchurch, London?

18 Which English tennis player was the first ever female Olympic champion?

19 The Molson family owns which Canadian NHL ice hockey club?

20 What is the pictured English breed of draught horse?

Answers to QUIZ 114 – France

1   Jacques-Louis David
2   Gérard Depardieu
3   Electrical supplies
4   *Hector's House*
5   Goyard
6   Citroën
7   Hugh Capet
8   Colette
9   DGSE (*Direction Générale de la Sécurité Extérieure*)
10 Jules Verne
11 Grated cheese (Gruyère and Parmesan)
12 Accor
13 *Roméo et Juliette*
14 *The Flowers of Evil* (*Les Fleurs du mal*) by Charles Baudelaire
15 Georges Bizet
16 Razzie or Golden Raspberry award
17 A lance fragment inflicted a mortal head wound during a jousting tournament
18 Jacques Cartier
19 Roger Vergé
20 Claude Debussy

1   Which Scottish-born scientist developed the HD-4 hydrofoil?

2   Which Soviet author published the novel *Envy* in 1927?

3   Which sculpture was discovered with only one wing by Charles Champoiseau in 1863?

4   In 1938, which clarinettist played the first jazz concert at Carnegie Hall?

5   Which Soviet official was shot and killed at the Smolny Institute on December 1, 1934?

6   The popular title of which song by Franco Migliacci and Domenico Modugno means 'to fly'?

7   Found in Buddhist temples throughout Japan, what are *bonshō*, also known as *tsurigane*?

8   Last erupting in 1917, what is the southernmost active volcano in the Cascade Range?

9   Which actress is married to Marcus Mumford of Mumford & Sons?

10 Davy Crockett helped thwart an 1835 assassination attempt on which US President?

11 CFCs contain carbon and which two halogens?

12 Who is the oldest ever winner of the Best Director Oscar?

13 Set up by Ramón Areces, what is Spain's only remaining department store chain?

14 Georges Polti is best known for his list of how many dramatic situations?

15 Which rap mogul bought the luxury champagne brand Armand de Brignac?

16 Which vitamin is also known as retinol?

17 Found in nail polish remover, which volatile liquid is the simplest ketone?

18 From 1756 to 1782, Broadhalfpenny Down was the home venue of which cricket club?

19 Which tennis rivalry began in round three of the Miami Masters in March 2004?

20 The Kukulkan Pyramid, known as "El Castillo" is located where?

Answers to QUIZ 115 – General Knowledge

1 Stuckism
2 *Marley & Me*
3 Dutch Republic or the Netherlands
4 *The Taking of Pelham One Two Three*
5 Rub' al-Khali – in the southern Arabian Peninsula
6 Pane carasau
7 J.R.R. Tolkien
8 Marburg virus
9 Casablanca, Morocco
10 Abdus Salam – in 1979
11 First female ballet dancer
12 Edward III
13 Yazidis or the Yezidi
14 Piaggio
15 Swedish House Mafia
16 King Louis-Philippe
17 A skatepark
18 Charlotte Cooper (in 1900)
19 Montreal Canadiens
20 Suffolk Punch

1   What is the longest medieval cathedral in Europe?

2   Which Biblical queen is known as *Bilqis* in the Islamic tradition?

3   In 1985, the Getty Museum paid a then world record $10.5m for which Mantegna painting?

4   Consecrated in 1958, the Basilica of St. Pius X is in which town in south-west France?

5   Canonised in 2009, Father Damien cared for the lepers of Kalaupapa on which island?

6   St. Machar's Cathedral is a Church of Scotland church in which city?

7   Opened in 1701, which City of London synagogue is the UK's oldest such place of worship?

8   The song *Dayenu* ('it would have sufficed') is part of which Jewish holiday?

9   Which "burial garment" is known in Italy as the *Santa Sindone*?

10 In Islam, *umrah* is a type of what?

11 Which Swede played Christ in the 1965 film *The Greatest Story Ever Told*?

12 Which Biblical king cried: "O my son Absalom, my son, my son Absalom!"?

13 Which 6th century saint allegedly encountered the Loch Ness Monster?

14 In religion, what is a doxology?

15 Which pope sent St. Augustine of Canterbury to convert England to Christianity?

16 The Trinity Lavra of St. Sergius monastery is the spiritual centre of which church?

17 Vaisakhi, aka Baisakhi, is a major festival in which religion?

18 Monte Cassino Abbey was the birthplace of which monastic order?

19 Where on a buddha is the ushnisha found?

20 Which Paris church is pictured?

Answers to QUIZ 116 – General Knowledge

1. Alexander Graham Bell
2. Yuri Olesha
3. The *Winged Victory of Samothrace* or *Nike of Samothrace*
4. Benny Goodman
5. Sergei Kirov
6. *Volare* – the song is alternately titled *Nel blu dipinto di blu*
7. Large bronze bells
8. Lassen Peak or Mount Lassen
9. Carey Mulligan
10. Andrew Jackson
11. Chlorine and fluorine – CFC stands for chlorofluorocarbon
12. Clint Eastwood – who was 74-years-old when he won for *Million Dollar Baby*
13. El Corte Inglés
14. 36
15. Jay Z
16. Vitamin A
17. Acetone or propanone
18. Hambledon Cricket Club
19. Roger Federer versus Rafael Nadal
20. Chichen Itza in Yucatan state, Mexico

1 Which 1988 Tom Stoppard play centres on a titular female spymaster?

2 Indian Prime Minister Narendra Modi served as chief minister (2001-2014) of which state?

3 The supreme being Eru is which fantasy world's version of God?

4 The London-based painter Oscar Murillo (b.1986) was born in which country?

5 In the book of Genesis, who stole the first-born birthright from his twin brother Esau?

6 Illustrated by Pamela Colman Smith, the Rider-Waite is a deck of which cards?

7 Introduced in 1955 by Bill Russell and Peter Hobbs, what was the vapour-controlled K1?

8 Ricky Gervais played a care worker at the nursing home Broad Hill in which TV show?

9 Created by Smedley's of Wisbech, which vegetable became Britain's first frozen food in 1937?

10 Held in Montreal, what type of event is *L'International des Feux Loto-Québec*?

11 The TV drama *Black Sails* is a prequel to which Robert Louis Stevenson novel?

12 What is the only nuclear-powered submarine known to have sunk an enemy ship using torpedoes?

13 In 1967, Gerald Feinberg coined which term for hypothetical faster-than-light particles?

14 Harland and Wolff's chief designer Thomas Andrews went down with which of his ships?

15 Once used for food, the Hawaiian poi is an extinct breed of what?

16 Rob Law got the idea for which children's ride-on suitcase in 1997?

17 Which French chef (c.1615-78) wrote the influential cookbook *Le Cuisinier françois*?

18 Which weights were held by athletes in the ancient long jump to push themselves further?

19 France's Thierry Gueorgiou is a 13-time world champion in which outdoor adventure sport?

20 The pictured helmet was found at which Anglo-Saxon royal burial site?

Answers to QUIZ 117 – Religion

1 Winchester Cathedral

2 Queen of Sheba

3 *The Adoration of the Magi* (c.1495-1505)

4 Lourdes

5 Molokai

6 Aberdeen

7 Bevis Marks Synagogue

8 Passover or *Pesach*

9 Turin Shroud

10 Pilgrimage – the 'minor pilgrimage' undertaken by Muslims whenever they enter Mecca

11 Max von Sydow

12 King David – on hearing of his third son's death

13 St Columba

14 An expression of praise to God

15 Gregory I 'the Great'

16 Russian Orthodox Church

17 Sikhism

18 Benedictine Order aka the Black Monks

19 The top of the head – it is the knot of hair

20 Sacré-Cœur or the Basilica of the Sacred Heart of Paris

1 Which First World War veteran's poem *Mattina / Morning* consists entirely of the lines: "M'illumino / D'immenso"?

2 In 1819, which German chemist isolated pure caffeine for the first time, calling it *Kaffebase*?

3 Which largely instrumental 1972 song is the only British no.1 to feature a mother and her son?

4 What is the largest Asian antelope? The mature male is known as a blue bull.

5 Labour's only Scottish MP, Ian Murray, represents which constituency?

6 The Gran Sasso raid rescued which man on September 12, 1943?

7 Which "Father of the Delta Blues", who died in 1934, is famed for his song *Pony Blues*?

8 In 1101, Ranulf Flambard, Bishop of Durham, made a bold escape from which fortress?

9 What is the most malleable and ductile metal?

10 "*Ouistiti*" is the French version of "Say 'cheese'". It is which monkey's name?

11 The James Beard Foundation Awards have been called "The Oscars of..." which industry?

12 Co-written by Rick James, *Party All the Time* was a 1985 US hit for which film star?

13 In 1986, the Rutan Model 76 Voyager became the first aircraft to do what?

14 The Coco Chanel, Windsor, Elton John and Vendôme are "Prestige Suites" in which hotel?

15 Taylor Swift named her pet cats, Meredith and Olivia, after which two TV characters?

16 More mathematical concepts and theorems are named after which Frenchman (1789-1857) than any other mathematician?

17 George Orwell devised 11 golden rules for making which drink?

18 Aged 14 years 286 days, which US figure skater became the youngest women's world champion in 1997?

19 What is English football's most-played league fixture?

20 Name the pictured American dancer –

Answers to QUIZ 118 – General Knowledge

1	*Hapgood*	11	*Treasure Island*
2	Gujarat	12	HMS *Conqueror* – which sank the *General Belgrano*
3	J.R.R. Tolkien's Middle-earth	13	Tachyon
4	Colombia	14	RMS *Titanic*
5	Jacob	15	Dog
6	Tarot cards	16	Trunki
7	The first automatic electric kettle	17	La Varenne or François Pierre de la Varenne
8	*Derek*	18	*Halteres*
9	Asparagus	19	Orienteering
10	Fireworks competition – said to be the most prestigious in the world	20	Sutton Hoo

1   Which toy inventor was elected as Conservative MP for Everton in 1931?

2   *Quotations from Chairman Mao Tse-Tung* is better known by which title?

3   Founded in 1988, Fidesz is a major political party in which country?

4   Which late Labour politician was the founding First Minister of Scotland?

5   What did the MP David Lloyd George call "Mr Balfour's poodle"?

6   Which socialist (1771-1858) created a model community at New Lanark?

7   In US politics, what is a 'Kinsley gaffe'?

8   The Christiansborg Palace houses which country's parliament?

9   What is the smallest republic in Europe?

10 Who succeeded Clement Davies as Liberal Party leader in 1956?

11 Joseph Estrada resigned from which country's presidency in 2001?

12 "United in diversity" is the motto of which organisation?

13 The *Estelada* is an unofficial flag flown by separatists in which region?

14 In 2013, Park Geun-hye assumed office as the first female president of which country?

15 From 2009 to 2014, when he became Italian prime minister, Matteo Renzi, was mayor of which city?

16 Who succeeded Jacques Santer as Prime Minister of Luxembourg in 1995?

17 In 2014, Anne Hidalgo became the first ever female mayor of which capital city?

18 Which accountant was Prime Minister of New Zealand from 1975 to 1984?

19 In 1872, Victoria Woodhull became the first woman to run for which office?

20 Name the pictured Tory MP for Windsor –

Answers to QUIZ 119 – General Knowledge

1 Giuseppe Ungaretti

2 Friedlieb Ferdinand Runge

3 *Mouldy Old Dough* by Lieutenant Pigeon – featuring Rob Woodward and his mother Hilda on piano

4 Nilgai (*Boselaphus tragocamelus*)

5 Edinburgh South

6 Benito Mussolini

7 Charley Patton

8 The Tower of London

9 Gold

10 Marmoset

11 Food or culinary industry

12 Eddie Murphy

13 Fly around the world without stopping or refuelling

14 Ritz Paris

15 Dr. Meredith Grey from *Grey's Anatomy* and Detective Olivia Benson from *Law and Order: Special Victims Unit*

16 Augustin-Louis Cauchy

17 Tea or, as in the title of his 1946 essay, *A Nice Cup of Tea*

18 Tara Lipinski

19 Aston Villa versus Everton

20 Isadora Duncan

QUIZ 121 – General Knowledge

1 Which capital city began work on the covering of the river Senne in 1867?

2 What was Catherine Cornaro forced to sell to Venice in 1489?

3 Which Tory MP for Congleton shares her name with a *Fake or Fortune?* TV presenter?

4 On April 3, 1973, Joel S. Engel of Bell Labs received the first ever what?

5 Defeating Pompey's sons, Julius Caesar's last victory was which March 45 BC battle?

6 Who is famed for his rendition of *Ol' Man River* as Joe in the 1936 film *Show Boat*?

7 Which Russian composer intended his unrealised Himalayan extravaganza *Mysterium* to be performed over a week?

8 In 1908, the Swiss chemist Jacques Brandenberger invented which clear, waterproof film?

9 Which school of yoga, whose name means 'eight limbs', was popularised by Krishna Pattabhi Jois?

10 What includes 8 kings, 8 queens, 16 bishops, 15 knights, 12 warders, 19 pawns, 14 tablemen and a belt buckle?

11 Churchill (the "Polar Bear Capital of the World"), Gimli, Ethelbert and Winkler are places in which Canadian province?

12 The cause of which disease, affecting domestic and wild bovids, was first shown to be viral in 1897 by Friedrich Loeffler?

13 Mount Marcy is which US state's highest point?

14 Mark McCormack founded which global talent agency in 1960?

15 Who topped the UK singles chart in 1955 with *Give Me Your Word*?

16 Which Scottish artist created *24 Hour Psycho* in 1993?

17 Who composed the TV theme tunes for *Howard's Way, Eldorado* and *EastEnders*?

18 Known as "the Boston Strong Boy", who is recognised as the first Heavyweight Champion of gloved boxing?

19 Great Britain plays the USA for the Westchester Cup in which sport?

20 What is the pictured bridge?

Answers to QUIZ 120 – Politics

1   Frank Hornby
2   The 'Little Red Book'
3   Hungary
4   Donald Dewar
5   The House of Lords
6   Robert Owen
7   The occurrence of someone telling the truth by accident
8   Denmark – it is the seat of the Folketing
9   San Marino
10 Jo Grimond
11 Philippines
12 European Union
13 Catalonia
14 South Korea
15 Florence
16 Jean-Claude Juncker, current European Commission president
17 Paris
18 Robert Muldoon
19 The Presidency of the United States
20 Adam Afriyie

1   Who won the 1991 Whitbread prize for his debut novel *Alma Cogan*?

2   Bran, Porsha, Erin, Merlina, Munin, Hugine, Rocky, Gripp and Jubilee act as traditional guardians where?

3   Job Charnock is traditionally credited with founding which Asian city?

4   Founded by Simon Woodroffe, which company opened its first restaurant in Soho, London in January 1997?

5   Which religious group abides by church rules of day-to-day living called the *Ordnung*?

6   Identified by its Orb trademark, what handwoven cloth is called *Clo Mhoris* in Gaelic?

7   What did Mr Micawber call the borderline between happiness and misery?

8   Which Poet Laureate "deeply loved 31 West Hill" in Highgate?

9   What Japanese musical instrument, played with a plectrum called a *bachi*, is also called *sangen* ('three strings')?

10 Professor Albert H. Munsell created an eponymous system in an early attempt at creating what?

11 The ship's surgeon, William Beatty (1773-1842), reported whose famous last words?

12 Edinburgh, Birmingham, Bristol and Rustington, West Sussex, have all won gold in which international horticultural competition?

13 Which Dominican fashion designer (1932-2014) was famous for his Pink Label products?

14 In which 1932 film did Greta Garbo (playing the Russian ballerina Grusinskaya) say: "I want to be let alone"?

15 Zymurgy is the art and practice of what?

16 Who said he was made a revolutionary by reading the Chekhov story *Ward 6*?

17 *Scolopendra gigantea*, the Amazonian giant, is the largest existing species of which arthropod in the world?

18 Bobby Moore ended his playing career with which football club in 1977?

19 Which New Zealand golfer won the US Open and the £1,000,000 HSBC World Match Play in 2005?

20 Which royal residence is pictured?

Answers to QUIZ 121 – General Knowledge

1 Brussels
2 The kingdom of Cyprus – she was its last queen
3 Fiona Bruce
4 Handheld mobile phone call in public – Martin Cooper of Motorola made the call
5 Battle of Munda (in southern Hispania)
6 Paul Robeson
7 Alexander Scriabin
8 Cellophane
9 Ashtanga yoga
10 The 93 pieces that are the Lewis Chessmen

11 Manitoba
12 Foot-and-mouth disease or hoof-and-mouth disease (*Aphthae epizooticae*)
13 New York State (part of the Adirondacks range)
14 IMG or International Management Group
15 Tennessee Ernie Ford
16 Douglas Gordon
17 Simon May
18 John L. Sullivan (1858-1918)
19 Polo
20 Sydney Harbour Bridge

QUIZ 123 – Fashion

1 Which British company launched its "iconic and timeless" suede Desert Boot in 1950?

2 The fashion house Versace is headquartered in which city?

3 Which split-toe socks are worn with traditional Japanese footwear such as *zori* and *geta*?

4 In 2005, Riccardo Tisci became the creative director of which French fashion house?

5 Who replaced Grace Mirabella as editor-in-chief of US *Vogue* in 1988?

6 Also called sea silk, which ancient cloth is woven from filaments secreted by the clam *Pinna nobilis*?

7 Which hats are known as *sombreros de paja toquilla* in Ecuador, their country of origin?

8 Once an important rite of passage in a boy's life, what was breeching?

9 Guido Palau has been described by *Vogue* as "The World's most in-demand..." what?

10 Retiring in 2005, twins John and Harry Greenhough were renowned makers of which fashion items?

11 In 1948, which high street fashion brand was started by Bernard Lewis and his brothers in London?

12 Who was Model of the Year at the British Fashion Awards in 2012 and 2014?

13 The French model Amanda Lear was a later muse of which Spanish painter?

14 Based in Paris, Marie Mercié and Anthony Peto are known for designing what?

15 Which hat was a trademark of musical-comedy star Maurice Chevalier?

16 Launched in 2001, which dolls are "girls with a passion for fashion"?

17 Aged 21, Yves Saint Laurent became head designer of which fashion house?

18 Which Abercrombie & Fitch spin-off clothing brand uses a flying seagull logo?

19 Which English designer created the £3,125 'Saskia' stretch-cady and mesh gown?

20 Name the pictured model –

Featureflash Photo Agency / Shutterstock.com

Answers to QUIZ 122 – General Knowledge

1 Gordon Burn
2 The Tower of the London (they are ravens)
3 Calcutta or Kolkata
4 YO! Sushi
5 The Amish
6 Harris Tweed
7 £20
8 John Betjeman
9 Shamisen
10 An accurate system for numerically describing colours – it is called the Munsell color system
11 Horatio Nelson
12 Entente Florale [Europe]
13 Oscar de la Renta
14 *Grand Hotel*
15 Fermentation
16 Lenin
17 Centipede
18 Fulham
19 Michael Campbell
20 Clarence House

1   Rising to 162 metres, what is Britain's highest chalk sea cliff?

2   Charlie Cheever and Adam D'Angelo founded which Q&A website in June 2009?

3   In which county did the Battle of Naseby take place in 1645?

4   Who altered the station names on a London Underground map in his artwork *The Great Bear*?

5   *The Barkleys of Broadway* was which duo's last film together?

6   The only father and son Archbishops of Canterbury shared which surname?

7   Roland Mouret introduced which £800 "dress of the season" in his Spring 2006 Collection?

8   Sir Arnold Bax said "one should try everything once" except for what?

9   Which king died from eating a surfeit of lampreys in 1135?

10 "Here Comes the Bride" features in which Wagner opera?

11 Where on your body are you most likely to find a diastema?

12 The cooking term *bretonne* denotes a dish garnished how?

13 Who was the first 20th century Pope to be canonised?

14 Who composed the music for the State Anthem of the Soviet Union that is now used for Russia's national anthem?

15 In 1908, Robert Ross commissioned the sculptor Jacob Epstein to carve which writer's tomb?

16 Which religion's symbol, the Khanda, depicts its *Deg Tegh Fateh* (Victory to Charity and Arms) doctrine?

17 Produced by cells exposed to the action of a virus, interferons belong to which class of immunoregulatory proteins?

18 What is the name of the light two-wheeled vehicle used in harness racing?

19 Which England spinner dismissed Donald Bradman most times in Tests?

20 Which preserved bog body at the British Museum is pictured?

Answers to QUIZ 123 – Fashion

1   Clarks
2   Milan
3   *Tabi*
4   Givenchy
5   Anna Wintour
6   Byssus
7   Panama hats
8   The occasion when a small boy was first dressed in breeches or trousers, rather than an infant's dress
9   Hair stylist
10 Hats – they worked for the Denton Hat Company, known for its Attaboy trilby hat
11 River Island
12 Cara Delevingne
13 Salvador Dalí
14 Hats
15 A straw hat
16 Bratz
17 The House of [Christian] Dior
18 Hollister
19 Stella McCartney
20 Helena Christensen

1   In 2010, DNA test results confirmed that Tutankhamun was the son of which pharaoh?

2   Which dictator built the tiny town of Gbadolite into a place dubbed the "Versailles of the Jungle"?

3   The Zika virus was first isolated in 1947 from a rhesus macaque in the Zika Forest of which country?

4   Relative to the mother, which animals produce the smallest offspring of any placental mammal?

5   Produced by the S cells in the duodenum, which peptide hormone regulates body water homeostasis?

6   Depicted on the $10 bill, who was the first US secretary of the Treasury?

7   The Swedish-born actor Warner Oland played which Chinese-American detective in 16 films?

8   Which lake, Bolivia's second-largest, was declared evaporated in December 2015?

9   In 1953, which Italian company introduced its signature horsebit loafers?

10 What is the most common system of measurement in the world?

11 Established in 1805, Truefitt & Hill is reputedly the world's oldest what?

12 Which pope was stabbed by the Bolivian surrealist painter Benjamin Mendoza y Amor Flores?

13 Punggye-ri is which country's only known nuclear test site?

14 Frank Finlay guest-starred as the Witchsmeller Pursuivant on which sitcom?

15 In 1496, Andrea del Verrocchio's equestrian statue of Bartolomeo Colleoni was erected in which city?

16 Followers of which syncretic religion believe in the creator god Bondye?

17 The six-item Fagerstrom Test assesses the intensity of dependence on which drug?

18 Which US golfer chipped in to win the playoff for the 1987 Masters?

19 Nicknamed "The Professor", which Ghanaian boxer defeated Wilfredo Gómez to win the WBC featherweight title in 1984?

20 The Marine type of which lizard is pictured?

Answers to QUIZ 124 – General Knowledge

1	Beachy Head	**11**	Your mouth – it is the gap between your two front teeth
2	Quora		
3	Northamptonshire	**12**	With (haricot) beans
4	Simon Patterson	**13**	Pius X
5	Fred Astaire, Ginger Rogers	**14**	Alexander Alexandrov
6	[Frederick (1896-1902) & William (1942-44)] Temple	**15**	Oscar Wilde
		16	Sikhism
7	Galaxy dress	**17**	Cytokines
8	"incest and folk dancing"	**18**	Sulky
9	Henry I	**19**	Hedley Verity (eight times)
10	*Lohengrin*	**20**	Lindow Man, also nicknamed "Pete Marsh"

QUIZ 126 – Technology

1   Kayvon Beykpour and Joseph Bernstein developed which live video streaming app?

2   Which professor of animal science built a "squeeze machine" that calms patients with autism spectrum disorders?

3   Invented by Miller Reese Hutchison, the Akouphone may have been the first electric what?

4   Jules Verne named Captain Nemo's submarine *Nautilus* after which US inventor's real-life sub?

5   The material used to develop Kleenex tissue was originally intended for use as a filter in which devices?

6   Which Japanese corporation's 6500D battery-powered drill (1969) was the first rechargeable power tool?

7   Marconi shared the 1909 Nobel Prize in Physics with Karl Braun for the development of what?

8   What will be the last version of the Microsoft Windows operating system to be released?

9   Written by Harold Cohen, AARON is a software program that creates original what?

10 Launched in 2009, what type of service is Venmo?

11 Which Windows Phone personal assistant is named after a *Halo* video game series character?

12 Patented in 1997, what is Geobond?

13 What is the internet-based practice of "doxing"?

14 Which German is the founder and CEO of the Berlin-based "company-building-machine" Rocket Internet?

15 UCLA dropout Travis Kalanick started which app with Garrett Camp in 2009?

16 Created by Cody Wilson of Defense Distributed, what is the 3-D printed "Liberator"?

17 Introduced in London in the 1880s, the first modern coin-operated vending machines dispensed which items?

18 Marion Donovan invented the first waterproof type of which disposable item?

19 Launched in 1961, what type of machine is the Faema E61 Legend S?

20 Which 8-bit home computer is pictured?

Answers to QUIZ 125 – General Knowledge

1 Akhenaten aka Amenhotep IV
2 Mobutu Sese Seko, president of Zaire (now Democratic Republic of the Congo)
3 Uganda
4 Giant panda
5 Secretin
6 Alexander Hamilton
7 Charlie Chan
8 Lake Poopó
9 Gucci
10 SI system or modern metric system
11 Barbershop
12 Paul VI – during his 1970 visit to the Philippines
13 North Korea
14 *The Black Adder* or *Blackadder*
15 Venice
16 Haitian Voodoo or Vodou
17 Nicotine
18 Larry Mize
19 Azumah Nelson
20 Iguana

1   The titular boy in which animated TV series lives in the town of Beach City with the "Crystal Gems" – Garnet, Amethyst and Pearl?

2   Annie Edson Taylor was the first person to do what daredevil feat?

3   What was the first European country to give women the vote in 1906?

4   What did Bill W. and Dr Bob found in Akron, Ohio, in 1935?

5   Which country is home to the 20-km long Postojna Cave, a karst cave system created by the Pivka River?

6   Which general of King David ensured Uriah the Hittite's death in battle?

7   Which ballet begins with Prince Siegfried's 21st birthday celebrations?

8   Who had established her first *Casa di Bambini* by 1907?

9   What cooking device was invented by the Swedish scientist Gustav Dalen in 1922?

10 Which comet has the shortest known orbital period, of 3.3 years?

11 Which US TV drama featured the fictional countries of Equatorial Kundu and Qumar?

12 In 1997, Tomislav Uzelac of Advanced Multimedia Products invented the first successful type of which player?

13 Which palace is the largest museum complex in Florence?

14 Which French fashion designer was creative director of Hermès from 2003 to 2010?

15 The Norbulingka was the summer residence of which religious leader, from the 1780s to 1959?

16 Which x-ray crystallographer was played by Nicole Kidman in Anna Ziegler's play *Photograph 51*?

17 Who said that cricket "requires one to assume such indecent postures"?

18 Which French pioneer and legend of sport climbing, who died in 2012, was nicknamed "Le Blond"?

19 Which Mexican boxer defeated Manny Pacquiao by knockout in the "Fight of the Decade" on December 8, 2012?

20 Who is the pictured Bollywood star?

Answers to QUIZ 126 – Technology

1 Periscope
2 Temple Grandin
3 Hearing aid
4 Robert Fulton
5 Gas masks
6 Makita
7 "Wireless telegraphy"
8 Windows 10
9 Artistic images or art
10 Mobile payment service, now part of PayPal
11 Cortana
12 A practically indestructible and fire-resistant building material

13 Researching and broadcasting an individual's personally identifiable information – it derives its name from 'documents'
14 Oliver Samwer
15 Uber – founded as UberCab
16 One-shot plastic pistol – the world's first 3-D printable gun made available online
17 Postcards
18 Disposable nappy
19 Espresso coffee machine
20 Commodore 64

QUIZ 128 – General Knowledge

1   The Bill Douglas film *Comrades* (1986) is about which group of Dorset farm labourers?

2   Which Stephen Poliakoff TV drama centres on the fate of the Fallon Photo Library?

3   Which monatomic gas heads the noble gas group in the periodic table?

4   Enhanced with cream and a touch of curry, Lady Curzon soup features which meat?

5   Which Australian hyperrealist sculptor of such works as *Big Baby* is the son-in-law of painter Paula Rego?

6   Abbreviated IVC, what is the largest vein in the human body?

7   Named from the Nahuatl for 'oily', which seeds come from the plant *Salvia hispanica*?

8   Launched in 1994, what is the most successful racing video game series in the world?

9   Which Pacific nation is the world's smallest republic?

10 Named after a legendary beast, which maths term describes a surface with infinite genus but exactly one end?

11 *List of the Lost* is which English singer's 2015 debut novel?

12 Which mammals were called *āyōtōchtli*, Nahuatl for 'turtle-rabbit', by the Aztecs?

13 The USS *Yorktown* (CV-5) aircraft carrier was sunk at which battle in June 1942?

14 The US legal activist John F. Banzhaf III formed which anti-smoking pressure group?

15 Georges Perec wrote his 1969 novel *La Disparition* without using which letter?

16 The Contact process produces high concentrations of which acid?

17 The "martyrs of Giron" took part in which doomed invasion?

18 Which bands of fibrous tissue attach muscles to bones?

19 Which American's personal record of 18.21m is the second-longest ever triple jump?

20 Which Epsom Derby-winning horse is pictured?

Answers to QUIZ 127 – General Knowledge

1	*Steven Universe*	**12**	MP3 playback program – which was called the AMP MP3 Playback Engine
2	Go over Niagara Falls in a barrel and survive (in 1901)		
3	Finland	**13**	Palazzo Pitti
4	Alcoholics Anonymous	**14**	Jean Paul Gaultier
5	Slovenia	**15**	Dalai Lama
6	Joab	**16**	Rosalind Franklin
7	*Swan Lake*	**17**	Oscar Wilde
8	Maria Montessori	**18**	Patrick Edlinger
9	Aga cooker	**19**	Juan Manuel Márquez
10	Encke's Comet	**20**	Shah Rukh Khan
11	*The West Wing*		

1   Established in Vienna in 1869, the *Heeresgeschichtliches Museum* is a museum of what?

2   After its defeat in the Anglo-Zulu War, the Zulu Kingdom was absorbed into which British colony?

3   Which French aircraft manufacturer first flew its Mirage 2000 jet fighter in 1978?

4   Dubbed the "British Schindler", which stockbroker saved 669 mainly Jewish, Czech children on the *Kindertransport*?

5   Produced by Lockheed Martin, which naval defence system is named after the shield of Zeus that was also worn by Athena?

6   Alaa Hussein Ali was convicted of treason for heading the Iraqi puppet government where?

7   Famed for his military manual *The Science of Victory*, which last Generalissimo of the Russian Empire never lost a battle?

8   Britain used tanks for the first time in which battle on September 15, 1916?

9   Which country's flag is supposed to have fallen from heaven during the 1219 Battle of Lyndanisse?

10 Anton Romako's most famous painting portrays the Austrian admiral, Wilhelm von Tegetthoff, at which 1866 naval battle?

11 Admiral Sandy Woodward referred to which conflict as "a lot closer run than many would care to believe"?

12 Lord Salisbury won the 1900 'Khaki Election' in the midst of which war?

13 Which 1812 battle was the bloodiest single day of the Napoleonic Wars?

14 According to his official biography, Boris Gromov was the last Soviet soldier to leave which place?

15 The US journalist Lowell Thomas famously documented the exploits of which soldier?

16 Which Union Army general was defeated at the 1862 Battle of Fredericksburg?

17 The main action of which battle actually took place on Breed's Hill?

18 Who became the *shizoku* when they were pensioned off in 1871?

19 Which boxer defeated Thomas Hearns in the April 15, 1985 fight billed as "The War"?

20 Name the pictured war poet –

Answers to QUIZ 128 – General Knowledge

1	The Tolpuddle Martyrs	13	Midway
2	*Shooting the Past*	14	Action on Smoking and Health (ASH)
3	Helium		
4	Turtle	15	E
5	Ron Mueck	16	Sulphuric acid
6	Inferior vena cava	17	Bay of Pigs in 1961
7	Chia seeds	18	Tendons
8	*Need for Speed*	19	Christian Taylor – Jonathan Edwards is the world record holder
9	Nauru		
10	Loch Ness monster surface		
11	Morrissey	20	Shergar
12	Armadillos		

1   Rumoured to have had an affair with Hattie McDaniel, which US actress said: "I'm as pure as the driven slush"?

2   Which celebrity chimpanzee was originally called Jiggs?

3   What role links Donald Pleasence, Max von Sydow, Telly Savalas and Christoph Waltz?

4   Ferenc Molnar's 1909 play *Liliom* was adapted into which Rodgers & Hammerstein musical?

5   Which African capital city is located on Bioko Island?

6   Niklaus Wirth named which computer language after a French philosopher?

7   In 1926, who checked into a Harrogate hotel calling herself Mrs. Neele?

8   Who sculpted the Piccadilly Circus statue popularly known as "Eros"?

9   Walter Santesso played which photographer in the film *La Dolce Vita*?

10 Which Italian composer (1685-1757) is now known mainly for his 555 keyboard sonatas?

11 Nix, Hydra, Kerberos and Styx are moons of which dwarf planet?

12 Which country consumes more than 20 million cream-filled buns known as semla every year?

13 Fought on August 12, 1759, the Battle of Kunersdorf was which Prussian king's heaviest defeat?

14 Peter Hujar's photo *Candy Darling on Her Deathbed* is the cover of which Mercury Prize-winning album?

15 Arundells was the Salisbury home of which Conservative prime minister?

16 The once-secret Natanz uranium enrichment plant is in which country?

17 Colin Tennant, later the 3rd Baron Glenconner, bought which West Indian island in 1958?

18 An aquatic version of volleyball, the sport of biribol originated in which country?

19 In football, what technique is known as the 'Trivela'?

20 Which painter is pictured?

Answers to QUIZ 129 – War

1   Military history
2   Colony of Natal
3   Dassault Aviation
4   Nicholas Winton
5   Aegis Combat System
6   In Kuwait – after the Iraqi invasion of 1990
7   Alexander Suvorov
8   Battle of Flers-Courcelette – within the Somme Offensive
9   Denmark – the flag is known as the Dannebrog
10 Battle of Lissa
11 Falklands War
12 Second Boer War
13 Battle of Borodino – on September 7, 1812
14 Afghanistan – on February 15, 1989
15 T.E. Lawrence / Lawrence of Arabia
16 Ambrose E. Burnside
17 Bunker Hill – in 1775
18 400,000 Samurai
19 Marvin Hagler
20 Siegfried Sassoon

1   Which 2013 release is the fastest-selling entertainment product in history?

2   Diane de Poitiers (1499-1566) was the mistress of which French king?

3   Block H at Bletchley Park houses which national museum?

4   In 2004, which killer hymenopteran (*Vespa velutina*) is thought to have arrived in France in a container of pottery?

5   Nellie Belles was the American mother of which Tory prime minister?

6   Aged 34, who was appointed the UK's youngest-ever Chief Scout in 2009?

7   Which US singer's 1988 song *Goodbye Horses* features in the film *The Silence of the Lambs*?

8   *Ringworld* is a 1970 science fiction novel by which US author?

9   Saimaa is which country's largest lake?

10 Who finishes this sequence: George VI, George Valentin, Abraham Lincoln, Ron Woodroof, Stephen Hawking?

11 Finlandia, Svedka, Danzka and Belaya Rus are brands of which drink?

12 Abbreviated PCR, which technique for replicating DNA was developed by the US biochemist Kary Mullis?

13 What is the longest and widest single nerve in the human body?

14 Which *Grange Hill* actor played Hitler five times and Himmler three times?

15 The scientist George Washington Carver found more than 300 uses for which legume?

16 The Canadian alternative R&B act Abel Tesfaye uses which stage name?

17 The characters Lol, Woody, Milky, Smell and Combo first appeared in which 2006 film?

18 Which golf trophy is named after the Norwegian-born inventor of the PING putter?

19 Which Australian winner of eight Grand Slam singles tennis titles was jokingly nicknamed "Muscles"?

20 Name the pictured flowering plant –

Answers to QUIZ 130 – General Knowledge

1 Tallulah Bankhead
2 Cheeta
3 Ernst Stavro Blofeld (James Bond's nemesis)
4 *Carousel*
5 Malabo (in Equatorial Guinea)
6 Pascal
7 Agatha Christie
8 Sir Alfred Gilbert (though it depicts Anteros)
9 Paparazzo
10 Domenico Scarlatti
11 Pluto
12 Sweden
13 Frederick the Great or Frederick II – who was defeated by Russo-Austrian forces
14 *I am a Bird Now* by Antony and the Johnsons
15 Edward Heath
16 Iran
17 Mustique
18 Brazil – it originated in the city of Birigui
19 Kicking the ball with the outside of the foot
20 Francis Bacon

1 Corno Grande is the highest peak in which European mountain range?

2 Which sacred mountain is known in Tibetan as *Kang Rinpoche*, or 'Precious Jewel of Snow'?

3 Which Belgian king died in a mountaineering accident in Marche-les-Dames on February 17, 1934?

4 The name of which mountain in Rio de Janeiro is Portuguese for 'hunchback'?

5 What is North Africa's highest peak?

6 Which mountain is the highest point of the Karakoram Range?

7 Which Hindu goddess of love and devotion is named after the Sanskrit for 'daughter of the mountain'?

8 What is the only active volcano in mainland Europe?

9 Mount Mitchell, the highest peak of the Appalachian Mountains, is in which US state?

10 Pico de Orizaba or Citlaltépetl is the highest mountain in which Latin American country?

11 Located on the Argentina-Chile border, what is the world's highest active volcano?

12 Which diamond is named after the Persian for 'mountain of light'?

13 Ol Doinyo Lengai, Maasai for 'Mountain of God', is the only active volcano in which country?

14 Norgay Montes and Hillary Montes are mountain ranges on which dwarf planet?

15 Anamudi in Kerala, India, is the highest peak in which range?

16 St. Catherine's Monastery is situated on which Egyptian mountain?

17 Uhuru Peak is the highest point of which African mountain?

18 The Oracle of Delphi was consulted at the Temple of Apollo on which mountain's slopes?

19 Which Swiss mountain above Wengen hosts the world's longest downhill ski course in World Cup racing?

20 Which Sri Lankan mountain is pictured?

Answers to QUIZ 131 – General Knowledge

1   *Grand Theft Auto V*
2   Henri II
3   The National Museum of Computing
4   Asian hornet or Asian predatory wasp
5   Harold Macmillan
6   Bear Grylls
7   Q. Lazzarus
8   Larry Niven
9   Finland
10 Hugh Glass – they are the roles that have won the last six Best Actor Oscars
11 Vodka
12 Polymerase chain reaction
13 Sciatic nerve or ischiadic nerve
14 Michael Sheard
15 Peanut
16 The Weeknd
17 *This is England*
18 Solheim Cup – named after Karsten Solheim
19 Ken Rosewall
20 Peony

1   *Strutter* was the first song on which US rock band's 1974 debut album?

2   Which religion derives its name from the Old English for 'sorcerer'?

3   Who succeeded Theobald of Bec as Archbishop of Canterbury?

4   The epigraph "Only Connect" features in which 1910 E.M. Forster novel?

5   Which port city is known as "The Golden Gate of Colombia"?

6   A villanelle is a poetic form containing how many lines?

7   Wizard Island is found in which American body of water?

8   Which film festival hands out the Golden Puffin?

9   *Nanuq* is the Inuit name for which animal?

10 Who installed *(Bodyspacemotionthings)* at the Tate in 1971?

11 Located in Oxfordshire, what is the largest station in the RAF?

12 In 2011, the last bottle of The Dalmore 62 was sold for £125,000. What is it?

13 Which heavy woollen fabric for coats is named after the army officer Charles Stanhope, 4th Earl of Harrington?

14 Which botanist published the 1480-page *Herball, or Generall Historie of Plantes* in 1597?

15 Tijuana is in which Mexican state, with its capital at Mexicali?

16 Known for its Washlet and Warmlet lines, Toto is a famous Japanese manufacturer of which fixtures?

17 *I am The Law* is Anthrax's musical ode to which comic book character?

18 Which Blackburn club won the FA Cup in 1883?

19 Which Swiss cyclist, who died on the road in mysterious, possibly suicide-related circumstances, was the first non-Italian Giro d'Italia winner?

20 Name the pictured king –

Answers to QUIZ 132 – Mountains

1 Apennines
2 Mount Kailash
3 Albert I
4 Corcovado
5 Mount Toubkal, Atlas Mountains
6 K2 or Mount Godwin-Austen or Chogori
7 Parvati – who is also called Uma
8 Mount Vesuvius
9 North Carolina
10 Mexico

11 Ojos del Salado
12 Koh-i-Noor
13 Tanzania
14 Pluto
15 Western Ghats
16 Mount Sinai
17 Mount Kilimanjaro
18 Mount Parnassus
19 Lauberhorn – it is 2.78 miles long
20 Adam's Peak or Sri Pada or *Samanalakanda* ('Butterfly Mountain')

QUIZ 134 – General Knowledge

1 Which French photographer is known for his 1953 image *Eiffel Tower Painter*?

2 Which band was formed in 1982 by former Generation X bassist Tony James?

3 Also called thrombocytes, which blood cells' function is to stop bleeding?

4 In 1908, which King of Portugal was assassinated in the Praça do Comércio, Lisbon?

5 Colin Pitchfork (b.1960) was the first person to be convicted of murder based on which evidence?

6 As a last resort defence against predators, what does a Texas horned lizard squirt from its eyes?

7 In Italy, the term *pentito* is used for which type of criminal?

8 Leo Amery gave the "In the name of God, go!" speech attacking which prime minister?

9 Popular in the Alpine regions of Bavaria and Austria, what is the Schuhplattler?

10 Flying by in 1986, what is the only spacecraft to have visited Uranus?

11 Ralph Vaughan Williams' musical work *The Lark Ascending* is based on a poem by who?

12 What is the only kingdom in Polynesia?

13 Which artist's *Pesaro Madonna* (1519-26) is in the Frari Church, Venice?

14 Starting in a tiny Bolton shop in 1876, what is the UK's largest family-owned bakery business?

15 In which German city is the Wallraf-Richartz Museum & Fondation Corboud?

16 The "Big Four" auditors are PwC, EY, KPMG and which company?

17 Located in the Indonesian province of Papua, what is the world's largest gold mine?

18 Which US athlete retained her 100m Olympic title in 1968?

19 Puig Aubert (1925-94) was arguably France's greatest ever player in which sport?

20 Name the German artist from the pictured sculpture –

Answers to QUIZ 133 – General Knowledge

1 Kiss

2 Wicca

3 Thomas Becket in 1162

4 *Howards End*

5 Barranquilla

6 19

7 Crater Lake

8 Reykjavik Film Festival (RIFF)

9 Polar bear

10 Robert Morris

11 RAF Brize Norton

12 A Scotch whisky

13 Petersham – as in Stanhope's other title, Viscount Petersham

14 John Gerard

15 Baja California or Baja California Norte

16 Toilets

17 Judge Dredd

18 Blackburn Olympic

19 Hugo Koblet – in 1950

20 Charles I

1   Which pedestrian Prague bridge on the Vltava is named after a 14th century Holy Roman Emperor?

2   Triumph-Palace, Europe's tallest apartment building, is in which capital city?

3   Which 368m-high Berlin landmark is Germany's tallest structure?

4   "Il Porcellino" ('piglet') is a Florentine nickname for which city landmark?

5   Which king ordered the building of the Tower of London's White Tower?

6   Which Brussels landmark is known in French as 'le Petit Julien'?

7   Which Arizona city is home to the 1831 London Bridge?

8   A tourist landmark in Barcelona, what is La Boqueria?

9   Designed by Ralph Erskine, the Byker Wall is a stretch of 620 maisonettes in which city?

10 Lorenzo Ghiberti created the *Gates of Paradise* bronze doors for which building?

11 The 126m-high Prime Tower is a new landmark in which Swiss city?

12 Southwark Towers, a 25-storey office block, was demolished to make way for which skyscraper?

13 Which city is home to the La Boca neighbourhood, Caminito street museum and Puente de la Mujer footbridge?

14 The "Welcome to Fabulous Las Vegas" sign is an example of which Space Age-inspired style, named after a West Hollywood coffee shop?

15 Which Spanish architect designed Dublin's Samuel Beckett Bridge and James Joyce Bridge?

16 Designed by César Pelli, the Torre Iberdrola is a skyscraper in which Basque city?

17 Which Italian architect designed New York's George Washington Bridge Bus Station (1963)?

18 Crescent Sign Company owner Thomas Fisk Goff designed which Los Angeles landmark in 1923?

19 The Hitchcock film *North by Northwest* climaxes at which landmark?

20 Identify the war memorial in the picture –

Answers to QUIZ 134 – General Knowledge

1   Marc Riboud
2   Sigue Sigue Sputnik
3   Platelets
4   Carlos I
5   DNA fingerprinting
6   A stream of blood
7   A mafioso who has turned informer, literally 'he who has repented'
8   Neville Chamberlain
9   A traditional folk dance
10 Voyager 2
11 George Meredith
12 Tonga
13 Titian
14 Warburtons
15 Cologne
16 Deloitte
17 Grasberg mine
18 Wyomia Tyus
19 Rugby league
20 Katharina Fritsch – it is the Fourth Plinth commission titled *Hahn/Cock*

QUIZ 136 – General Knowledge

1   Anne of Bohemia and Isabella of Valois were the consorts of which king?

2   The novel *Titan* by Jean Paul inspired the nickname of which Austrian's first symphony?

3   The ruined Mayan cities of Seibal and Q'umarkaj are in which country?

4   The world's tallest volcanic stack, which erosional remnant supports the last known wild population of Lord Howe Island stick insect?

5   Ehrenfried Walther von Tschirnhaus invented the European form of what material?

6   What is the smallest Canadian province in terms of area?

7   *The Blinded Samson* (1912) is a self-portrait by which German painter and Berlin Secession president (1915-25)?

8   What is the S.I. base unit of thermodynamic temperature?

9   Which country's seven parishes include Encamp, Ordino and la Massana?

10 Patrizia von Brandenstein procured John Travolta's famous white suit for which film?

11 Which Pope crowned Charlemagne as Holy Roman Emperor in 800?

12 Which English-born photographic pioneer created the zoopraxiscope in 1879?

13 Which English poet (1793-1864) is the subject of Edward Bond's play *The Fool*?

14 Marcus Fenix is the main protagonist of which video game series?

15 Who was *Time* magazine's Man of the Year in 1939 and 1942?

16 Which Sondheim musical features the songs *Not a Day Goes By* and *Our Time*?

17 The rum company Barbancourt was founded in which Caribbean country?

18 *Blazing Saddles* actor Alex Karras, aka Mongo, played for which NFL team?

19 Bobble hat-wearing goalkeeper Jens Martin Knudsen played for which island group?

20 Name the pasta variety –

Answers to QUIZ 135 – Landmarks

1 Charles Bridge – named after Charles IV
2 Moscow
3 Berliner Fernsehturm or Berlin TV Tower
4 The bronze fountain of a boar
5 William the Conqueror
6 The *Manneken-Pis* statue
7 Lake Havasu City
8 Public market
9 Newcastle upon Tyne
10 Florence Baptistery
11 Zürich
12 The Shard
13 Buenos Aires
14 Googie architecture
15 Santiago Calatrava
16 Bilbao
17 Pier Luigi Nervi
18 The HOLLYWOOD sign
19 Mount Rushmore
20 Menin Gate or Menenpoort

1   Which US artist is famed for her photographic series *Untitled Film Stills* (1977-1980)?

2   Which male Pinta giant tortoise, the last of its subspecies, died in June 2012?

3   What title links albums by Bruce Springsteen, Emmylou Harris and Dead Confederate and songs by Neil Young and Miley Cyrus?

4   Which bitmap image format is abbreviated GIF?

5   Which British car marque was used for the Husky, Imp and Minx models?

6   Mount Semeru is the highest volcano on which Indonesian island?

7   Who was King of France during the 1572 St Bartholomew Day's massacre?

8   Which Argentine writer's 1995 novel *Santa Evita* is thought to have sold 10m copies?

9   Which German-language version of *Memories are Made of This* was a huge hit in 1956 for Austrian singer Freddy Quinn?

10 Which Hindu spring festival of colours is celebrated on the full moon day of Phalguna?

11 Which anthropologist once said: "Not a year goes by without my receiving an order for jeans"?

12 Which Austrian painted *Portrait of Wally* (1912) and *Death and the Maiden* (1915)?

13 The Kapellbrücke (Chapel Bridge) is which Swiss city's most famous symbol?

14 The city of Vila Nova de Gaia is the centre of production for which fortified wine?

15 Which Swedish-Danish TV drama stars Sofia Helin as cop Saga Norén?

16 The Catholic priest Josemaría Escrivá founded which organisation in 1928?

17 The American, Marion Tinsley, is considered which game's greatest ever player?

18 Which left-handed US golfer won the Masters in 2012 and 2014?

19 The Tokyo Yūshun is Japan's equivalent of which English sporting event?

20 Identify the pictured drummer –

Answers to QUIZ 136 – General Knowledge

1   Richard II
2   Gustav Mahler
3   Guatemala
4   Ball's Pyramid
5   Porcelain (specifically Meissen porcelain)
6   Prince Edward Island
7   Lovis Corinth
8   Kelvin
9   Andorra
10 *Saturday Night Fever*

11 Saint Leo III
12 Eadweard Muybridge
13 John Clare
14 *Gears of War*
15 Joseph Stalin
16 *Merrily We Roll Along*
17 Haiti
18 Detroit Lions
19 Faroe Islands
20 Conchiglie – meaning 'shells' or 'seashells"

QUIZ 138 – General Knowledge

1   In the 1960s, the Transfermium Wars began as a US-Soviet dispute over what?

2   Which Italian fashion designer (1914-92), whose first designs were for the Reed College (Oregon) skiing team, was Marchese di Barsento?

3   *Long Tall Sally* in 1957 and *Baby Face* in 1959 were Top 3 hits for which US singer?

4   *Darye* is the traditional Korean form of which ceremony?

5   Which German polymath built his 'Step Reckoner' calculating machine in 1673?

6   Which West German Chancellor employed the Stasi spy Günter Guillaume?

7   The baronet Sir Ruthven Murgatroyd is the hero of which Gilbert & Sullivan operetta?

8   A Chinese cultural icon, what type of vehicle is the 'Flying Pigeon'?

9   Which spice was called "török bors" ('Turkish pepper') at first by Hungarians?

10 Which bovine is one of Africa's Big Five game animals?

11 Victor is the red-horned mascot of which Montreal comedy festival?

12 Edinburgh of The Seven Seas is the capital of which South Atlantic island?

13 Ted Mosby told his kids Luke and Penny which rather expansive story in a US sitcom title?

14 Gagarin's Start is a launch site at which cosmodrome?

15 *Vera; or, The Nihilists* (1880) was the flop first play by which dramatist?

16 Which retailer began as a London drapers store founded by William Clark in 1778?

17 Cereology is the study of which mysterious patterns?

18 Which wrestler won his first 'world' title when he beat The Iron Sheik in 1984?

19 The winner of which NASCAR race receives the Harley J. Earl Trophy?

20 A statue of which reformer is seen in the picture?

360b / Shutterstock.com

Answers to QUIZ 137 – General Knowledge

1	Cindy Sherman	12	Egon Schiele
2	Lonesome George	13	Lucerne
3	*Wrecking Ball*	14	Port wine
4	Graphics Interchange Format	15	*The Bridge* / Danish: *Broen* / Swedish: *Bron*
5	Hillman	16	Opus Dei
6	Java	17	Draughts (aka checkers)
7	Charles IX	18	Bubba Watson
8	Tomás Eloy Martínez	19	Epsom Derby
9	*Heimweh* ('Homesickness')	20	Ginger Baker – of Cream and Blind Faith fame
10	Holi		
11	Claude Lévi-Strauss		

1   Which Welsh courtier and dynasty founder was beheaded at Hereford in 1461?

2   Born Angelo Correr, which Pope was forced to resign to end the Western Schism in 1415?

3   Ward Hill Lamon was the self-appointed bodyguard of which president?

4   Also known as water bears or moss piglets, which eight-legged micro-animals are perhaps the most durable of all known organisms?

5   Born Isabel Flores de Oliva, who was the first Catholic saint of the Americas?

6   The John Frost Bridge crosses the Lower Rhine at which Dutch city?

7   *Die Feen* ('The Fairies') was which German composer's first completed opera?

8   Nicknamed "Toom (empty) Tabard", who was king of Scotland from 1292 to 1296?

9   Douglas Hector teaches General Studies in which Alan Bennett play?

10 Which Italian neo-impressionist, who hanged himself in 1907 after the death of his wife and son, painted *The Fourth Estate / Il quarto stato* (1901)?

11 Which group of men avenged their master Asano Naganori in 1703?

12 The Gala and Braeburn apple varieties originated in which country?

13 Herman's Hermits had a US no.1 with a cover of which 1910 music hall song?

14 Who called his son the "miracle which God let be born in Salzburg"?

15 Founded in 797, the Gymnasium Paulinum is said to be Germany's oldest what?

16 Trysil is which country's largest ski resort?

17 Which Hancock Prospecting heiress is Australia's richest person?

18 In 1985, Jason Bunn became England's first world champion in which board game?

19 Who was the first US driver to win the Formula One world title?

20 Name the Istanbul mosque in the image –

Answers to QUIZ 138 – General Knowledge

1 Naming the chemical elements 104 to 106 – eventually named rutherfordium, dubnium and seaborgium

2 Emilio Pucci

3 Little Richard (Richard Wayne Penniman)

4 Tea ceremony

5 Gottfried Wilhelm von Leibniz

6 Willy Brandt (born Herbert Ernst Karl Frahm)

7 *Ruddigore; or, The Witch's Curse*

8 Bicycle

9 Paprika

10 Cape buffalo or African buffalo (*Syncerus caffer*)

11 Just for Laughs / *Juste pour rire*

12 Tristan da Cunha

13 *How I Met Your Mother* – the mother was Tracy McConnell (Cristin Milioti)

14 Baikonur Cosmodrome, Kazakhstan

15 Oscar Wilde

16 Debenhams

17 Crop circles

18 Hulk Hogan

19 Daytona 500

20 Martin Luther

QUIZ 140 – Olympics

1   In 1960, which German sprinter won the men's 100m in an Olympic record time of 10.2 seconds?

2   Denmark won their first and so far only Winter Olympic medal in 1988, a silver medal in which event?

3   Which Canadian was the first to win an Olympic gold for men's snowboarding, despite an initial disqualification for marijuana use?

4   Queen Sofia of Spain represented her native Greece in which sport?

5   Which Swedish winner of 42 World Cup races and seven world championship golds won her sole Olympic title in slalom in 2006?

6   Which Japanese athlete's 1928 triple jump win made him the first Asian Olympic champion in an individual event?

7   What were the first Winter Olympics held in a Communist state?

8   Which late athlete was the first Kenyan to win Olympic marathon gold (in 2008)?

9   Dr Benjamin Spock was an Olympic gold medallist at which sport?

10 Which Finnish vegetarian bricklayer set Olympic records in the 5,000m, 10,000m and cross country races in 1912?

11 Which US swimmer's four golds, including a 50m freestyle individual win, made her the most successful athlete at Atlanta?

12 Which 1960 Olympic 1500m champion ran in kangaroo-hide shoes?

13 Which British figure skater won gold at the 1980 Olympics?

14 Which 64-year-old, part of Sweden's single shot running deer team in 1912, remains the oldest gold medallist in Olympic history?

15 In 1984, which Senegalese man was the first black African skier to take part in the Olympics?

16 Who became the first American male to win Olympic gold in alpine skiing, winning the downhill in 1984?

17 Deon Hemmings' 1996 win in which athletics event made her the first Jamaican woman to win an Olympic gold?

18 In which event did rower Steve Redgrave win his first Olympic gold?

19 Who is the only woman to win four golds in alpine skiing at the Winter Olympics?

20 Which US wrestler, who beat odds of 2,000-1 to win gold, is pictured?

Answers to QUIZ 139 – General Knowledge

1   Owen Tudor – second husband of Catherine of Valois and Henry VII's grandfather
2   Gregory XII
3   Abraham Lincoln
4   Tardigrades
5   St. Rose of Lima (1586-1617)
6   Arnhem
7   Richard Wagner
8   John Balliol
9   *The History Boys*
10 Giuseppe Pellizza da Volpedo
11 The 47 Ronin (leaderless samurai)
12 New Zealand
13 *I'm Henery the Eighth, I am*
14 Leopold Mozart – of Wolfgang Amadeus
15 School
16 Norway
17 Gina Rinehart
18 Monopoly
19 Phil Hill – in 1961
20 Sultan Ahmed Museum, popularly known as the Blue Mosque

1   Located in North Carolina and Tennessee, what is the most visited US national park?

2   Which movie star's Forest Lawn gravestone reads: "She did it the hard way"?

3   Which traditional medicine derives its name from the Zulu word for 'tree'?

4   Which Spaniard wrote the 1941 surrealist play *Desire Caught by the Tail*?

5   Formed in 1949, what is the world's largest military alliance?

6   Arbroath and Forfar are in which historic county of Scotland?

7   Thomas Breakwell (1872-1902) was which religion's first English convert?

8   *Tug of War* and *Flowers in the Dirt* are solo albums by which Beatle?

9   Eaton Hall, Cheshire, is the principal home of which duke?

10 Luke Kelly and Ronnie Drew became founding members of which Irish folk band in 1962?

11 Polyandry is the practice of a woman having what?

12 The Tank Museum at Bovington Camp is in which county?

13 Marzolino cheese is so named because it is traditionally made when?

14 *The Crucifixion* is an 1887 oratorio by which English composer?

15 Who was lead singer of Iron Maiden from 1994 to 1999?

16 Comb, Chunk and Creamed are types of which sweet food?

17 Who became manager of Israel's national football team in 2002?

18 The Trinidad-born brothers Delon, Bevon and Steffon Armitage play which sport?

19 Kilkenny's D.J. Carey was a champion player of which sport?

20 Which Australian author of *Bliss, Illywhacker* and *Jack Maggs* is pictured?

Answers to QUIZ 140 – Olympics

1   Armin Hary
2   Women's curling
3   Ross Rebagliati
4   Sailing – in 1960
5   Anja Pärson
6   Mikio Oda
7   Sarajevo 1984
8   Samuel Wanjiru
9   Rowing – men's eight in 1924
10 Hannes Kolehmainen
11 Amy Van Dyken
12 Herb Elliott
13 Robin Cousins

14 Oscar Swahn
15 Lamine Guèye
16 Bill Johnson
17 400m hurdles
18 Coxed Four – in 1984
19 Janica Kostelić – in 2002 (Slalom, Giant slalom, Combined) and 2006 (Combined)
20 Rulon Gardner – who defeated Alexander Karelin (unbeaten in 13 years) to win 130kg Greco-Roman wrestling gold

1 Spica is the brightest star in which constellation, the largest of the zodiac?

2 George Gershwin heard which of his works as a "musical kaleidoscope of America"?

3 Native to Spain, Airén is said to be the world's most grown what?

4 What is unusual, among mammals, about a Cuban solenodon's saliva?

5 Which novelist set up the Diabetic Association with Dr. R.D. Lawrence in 1934?

6 Bornite, Azurite and Covellite are ores of which transition metal?

7 Which US novelist wrote *Suttree*, *Blood Meridian*, and *All the Pretty Horses*?

8 Popular in Latin America, what are *alfajores*?

9 Which Cyprus resort is named after a 16th century Venetian monastery?

10 Holkham National Nature Reserve – England's largest – is in which county?

11 Kirsten Mehr is the German-born wife of which politician?

12 Which Albanian city is the birthplace of communist leader Enver Hoxha and writer Ismail Kadare?

13 The 2014 film *The Riot Club* is based on which play by Laura Wade?

14 Native to South America, the smallest crocodilian is called Cuvier's what?

15 Located in Bolivia, what is the world's largest salt flat?

16 The Australian, Con Colleano (1899-1973), found fame as which type of circus performer?

ANSWERS ON PAGE **299**

17 Known for his *Veil* and *Unfurled* series, which Color Field artist painted the *Stripe* series works *No End* and *Equator* in the last year of his life?

18 Archery (*Dha*) is the national sport of which landlocked Asian kingdom?

19 Who was dubbed the "Brash Basher of Belleville" by tennis journalist Bud Collins?

20 What is the name of the fortified tower in the picture?

Answers to QUIZ 141 – General Knowledge

1 Great Smoky Mountains National Park
2 Bette Davis
3 Muti – from *umuthi*
4 Pablo Picasso
5 NATO / North Atlantic Treaty Organisation
6 Angus
7 Bahá'í Faith
8 Paul McCartney
9 Gerald Grosvenor, 6th Duke of Westminster
10 The Dubliners, initially called the Ronnie Drew Folk Group
11 More than one husband at the same time
12 Dorset
13 In the month of March (*Marzo*)
14 Sir John Stainer
15 Blaze Bayley
16 Honey
17 Avram Grant
18 Rugby union
19 Hurling
20 Peter Carey

QUIZ 143 – Literature

1 *The Sand Child* (1985) and *This Blinding Absence of Light* (2000) are novels by which Moroccan author?

2 The 1934 novel *A Man Lay Dead* introduced which Inspector of Scotland Yard?

3 Which Australian bush poet wrote *The Man from Snowy River* in 1890?

4 Which Italian director wrote the novels *The Ragazzi* (1955) and *A Violent Life* (1959)?

5 The British army officer Frederick Browning married which author in 1932?

6 Which Andrew Marvell poem claims that "the grave's a fine and private place"?

7 Who first self-published 60 pages of his sci-fi work *WOOL* in 2011?

8 Who wrote about a community of moles in *The Duncton Chronicles*?

9 Which Austrian wrote the 1970 novel *The Goalie's Anxiety at the Penalty Kick*?

10 Which tetralogy of novels begins with *Some Do Not...* (1924)?

11 What is the nickname of Irvine Welsh's literary character Simon Williamson?

12 Which English poet wrote *The Tragicall Historye of Romeus and Juliet* (1562)?

13 Born in Buon Me Thuot, Vietnam in 1971, whose debut novel, *The Sympathizer*, won the 2016 Pulitzer Prize for Fiction?

14 Which title character in a Thomas Hardy novel bears a child named Sorrow?

15 Which Greek-American crime author wrote *The Big Blowdown* and *Hell to Pay*?

16 Which US man of letters wrote *Axel's Castle*, *To the Finland Station* and *Patriotic Gore*?

17 Vacuum cleaner salesman James Wormold is which spy novel's title character?

18 *Some Tame Gazelle* (1950) was the first novel by which writer?

19 Said to be the second best-selling novel in Japan (behind Natsume Soseki's *Kokoro*), *No Longer Human* (1948) is which Japanese author's masterpiece?

20 Name the pictured Dame –

Answers to QUIZ 142 – General Knowledge

1	Virgo	**10**	Norfolk
2	*Rhapsody in Blue*	**11**	Nigel Farage
3	Grape	**12**	Gjirokastër
4	It is venomous	**13**	*Posh*
5	H.G. Wells – it was the forerunner of Diabetes UK	**14**	Dwarf caiman
		15	Salar de Uyuni
6	Copper	**16**	Tightrope walker or tight wire dancer
7	Cormac McCarthy		
8	Cookies, or more specifically, shortbread sandwich cookies with a dulce de leche filling	**17**	Morris Louis
		18	Bhutan
		19	Jimmy Connors
9	Ayia Napa	**20**	Belem Tower or Torre de Belém, Lisbon

1 Created by Aki Kondo, what is the Japanese character Rilakkuma?

2 According to legend, which pasta represents Venus's navel (*ombelico di Venere*)?

3 San Quentin and Folsom are the two oldest prisons in which US state?

4 In 1933, which Budapest-born physicist conceived the idea of a nuclear chain reaction while crossing a London street?

5 A view of his estate, *Le Gras*, the oldest surviving camera photograph was taken by which Frenchman?

6 In which film was Leonardo DiCaprio asked to "draw me like one of your French girls"?

7 The Mole Antonelliana houses the world's tallest museum, the Museo Nazionale del Cinema, in which city?

8 Which Spanish church is the world's largest Gothic cathedral?

9 Located in South Australia, Anna Creek Station is the world's largest working what?

10 Which 1978 Len Deighton novel is set in a world where the Nazis won World War Two?

11 Which Australian birds are so-called because they often travel in groups of twelve?

12 Which TV period drama was set at 165 Eaton Place in Belgravia?

13 The Chicxulub crater is buried underneath which peninsula in Mexico?

14 Founded in 1845, Tsukiji Masamoto is a leading Japanese maker of which high-end items?

15 Which American wrote the 1864 song *If You've Only Got a Moustache*?

16 The largest congregation in the US, Lakewood Church is in which Texas city?

17 The Chapman cycle explains how which molecule is continually regenerated in Earth's stratosphere?

18 Canada's Patrick Anderson is widely considered the world's best player in which Paralympic sport?

19 Who was the first man to win both an Olympic gold and a Super Bowl ring?

20 Which British scientist is pictured?

Answers to QUIZ 143 – Literature

1 Tahar Ben Jelloun
2 Inspector Roderick Alleyn – in Ngaio Marsh's first detective story
3 Andrew Barton 'Banjo' Paterson
4 Pier Paolo Pasolini
5 Daphne du Maurier
6 *To His Coy Mistress*
7 Hugh Howey
8 William Horwood
9 Peter Handke
10 *Parade's End* by Ford Madox Ford
11 'Sick Boy' – as featured in *Trainspotting*, *Porno* and *Skag Boys*
12 Arthur Brooke
13 Viet Thanh Nguyen
14 Tess of the d'Urbervilles / Tess Durbeyfield
15 George Pelecanos
16 Edmund Wilson
17 *Our Man in Havana* by Graham Greene
18 Barbara Pym
19 Osamu Dazai
20 Catherine Cookson

1   What was the largest battle ever fought between Scotland and England?

2   Yvonne Vendroux ("Tante Yvonne") married which Frenchman in 1921?

3   Which French painter's *Melun Diptych* supposedly portrays Charles VII's mistress Agnès Sorel?

4   In 363, Jovian was declared Roman Emperor upon the death of which pagan?

5   Emperor Taizu (927-976) founded which Chinese dynasty?

6   In 1802, engineer Albert Mathieu-Favier put forward an idea for which tunnel?

7   Who was William Warham's successor as Archbishop of Canterbury?

8   The Doolittle Raid was an April 18, 1942 US air attack on which city?

9   Lord Chelmsford was commander-in-chief of the British forces during which 1879 war?

10 What links B.J. Vorster in 1966, Rajiv Gandhi in 1984, Ingvar Carlsson in 1986 and Shimon Peres in 1995?

11 Which Swedish king was victorious at the Battle of Breitenfeld, just north of Leipzig, in September 1631?

12 Which two future US presidents signed the Declaration of Independence?

13 The Shah dynasty ruled which Asian kingdom from 1768 to 2008?

14 Which king ascended the throne upon the murder of his half-brother Edward the Martyr in 978?

15 Emile Zola published which open letter to the president of the French Republic in the newspaper *L'Aurore* on January 13, 1898?

16 The Dutch communist Marinus van der Lubbe was found guilty of causing which 1933 event?

17 A raid on Holbeche House, Staffordshire, resulted in most of which plot's principals being killed or arrested?

18 Which king of Qin and "First Emperor" unified China in 221 BC?

19 The 1328 Treaty of Edinburgh-Northampton recognised which man's title as king of Scots?

20 Which British statesman is pictured?

Answers to QUIZ 144 – General Knowledge

1   A soft toy bear
2   Tortellini
3   California – the former opened in 1852; the latter in 1880
4   Leo Szilard
5   Joseph Nicéphore Niépce – *View from the Window at Le Gras* was taken in 1826 or 1827
6   *Titanic* – his character Jack was asked to do so by Rose (Kate Winslet)
7   Turin
8   Seville Cathedral
9   Cattle station
10 *SS-GB*

11 Apostlebird (*Struthidea cinerea*)
12 *Upstairs, Downstairs*
13 Yucatán Peninsula
14 Knives – for professional chefs, cooks and butchers
15 Stephen Foster
16 Houston
17 Ozone
18 Wheelchair basketball
19 Bob Hayes – the 1964 100m Olympic champion and Super Bowl VI winner with the Dallas Cowboys
20 Susan Greenfield or Baroness Greenfield

1 Which 2015 Pixar film is partly set in the mind of the young girl Riley Andersen?

2 Which Bristol-born physicist is known for his 1928 relativistic quantum theory of the electron?

3 In the *Asterix* comics, who is the oldest inhabitant of Asterix's village?

4 What type of fish is the wels (*Silurus glanis*), Europe's largest freshwater fish?

5 Which Frenchman wrote the decadent novel *The Diary of a Chambermaid* (1900)?

6 Which Austrian composed a Symphony "No. 0" in D Minor and *Wagner Symphony*?

7 Istanbul's Selimiye Army Barracks houses a museum named after which nurse?

8 In Japan, Kampo is a traditional system of what?

9 Initially called the Creola, which chocolate biscuit was introduced in 1910 by the company Peek Freans?

10 Just north of Copenhagen, Dyrehavsbakken – in short Bakken – is the world's oldest what?

11 Which Indian state is the country subdivision with the largest population in the world?

12 Made in 1962, the Marshall JTM45 was the first what?

13 Built on the world's first offshore oil platform, Neft Daşları is a man-made island in which body of water?

14 In an E4 drama's first two series, who are Kelly, Curtis, Alisha, Simon and Nathan?

15 Officially opened in 2009, the visitors' centre Hafod Eryri is located on which mountain's summit?

16 In ancient Rome, *samnite*, *murmillo*, *thraex* and *secutor* were types of what?

17 Which Frenchman hand-built his first bicycle, the *Le Grand Bi* penny-farthing, in 1882?

18 Which British athlete's 50km walk Olympic gold medal was presented to him by Hitler in 1936?

19 Which Sri Lankan cricketer ended his career with 28,016 international runs?

20 Which US make of trailer is pictured?

Answers to QUIZ 145 – History

1 Battle of Flodden (1513) – it was the largest in terms of troop numbers

2 Charles de Gaulle

3 Jean Fouquet

4 Julian the Apostate

5 Song dynasty

6 A cross-Channel fixed link or two-level tunnel under the English Channel

7 Thomas Cranmer – in 1533

8 Tokyo

9 Anglo-Zulu War or Zulu War

10 They all succeeded assassinated prime ministers in those years – Hendrik Verwoerd, Indira Gandhi, Olof Palme, Yitzhak Rabin

11 Gustavus Adolphus or Gustav II Adolf

12 John Adams, Thomas Jefferson

13 Nepal

14 Ethelred II or Ethelred the Unready

15 *J'accuse* – with regards to the Alfred Dreyfus affair

16 Reichstag fire

17 Gunpowder Plot

18 Qin Shi Huang or Shihuangdi – who was born Ying Zheng

19 Robert I or Robert the Bruce

20 Sir Robert Walpole, 1st Earl of Orford and the *de facto* first prime minister of Great Britain

1   Who formed the ill-fated pop duo Seona Dancing with Bill Macrae?

2   Ponta Delgada is the capital of which Atlantic island group?

3   Which Englishman patented the calotype photographic process in 1841?

4   Radiohead are named after the 1986 song *Radio Head* by which US band?

5   Carmen Callil founded which publishing company in 1973?

6   Who opened his first holiday camp at Skegness in 1936?

7   Which Caribbean country's flag features a Sisserou parrot?

8   Edmund of Langley (1341-1402) founded which English royal dynasty?

9   What are you doing if you are engaging in "static apnea"?

10 Which psychoanalyst praised cocaine in his 1884 essay *Uber Coca*?

11 Who called his work "light writing" in the 1957 memoir *Over Seventy*?

12 In 1964, Alec Guinness won a Tony award for playing which Welsh poet?

13 Set in the fictional Dublin suburb of Carrigstown, what is Ireland's most popular and longest running TV soap?

14 Which theoretical physicist discovered the law of the photoelectric effect in 1905?

15 Robert the Bruce split Henry de Bohun's head with a battle-axe at which 1314 clash?

16 Which Flemish artist's altarpiece, *The Last Judgement* (1446-52), is in the Hôtel-Dieu, Beaune?

17 In 2010, David Cameron, aged 43, became the youngest prime minister since which man in 1812?

18 The Scottish Grand National is run where every April?

19 Arthur Wint was Jamaica's first Olympic gold medallist, winning which athletics event in 1948?

20 Which nuclear power plant features in the image?

Answers to QUIZ 146 – General Knowledge

1 *Inside Out*
2 Paul Dirac – it is named the Dirac equation
3 Geriatrix
4 Catfish
5 Octave Mirbeau
6 Anton Bruckner
7 Florence Nightingale
8 Medicine
9 Bourbon biscuit – the first cream sandwich biscuit
10 Amusement park
11 Uttar Pradesh
12 Guitar amplifier made by Marshall Amplification
(the company founded by Jim Marshall in 1962)
13 Caspian Sea – it is part of Azerbaijan
14 *Misfits*
15 Snowdon – *Hafod* is Welsh for upland summer residence; *Eryri* is the Welsh name for Snowdonia
16 Gladiator
17 Armand Peugeot
18 Harold Whitlock
19 Kumar Sangakkara
20 Airstream

1 *The Notebooks of Malte Laurids Brigge* (1910) is which German-language poet's only novel?

2 The *Taddei Tondo* is the UK's only marble sculpture by which artist?

3 The Buggles had their sole no.1 with which 1979 debut single?

4 Scott Carpenter's death in October 2013 left which man as the sole surviving Mercury 7 astronaut?

5 Which Suffolk nuclear power station is the UK's only pressurised water reactor (PWR)?

6 What was the only European communist state not to sign the Warsaw Pact?

7 The 1961 Western *One-Eyed Jacks* is the only film directed by which US actor?

8 Which "Islamic Republic" is the world's sole Shi'ite state?

9 Which 94-year-old actress is the last surviving *Golden Girl*?

10 Jamal Al-Gashey is the lone surviving terrorist perpetrator of which event?

11 What is the sole official language in the Swiss cantons of Jura and Vaud?

12 Which stand-up comedian's only film as a director was *Jo Jo Dancer, Your Life is Calling* (1986)?

13 Covered in conical spines, which Australian lizard is the sole species in the genus *Moloch*?

14 Where is the only official state residence of royalty in the US?

15 Who is the only actor seen on-screen in the 2013 film *Locke*?

16 *Les Plaideurs* was the sole comedy by which French dramatist, who also wrote the play *Andromaque*?

17 What is the only Asian country that has not officially adopted the metric system?

18 From 1966, which Nazi was the sole inmate in Berlin's Spandau prison?

19 Winston Churchill Avenue is the only road in and out of which British overseas territory?

20 Name the "UK based pop-rock artist" in the image –

Helga Esteb / Shutterstock.com

Answers to QUIZ 147 – General Knowledge

1	Ricky Gervais	13	*Fair City*
2	Azores	14	Albert Einstein
3	William Fox Talbot	15	Battle of Bannockburn
4	Talking Heads	16	Rogier van der Weyden
5	Virago Press	17	Lord Liverpool or Robert
6	Billy Butlin		Jenkinson, 2nd Earl of
7	Dominica		Liverpool
8	House of York – he was the	18	Ayr Racecourse
	1st Duke of York	19	400m
9	You are holding your breath	20	Three Mile Island Nuclear
10	Sigmund Freud		Generating Station – on the
11	P.G. Wodehouse		namesake island in the
12	Dylan Thomas – in the play		Susquehanna River, near
	Dylan by Sidney Michaels		Harrisburg, Pennsylvania

1   Chow Yun-Fat played the Hong Kong assassin Ah Jong in which 1989 film?

2   One of three he described as "the merriest, the wiliest and the holiest harlots" in his realm, Jane Shore was a mistress of which king?

3   The American Ornithologists' Union named its scientific journal in honour of which extinct, flightless bird, also called the garefowl?

4   Who is chased by Blinky, Inky, Pinky and Clyde?

5   The hyoid bone is so-named because it is "shaped like" which Greek letter?

6   Which cathedral church of Rome houses the Cathedra (ecclesiastical seat) of the Roman Pontiff (Pope)?

7   Which operatic title character abandons Donna Elvira, a lady of Burgos?

8   Brass mainly consists of which two metals?

9   Handel's *Music for the Royal Fireworks* celebrated the end of which war?

10 Thor Heyerdahl's boat *Ra II* was made of what material?

11 Which Jewish festival, occurring on the sixth day of Sivan, is also known as the Feast of Weeks?

12 What common household pet has the scientific name *Carassius auratus*?

13 The Falklands celebrate which woman's "Day" on January 10?

14 In *Hamlet*, which character's last words are "I am slain!"?

15 Sharing its name with a 'Sea', what is the largest species of tern in the world?

16 The herb-flavoured Polish drink Żubrówka is known by which English name?

17 Ochre brittlegill, pig's ear and shaggy parasol are types of what?

18 Which German's 27-year reign as world chess champion began in 1895?

19 Dame Sarah Storey was a Paralympic champion in which two sports?

20 Which American celebrity chef is pictured?

Answers to QUIZ 148 – The One and Only...

1 Rainer Maria Rilke
2 Michelangelo
3 *Video Killed the Radio Star*
4 John Glenn
5 Sizewell B
6 Yugoslavia
7 Marlon Brando
8 Iran
9 Betty White
10 Munich massacre in 1972
11 French
12 Richard Pryor
13 Thorny devil or thorny dragon (*Moloch horridus*)
14 Honolulu, Oahu (the Iolani Palace, home to the last two of the Hawaiian Kingdom's monarchs)
15 Tom Hardy – who played Ivan Locke
16 Jean Racine
17 Myanmar (Burma)
18 Rudolf Hess
19 Gibraltar
20 Chesney Hawkes – who had a 1991 no.1 single with ... *The One and Only*

1   Which US duo had a worldwide hit with *Love Will Keep Us Together* in 1975?

2   Which nebula is classified with the Messier number, M1?

3   The Mantoux test is used to diagnose which infectious disease?

4   Which 1854 opera is the first in Wagner's "Ring Cycle"?

5   Who was the first female winner of the Perrier Comedy Award?

6   Begun in around 1803, *The Watsons* is an incomplete novel by which author?

7   Who was elected president of the Royal Society in 1703?

8   The 1960 film *Scent of Mystery* introduced which viewer gimmick?

9   Which bookshop chain was founded in 1987 by James Heneage?

10 Which soul star released the album *Hot Buttered Soul* in 1969?

11 In which novel does Farmer Boldwood shoot Sergeant Troy?

12 Who founded the Severn Wildfowl Trust at Slimbridge in 1946?

13 *Postcards from God* is a musical about which unlikely art critic?

14 In Japanese cuisine, what sort of marine delicacy is *uni*?

15 Sacred Heart Hospital was the setting for which US sitcom?

16 *Le Boudin* is the official march of which elite military unit?

17 What type of team features Beaters, Chasers, a Keeper and a Seeker?

18 Which five-time Tour de France winner has the most career stage wins ever?

19 In 1970, who became the last player to score in every FA Cup round?

20 Native to Africa, which type of noct...

Answers to QUIZ 149 – General Knowledge

1 *The Killer*
2 Edward IV
3 Great auk (*Pinguinus impennis*) – the journal is named *The Auk*
4 Pac-Man
5 Upsilon
6 Papal Archbasilica of St. John in Lateran or St. John Lateran, Rome
7 Don Giovanni – in the opera by Mozart
8 Copper and zinc
9 War of Austrian Succession (1740-48) – it also celebrated the signing of the Treaty of Aix-la-Chapelle
10 Papyrus
11 Shavuot
12 Goldfish
13 Margaret Thatcher
14 Polonius
15 Caspian tern (*Hydroprogne caspia*) – known in New Zealand as the *taranui*
16 Bison Grass Vodka
17 Mushroom
18 Emanuel Lasker
19 Cycling and swimming
20 Mario Batali

ANSWERS ON PAGE 315

...ich country?

...e British Isles?

...ndreds including

...red the countries of Freedonia

...s are resorts on which "Costa"?

6 W...   ...nland country on the African
   contin...

7 What anim... ...ents a zoo on an Ordnance Survey map?

8 Mount Whitney is the highest peak in which Californian
   range?

9 Splott and St. Mellons are districts in which British city?

10 Puncak Jaya is the highest peak on which island?

11 Gruyère cheese is named after a town in which Swiss canton?

12 Northern Europe's largest castle ruin, Hammershus is on
   which Danish island?

13 Mount Paektu is the highest mountain in which Asian
   country?

14 Charlotte is the largest city in which US state?

15 The Uffington White Horse is a chalk hill figure in which
   county?

16 The Salton Sea is the largest lake in which US state?

17 Büsingen am Hochrhein is an exclave of Germany surrounded
   by which country?

18 Mies van der Rohe named which chair after the largest city in
   Moravia?

19 Which island is known as *Ellan Vannin* in its native language?

20 Name the pictured volcano –

Answers to QUIZ 150 – General Knowledge

	Captain & Tennille	**12**	Peter Scott
	Crab Nebula – in Taurus	**13**	Sister Wendy Beckett
	Tuberculosis	**14**	Sea urchin roe
	Das Rheingold	**15**	*Scrubs*
	Jenny Eclair (in 1995)	**16**	French Foreign Legion
	Jane Austen	**17**	Quidditch team
	Sir Isaac Newton	**18**	Eddy Merckx – with 34 stage
	Smell-O-Vision		wins
	Ottakar's	**19**	Peter Osgood – for Chelsea
0	Isaac Hayes	**20**	Galago or bushbaby or
1	*Far from the Madding Crowd*		nagapie
	by Thomas Hardy		

QUIZ 152 – General Knowledge

1   Which swimwear brand is named after the French word for crankshaft?

2   Which metal is common to the alloys Monel, Invar and Nitinol?

3   Which US painter depicted restaurants in *Automat* (1927) and *Chop Suey* (1929)?

4   What one-word name was adopted by the US photographer Arthur Fellig?

5   Cousin Jerez was the villain in which spoof soap?

6   Which reporter's first adventure took place *in the Land of the Soviets*?

7   Which German wrote the tragic play *Maria Stuart* (1800)?

8   Joyce Cansfield won the first series of which game show in 1982?

9   Which Ari Folman film deals with the 1982 Sabra & Shatila massacre?

10 What is the Lord Mayor of the City of London's official residence?

11 Which 2008 Bernard Cornwell novel recounts a 1415 battle?

12 Which comedy duo were *The Magnificent Two* in a 1967 film?

13 Rising to almost 370m, Cave Hill overlooks which UK city?

14 Which artist directed the video for Blur's no.1 single *Country House*?

15 Which London clockmaker invented an eponymous brass alloy?

16 Which comedy character has three children: Valmai, Bruce and Kenneth?

17 Nicholas Lanier became the first holder of which Royal Household title in 1626?

18 Who won his fourth and final World Superbike Championship in 1999?

19 Philippe Jeantot founded which round-the-world yacht race in 1989?

20 Which US president is depicted on the pictured coin?

Answers to QUIZ 151 – Geography

1	Spain	12	Bornholm
2	Lough Neagh	13	North Korea
3	Staffordshire	14	North Carolina
4	*Duck Soup*	15	Oxfordshire
5	Costa del Sol	16	California
6	The Gambia	17	Switzerland
7	Elephant	18	Brno chair
8	Sierra Nevada	19	Isle of Man – the language is Manx
9	Cardiff		
10	New Guinea	20	Mount Etna or Mongibello or *Mungibeddu*
11	Canton of Fribourg (as in the town of Gruyères)		

1 Which red grape variety is the main component in a Chianti wine blend?

2 Which family resides in a gothic mansion at 1 Cemetery Ridge?

3 As in the cinemas, IMAX is a blend of which two words?

4 Which German physicist's constant is denoted by the letter h?

5 Carlo Petrini began which culinary movement in 1986?

6 Opened in 1965, what was Britain's first long-distance footpath?

7 Which writer was called "English literature's performing flea" by Sean O'Casey?

8 David Cameron was head of corporate communications at which TV company?

9 Jaime Sin (1928-2005) was the 30th Roman Catholic Archbishop of which Asian capital?

10 The American biologist Gregory Pincus is best known for developing what?

11 Both Picasso and Matisse have been credited with calling which French painter "the father of us all"?

12 Which Michael Jackson song about a boy and his rat comes from a 1972 sequel to the horror film *Willard*?

13 Which southern sky constellation features the Coalsack Nebula and Jewel Box star cluster?

14 Who is the Labour MP for Islington North?

15 Launched in 2003, which saloon car is Rolls Royce's flagship model?

16 What did Ermal Fraze invent after he used a car bumper to open a can?

17 Which spy was the subject of George Steiner's 1980 *New Yorker* essay *The Cleric of Treason*?

18 In 1900, fencer Ramon Fonst won which Caribbean country's first Olympic gold?

19 Jason Robinson began his rugby league career at which South Leeds club?

20 Which Los Angeles observatory is pictured?

Answers to QUIZ 152 – General Knowledge

1	Vilebrequin	12	Morecambe & Wise
2	Nickel	13	Belfast
3	Edward Hopper	14	Damien Hirst
4	Weegee	15	Christopher Pinchbeck
5	*Acorn Antiques*	16	Dame Edna Everage
6	Tintin	17	Master of the King's Musick
7	Friedrich von Schiller	18	Carl Fogarty
8	*Countdown*	19	Vendée Globe
9	*Waltz with Bashir*	20	Thomas Jefferson – on a
10	Mansion House		Jefferson nickel
11	*Azincourt*		

QUIZ 154 – Popular Music

1 Which star of *The Rocky Horror Show* released the albums *Read My Lips* and *Fearless*?

2 Teenagers Suzuka Nakamoto, Yui Mizuno and Moa Kikuchi formed which Japanese metal idol band in 2010?

3 Which cheese-making bassist wrote the memoir *Bit of a Blur*?

4 Alison Moyet formed which pop duo with Vince Clarke?

5 Which Christmas no.1 first appeared on the 1984 LP *Various Positions*?

6 Who topped the charts in 1955 with her single *Mambo Italiano*?

7 *The Kick Inside* (1978) was which female musician's debut album?

8 The musician Manfred Mann was born in which African city?

9 Tom Chaplin, Tim Rice-Oxley and Richard Hughes form which band?

10 Which American singer "kissed a girl" and "liked it"?

11 Which Canadian singer had a 1995 no. 1 with *Think Twice*?

12 Peter Gabriel quit as which band's lead singer in 1975?

13 Fedde Le Grand had a 2006 no. 1 with *Put Your Hands Up For...* where?

14 Which Pink Floyd album studio features the tracks *Money*, *Breathe* and *Eclipse*?

15 Which chart-topping pop group was originally called Touch?

16 Which English band was founded in 1965 by Steve Marriott, Ronnie Lane, Kenney Jones and Jimmy Winston?

17 Which 1980s pop star was born Stuart Leslie Goddard?

18 Formed in 1971, which British pub rock band had top 40 hits with *She's a Windup* and *Milk and Alcohol*?

19 The name of which industrial band, formed in West Berlin in 1980, means 'Collapsing New Buildings'?

20 Which *King Kunta* rapper is pictured?

Christian Bertrand / Shutterstock.com

Answers to QUIZ 153 – General Knowledge

1   Sangiovese
2   The Addams Family
3   Image, maximum
4   Max Planck
5   Slow Food
6   The Pennine Way
7   P.G. Wodehouse
8   Carlton
9   Manila – he was known as Cardinal Sin
10 The oral contraceptive known as "the pill"
11 Paul Cézanne
12 *Ben*
13 Crux ('Cross')
14 Jeremy Corbyn
15 Rolls-Royce Phantom
16 The ring-pull on drink cans or pull-tab
17 Anthony Blunt
18 Cuba – it came in the épée event
19 Hunslet
20 Griffith Observatory

QUIZ 155 – General Knowledge

1   Which French company made the £23,484 *Patchwork Tribute* bag?

2   What flaked fish traditionally features in the dish kedgeree?

3   Henry and Helal Hassenfeld founded which toy company in 1923?

4   Who was the Labour candidate at the 1982 Beaconsfield by-election?

5   Elsanta is the most sold variety of which fruit in supermarkets?

6   The manat is the currency of which two former Soviet republics?

7   Rear Admiral Charles Davis Lucas was the first recipient of which award?

8   Consecotaleophobia is the fear of which dining implements?

9   Which Miller beverage is "The Champagne of Beers"?

10 Which 1969 Samuel Beckett play lasts about 35 seconds?

11 Baby Spencer Elden features on the cover of which rock album?

12 Horace Saussure made the first ascent of which mountain in 1787?

13 The Manchester-born computer programmer Col Needham created which online database in 1990?

14 Which town in the Altötting district of Upper Bavaria is home to Europe's longest castle at 1,043m?

15 Which of the Galápagos Islands was named after Ecuador's first president?

16 Which iron-rich protein enables red blood cells to carry oxygen from your lungs to the rest of the body?

17 Largely black except for a white facial shield, which plump water bird of the rail family is *Fulica atra*?

18 Each player begins a game of draughts with how many playing pieces?

19 Denis Ten is the first person from which country to win a world or Olympic medal in figure skating?

20 Which Lockheed Martin fighter aircraft is pictured?

Answers to QUIZ 154 – Popular Music

1 Tim Curry
2 Babymetal – their band aliases are, respectively, "Su-metal", "Yuimetal" and "Moametal"
3 Alex James
4 Yazoo
5 *Hallelujah* by Leonard Cohen
6 Rosemary Clooney
7 Kate Bush
8 Johannesburg

9 Keane
10 Katy Perry
11 Celine Dion
12 Genesis
13 Detroit
14 *The Dark Side of the Moon*
15 Spice Girls
16 Small Faces
17 Adam Ant
18 Dr. Feelgood
19 Einsturzende Neubauten
20 Kendrick Lamar

1 In biology, what is the smallest unit of life that can exist independently?

2 Which amphibians are the most poisonous animals alive?

3 Which French composer's *Messagesquisse* (1977) is scored for seven cellos (one soloist)?

4 Which French author wrote the 1952 novel *The Bridge over the River Kwai*?

5 Which title links a Taylor Swift single, Bastille's debut album, and a memoir by Lorna Sage?

6 Which RAF station is the home of the Royal Air Force's HQ Air Command?

7 Which bird (*Alectoris philbyi*) was named after the father of double agent Kim Philby?

8 Janette and Ian Tough perform as which Scottish comedy duo?

9 *Vogue* magazine dubbed the French chef Pierre Hermé "The Picasso of..." what?

10 Which 1993 Wallace & Gromit film features the villainous penguin Feathers McGraw?

11 Which US TV comedy centres on the troubled internet startup Pied Piper?

12 Odysseus fooled the cyclops Polyphemus by saying his name was what?

13 Henry the Young King (1155-83) was the son of which king?

14 Which Astor was the richest passenger on board *Titanic*?

15 What is the first astrological sign in the zodiac?

16 What is the biggest selling Scotch whisky brand worldwide?

17 The Special Boat Service (SBS) is based in which Dorset seaport?

18 The Larry O'Brien trophy is awarded to the winner of which championship series?

19 Who is the only swimmer to win back-to-back Olympic 50m and 100 freestyle titles?

20 Who is the pictured Labour politician?

Answers to QUIZ 155 – General Knowledge

1 Louis Vuitton
2 Haddock
3 Hasbro
4 Tony Blair
5 Strawberry
6 Azerbaijan and Turkmenistan
7 Victoria Cross
8 Chopsticks
9 Miller High Life
10 *Breath*
11 *Nevermind* by Nirvana
12 Mont Blanc
13 Internet Movie Database (IMDb)
14 Burghausen
15 Floreana Island – named after Juan José Flores
16 Haemoglobin
17 Eurasian coot or coot
18 12
19 Kazakhstan
20 F-22 Raptor

1 Which Assam-born actress won an Oscar for the title role in *Darling*?

2 Mel Gibson's film *Apocalypto* is in which Mayan language?

3 Which 1994 film centres on the wrongly jailed prisoner Andy Dufresne?

4 Who directed *The Lady Eve* and *The Palm Beach Story*?

5 The "Sin" in the title of the 2005 film *Sin City* is short for what word?

6 Who won her first Best Actress Oscar for *Morning Glory* in 1934?

7 Dame May Whitty played the title role in which 1938 film?

8 Professor Marcus led which gang of titular crooks in an Ealing comedy film?

9 Costume designer William Travilla created the iconic ivory cocktail dress seen in which 1955 film?

10 Who wrote, co-directed and starred in the 1942 war film *In Which We Serve*?

11 Who won Oscars for directing *Mrs Miniver* and *The Best Years of Our Lives*?

12 Which role was played by Laurence Olivier in the 1941 film *That Hamilton Woman*?

13 *Desperado* was Robert Rodriguez's 1995 sequel to which low-budget film?

14 Which 1984 film, with a Christmastime setting, is set in the town of Kingston Falls?

15 Which 1946 film, with a Christmastime setting, is set in the town of Bedford Falls?

16 Anil Kapoor played the quiz show host Prem Kumar in which Oscar-winning film?

17 Which Harlen Coben novel was adapted into a 2006 French film by director Guillaume Canet?

18 The film *The Blair Witch Project* was set in which state?

19 Cyrus "The Virus", "Diamond Dog", "Billy Bedlam" and Cameron Poe flew with which airline?

20 Which movie award is pictured?

Answers to QUIZ 156 – General Knowledge

1 Cell

2 Golden poison frogs or golden dart frogs – a single frog harbours enough toxin to kill 10 grown men

3 Pierre Boulez

4 Pierre Boulle

5 *Bad Blood*

6 RAF High Wycombe

7 Philby's partridge, named after the British explorer St. John Philby

8 The Krankies or Wee Jimmy Krankie & Ian Krankie

9 Pastry

10 *The Wrong Trousers*

11 *Silicon Valley*

12 "Nobody" or "No man"

13 Henry II

14 John Jacob Astor IV

15 Aries

16 Johnnie Walker

17 Poole

18 NBA Finals

19 Alexander Popov (in 1992 and 1996)

20 Sadiq Khan – former MP for Tooting now Mayor of London

1   Worn by the Queen as a skirt, the Balmoral Tartan was designed by which man?

2   Assassinated in 1961, Patrice Lumumba was which country's first Prime Minister?

3   Which duo made the 1895 film *The Arrival of a Train at La Ciotat Station*?

4   Ruben Rausing founded which Swedish packaging company in 1951?

5   The London shop Paxton & Whitfield specialises in which food?

6   Worn in cold weather, what is a Chullo?

7   Dr. Harlan Tarbell created a renowned course in which subject?

8   Trevor Wilkinson founded which sports car company in 1947?

9   In France, which economic problem is known as *chômage*?

10   Citizen Chauvelin is the chief enemy of which literary hero?

11   The Syrian philosopher Michel Aflaq was the ideological founder of which Arabic political party?

12   At which 1265 battle was Simon de Montfort killed?

13   Opened by António Salazar in 1936, Tarrafal was a notorious prison camp in which Portuguese colony?

14   Which horror movie villain wears an altered Captain James T. Kirk mask?

15   The male of which national bird of Antigua and Barbuda inflates its bright red throat pouch to attract mates?

16   Which 1850-64 Chinese rebellion was the bloodiest civil war in history?

17   In sumo wrestling, what role is performed by a *tokoyama*?

18   The Argentine football club Newell's Old Boys is based in which city?

19 What is the 8th hole at Royal Troon's Old Course called?

20 Co-designed by Rem Koolhaas, what is the name of the pictured building in Beijing?

Answers to QUIZ 157 – Film

1 Julie Christie
2 Yucatec
3 *The Shawshank Redemption*
4 Preston Sturges
5 Basin
6 Katharine Hepburn
7 *The Lady Vanishes*
8 *The Ladykillers*
9 *The Seven Year Itch* – the dress was worn by The Girl (Marilyn Monroe)
10 Noël Coward
11 William Wyler
12 Horatio Nelson
13 *El Mariachi*
14 *Gremlins*
15 *It's a Wonderful Life*
16 *Slumdog Millionaire*
17 *Tell No One*
18 Maryland
19 Con Air – in the 1997 film of the same name
20 César Award – the French equivalent of the BAFTA or Oscar

1   Known by the Latin name *Acherontia atropos*, what is the largest moth to appear in Britain?

2   A minaret in the town of Eger in Hungary marks the northernmost point of which empire's expansion?

3   Opening in 1998, Taipei's Cat Flower Garden was the first establishment of what type?

4   At Bayreuth, it is customary not to applaud at the end of which 1882 Wagner opera's first act?

5   Who invented bifocal glasses, the odometer and the lightning rod?

6   Which DIY products brand uses the strapline: "Does exactly what it says on the tin"?

7   If Marcus Aurelius was the last of the Five Good Emperors of ancient Rome, who became the first in 96 AD?

8   Appleton Estate, Montilla, Cacique and Brugal are brands of which spirit?

9   The 169-seat Storting is the parliament of which country?

10 Which English grime MC, known for his hit *Wearing My Rolex*, was born Richard Kylea Cowie?

11 Founded in Los Angeles in 1934, what is the world's largest law firm by revenue?

12 Which 2005 film centres on changes at the Northampton shoe factory Price & Sons?

13 Which crime writer created the Luton private eye Joe Sixsmith?

14 The Belavezha Accords effectively dissolved which State?

15 Which French designer (b.1951) invented the puffball or *pouf* skirt?

16 The Norwegian artist Lise Myhre created which comic strip goth?

17 Which Italian company released the A6 Gran Turismo in 1947?

18 Swapping shirts is a tradition that dates back to a 1931 football game that saw which team first beat England?

19 Which driver won his first Formula One world championship in 1951?

20 What is the pictured London museum?

Answers to QUIZ 158 – General Knowledge

1   Prince Albert
2   The [Democratic Republic of the] Congo
3   Auguste & Louis Lumière
4   Tetra Pak
5   Cheese – it is a cheesemongers
6   Peruvian hat with ear-flaps
7   Magic, as in the *Tarbell Course in Magic*
8   TVR
9   Unemployment
10 "The Scarlet Pimpernel"
11 Ba'ath Party
12 Evesham
13 Cape Verde – on the island of Santiago
14 Michael Myers – in the *Halloween* movies
15 Magnificent frigatebird (*Fregata magnificens*)
16 Taiping Rebellion – which took an estimated 20 million lives
17 The wrestlers' hairdresser
18 Rosario
19 The Postage Stamp
20 CCTV Headquarters – as in China Central Television

1   What is alopecia totalis?

2   The rotator cuff is a muscle group that stablises which part of the body?

3   Which mathematician was known as the 8th Laird of Merchiston?

4   The Higgs boson was named after a British physicist with which first name?

5   Olericulture is the science of growing of what?

6   Which German mathematician (1845-1918) founded set theory?

7   What are simple, comminuted and greenstick types of?

8   The National Physical Laboratory is in which London suburb?

9   Born in 2001, CC was the first clone of which animal?

10 The Scottish chemist Daniel Rutherford isolated which gaseous element in 1772?

11 Which gas law is expressed as $PV = k$?

12 Luc Montagnier and Françoise Barré-Sinoussi won the 2008 Nobel prize in medicine for their discovery of which lentivirus?

13 In 1967, which South African surgeon performed the first successful human-to-human heart transplant?

14 In 1995, theoretical physicist Edward Witten proposed M-theory as a unification of what?

15 What is the hardest substance in the human body?

16 Which group of sheet silicate minerals are named after the Latin word for 'crumb'?

17 Which process depends on the glycoprotein, von Willebrand factor, to bind to Factor VIII?

18 Which two metals are extracted from the black metallic ore, coltan?

19 Which US astronomer was the first to describe the redshift phenomenon and tie it to an expanding universe?

20 Which Australian mathematician is pictured?

Answers to QUIZ 159 – General Knowledge

1 Death's-head hawk moth
2 Ottoman empire
3 Cat café
4 *Parsifal*
5 Benjamin Franklin
6 Ronseal
7 Nerva
8 Rum
9 Norway
10 Wiley
11 Latham & Watkins
12 *Kinky Boots*
13 Reginald Hill
14 Soviet Union
15 Christian Lacroix
16 Nemi
17 Maserati
18 France – who won 5-2
19 Juan Manuel Fangio
20 Sir John Soane's Museum
   – in Lincoln's Inn Fields

1   The Spinnaker Tower overlooks which English city's harbour?

2   The 2.55 is a classic bag produced by which fashion house?

3   Who painted the Queen's first portrait when she was aged just seven?

4   Altair is the brightest star in which constellation?

5   Dementia praecox was an early name for which mental illness?

6   Picasso said: "We have learned nothing" after viewing which paintings?

7   In the food industry, what paste-like product is MRM?

8   Which antelope-like artiodactyl mammal is North America's fastest land mammal?

9   Who became the first King of Romania in 1881?

10 Henry Perky invented which breakfast cereal in 1893?

11 Which Swiss modernist wrote the 1925 book *The Robber*?

12 At which battle did Rudyard Kipling's only son, John, die in 1915?

13 In a poem by Amy Lowell, which flowers are repeatedly described as "False blue, / White, / Purple"?

14 Which organ accounts for 75 per cent or more of the body's cholesterol synthesis?

15 The poet William Ernest Henley was Robert Louis Stevenson's model for which character?

16 Situated on the Huddersfield Narrow Canal, what is the longest, highest and deepest canal tunnel in Britain?

17 Held in September and October, what are *les vendanges*?

18 Which Jewish pugilist published *The Art of Boxing* in 1789?

19 South African rugby star Bryan Gary Habana is named after which two Manchester United footballers?

20 Which Hindu god is depicted in the image?

Answers to QUIZ 160 – Sciences

1   The complete loss of scalp hair
2   Shoulder or shoulder joint
3   John Napier
4   Peter
5   Vegetables
6   Georg Cantor
7   Fracture
8   Teddington
9   Cat (short for CopyCat)
10 Nitrogen
11 Boyle's law or Boyle-Mariotte law or Mariotte's law – where P is the pressure of the gas, V is the volume of gas, and k is a constant
12 HIV (human immunodeficiency virus)
13 Christiaan Barnard
14 Superstring or string theories
15 Tooth enamel
16 Mica
17 Blood clotting or coagulation
18 Niobium & tantalum – coltan is short for columbite-tantalite
19 Edwin Hubble
20 Terence Tao – first Australian to win Fields Medal, in 2006 for contributions to "partial differential equations, combinatorics, harmonic analysis and additive number theory"

QUIZ 162 – Theatre

1   The T-Birds and the Pink Ladies are gangs in which musical?

2   Daron Hagen's 1999 opera *Bandanna* is based on which Shakespeare tragedy?

3   Who was the first director of the Royal Shakespeare Company?

4   Which mime artist used the stage persona "Bip"?

5   Who wrote the plays *Top Girls* (1982) and *The Skriker* (1994)?

6   Alceste is the painfully honest hero of which Molière play?

7   Later to play Private Godfrey in *Dad's Army*, who wrote the 1923 play *The Ghost Train*?

8   The film *Mrs. Henderson Presents* centred on which London theatre?

9   Sir Bernard Miles founded which London theatre in 1959?

10 Which 1959 musical was Rodgers and Hammerstein's last collaboration?

11 The musical *Five Guys Named Moe* celebrates which man's music?

12 Laura Michelle Kelly originated which musical's title role in 2004?

13 Which French dramatist wrote *The Moods of Marianne*, *Lorenzaccio* and *Le Chandelier*?

14 Who has won Tonys for his roles in *Boeing-Boeing*, *Jerusalem* and *Twelfth Night*?

15 Which US dramatist wrote the 1985 play *The Normal Heart*?

16 Which word for a pompous person was coined in 1755 by the English playwright Samuel Foote?

17 *My Shot* and *Wait for It* are songs from a 2015 musical about which US Founding Father?

18 Which Restoration dramatist wrote *The Plain Dealer* and *The Country Wife*?

19 *House of Cards*, written by the "40-ish" playwright Henry, is a comedy within which Tom Stoppard play?

20 Which theatre structure on the southwest slope of the Acropolis of Athens is pictured?

Answers to QUIZ 161 – General Knowledge

1   Portsmouth
2   Chanel
3   Philip de László
4   Aquila
5   Schizophrenia
6   Lascaux cave paintings
7   Mechanically Recovered Meat
8   Pronghorn (*Antilocapra americana*)
9   Carol I
10 Shredded Wheat
11 Robert Walser
12 Battle of Loos
13 *Lilacs*
14 Liver
15 Long John Silver
16 Standedge Tunnel
17 France's grape harvests
18 Daniel Mendoza
19 Bryan Robson and Gary Bailey
20 Shiva

1 The performing killer whale Keiko starred in which 1993 film?

2 Tom Stoppard's play *The Invention of Love* is about which English poet?

3 What did Lord Byron call "The Monarch of the mountains"?

4 Which Inca creator god destroyed the world with the Unu Pachakuti flood?

5 Patrick Nagel designed the 1982 *Rio* album cover for which band?

6 Which *Carry On* film features a search for the legendary Oozlum bird?

7 In June 1942, who took Tobruk in an attack that became known as the Battle of Gazala?

8 Released in 1972, Magnavox Odyssey was the first commercial what?

9 The trapezium bone is a carpal bone located where in the body?

10 In 1980, Paul Goresh took a photo of which man signing an autograph for his killer?

11 Couscous is made of crushed and steamed what?

12 The boll weevil feeds on the buds and flowers of which plant?

13 Charlie and Craig Reid comprise which Scottish band?

14 Jacob Schick patented which aid to personal hygiene in 1928?

15 Dave Hampton of Sounds Amazing invented which furry virtual animal?

16 Who surrendered to Captain Frederick Maitland on the *HMS Bellerephon*?

17 Which chemical element is named after the Latin name for Copenhagen ?

18 What is the largest stadium in Europe not primarily used for association football?

19 Which boxer lost 'The Showdown' with WBC champion Sugar Ray Leonard in 1981?

20 Who created the pictured Rover chair from a red leather car seat he salvaged from a rusting Rover 200?

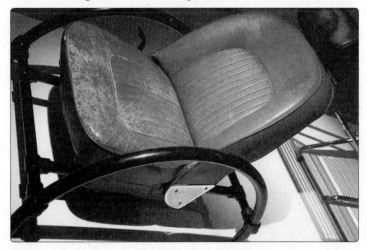

Answers to QUIZ 162 – Theatre

1   *Grease*
2   *Othello*
3   Peter Hall
4   Marcel Marceau
5   Caryl Churchill
6   *The Misanthrope* – full title: *The Misanthrope, or the Cantankerous Lover*
7   Arnold Ridley
8   The Windmill Theatre
9   The Mermaid Theatre
10 *The Sound of Music*
11 Louis Jordan's
12 *Mary Poppins*
13 Alfred de Musset
14 Mark Rylance
15 Larry Kramer
16 Panjandrum
17 Alexander Hamilton – the musical is titled *Hamilton*
18 William Wycherley
19 *The Real Thing*
20 Odeon of Herodes Atticus or Herodes Atticus theatre

1   Which news channel's motto is "'The opinion and the other opinion"?

2   Who won an Oscar for playing Iris Murdoch's husband, John Bayley?

3   Epomeo wine comes from which Bay of Naples island?

4   What is the world's largest flatfish?

5   What is the chief town on Mull in the Inner Hebrides?

6   Sir Edmund Barton was the first prime minister of which country (1901-03)?

7   Which Tory politician was called "a semi house-trained polecat" by Michael Foot?

8   Formally opened in 1914, what is Edinburgh's main concert hall?

9   Which French printer and classical scholar wrote in 1594: "If youth knew; if age could"?

10 Which vice president ousted his cousin, president Ahmed Hassan al-Bakr, in 1979?

11 Which London restaurant was opened by Rose Gray and Ruth Rogers in 1987?

12 Thomas Cook's first package tour in 1841 took 600 people where?

13 Helen Duncan was the last Briton convicted of which offence, in 1944?

14 Which Gerry & The Pacemakers debut single went to no.1?

15 Sir Edward Dalyngrigge built which moated Sussex castle?

16 What does the phrase 'Punic faith' describe?

17 The Queen's eldest grandson, who is married to Autumn Kelly?

18 The Kinnaird Cup is contested in the Eton form of which game?

19 Which Italian was disqualified after he was helped to the finish of the 1908 Olympic marathon?

20 Which "body-con" dress style, the signature item of the French label Hervé Leger, is pictured?

Answers to QUIZ 163 – General Knowledge

1	*Free Willy*	11	Semolina or durum wheat
2	A.E. Housman	12	Cotton
3	Mont Blanc	13	The Proclaimers
4	Viracocha	14	Electric razor
5	Duran Duran	15	Furby
6	*Carry On Up the Jungle*	16	Napoleon Bonaparte
7	Erwin Rommel (and the Axis powers)	17	Hafnium
8	Home video game console	18	Croke Park, Dublin
9	Wrist	19	Thomas "The Hitman" Hearns
10	John Lennon – Lennon was signing a copy of his LP *Double Fantasy* for Mark David Chapman	20	Ron Arad – the Israeli designer who also created the Bookworm bookshelf

1   Anchises' affair with which Greek goddess resulted in the birth of Aeneas?

2   In Greek myth, who married Theseus and then fell in love with her stepson Hippolytus?

3   Aurora is the Roman goddess of what?

4   Which Norse god fathered the evil serpent Jörmungand and Hel, the goddess of death?

5   In Greek myth, which youth rejected the nymph Echo and fell in love with his own reflection?

6   Wielded by the Norse god Odin, what sort of weapon is Gungnir?

7   What is the only planet in the solar system named after a Greek god rather than a Roman one?

8   Which Volkswagen car model is named after a goddess of the dawn?

9   The Egyptian goddess Bastet was worshipped in the form of a lioness and, later, which animal?

10   Which Greek god was the son of Zeus and the nymph Maia, one of the Pleiades?

11   Which Aztec god was known as "the Feathered Serpent"?

12   Which Roman goddess leant her name to a D-Day landing beach?

13   Named after a Roman goddess, what is the brightest asteroid?

14   Who was the muse of tragedy in Greek mythology?

15   Jimmu was the mythical founder of which country?

16   Who was the mythical sister of Euryale and Stheno?

17   Dedicated to the Phoenician god of healing, the Temple of Eshmun is in which country?

18 The Egyptian goddess Serket took the form of which arachnid?

19 Juventas is the Roman name of which Greek goddess of youth?

20 In Irish legend, who built the pictured Giant's Causeway in County Antrim?

Answers to QUIZ 164 – General Knowledge

1 Al Jazeera
2 Jim Broadbent
3 Ischia
4 Pacific halibut (*Hippoglossus stenolepis*)
5 Tobermory
6 Australia
7 Norman Tebbit
8 Usher Hall
9 Henri Estienne
10 Saddam Hussein
11 The River Café

12 Loughborough
13 Witchcraft
14 *How Do You Do It?*
15 Bodiam Castle
16 Treachery
17 Peter Phillips
18 Eton Fives
19 Dorando Pietri – US runner Johnny Hayes was the winner
20 Bandage dress or bender dress

1   Who reigned as the first King of the Belgians from 1831 to 1865?

2   Which Scot played Eli Gold in the US TV show *The Good Wife*?

3   Which type of pastry derives its name from the Greek word for 'leaf'?

4   Sligo, Mayo and Roscommon are counties in which Irish province?

5   Songkran is the New Year's Day festival in which Asian country?

6   What was defined by Susan Sontag as "melancholy minus its charms"?

7   Looted by Anglo-French forces in 1860, what was the *Yuanmingyuan*?

8   *Jump!* is a 2010 novel by which "Rutshire Chronicles" author?

9   Who named his Symphony No. 13 after the Ukrainian ravine, Babi Yar?

10 A Horse's Neck cocktail mixes brandy with which drink?

11 Launched in 1967, what was Britain's first mainland local radio station?

12 Which Gerard Manley Hopkins poem begins: "Glory be to God for dappled things"?

13 Native to Brazil, *Gauromydas heros* is the world's largest known species of which insect?

14 Which English historian became Baron Dacre of Glanton?

15 Nora Helmer is the protagonist of which Henrik Ibsen play?

16 Which Frenchman painted *Bonaparte at the Pont d'Arcole* (1796) and *Napoleon on the Battlefield of Eylau* (1808)?

17 John C. Frémont was which party's first ever candidate for US president?

18 Britain's Malcolm Cooper was a double Olympic champion in which sport?

19 Which English player won the 1993 BDO World Darts Championship, the last unified world championship?

20 Name the pictured computer scientist –

drserg / Shutterstock.com

Answers to QUIZ 165 – Mythology

1	Aphrodite	12	Juno
2	Phaedra	13	4 Vesta
3	Dawn	14	Melpomene
4	Loki	15	Japan
5	Narcissus	16	Medusa
6	Spear	17	Lebanon
7	Uranus	18	Scorpion
8	Eos	19	Hebe
9	Cat	20	Fionn mac Cumhaill or
10	Hermes		Finn MacCool
11	Quetzalcoatl		

1   Which 1971 David Bowie album features the tracks *Kooks*, *Andy Warhol* and *Song for Bob Dylan*?

2   Associated with Jesus as his boyhood home, what is the largest Arab city in Israel?

3   Which author of *The 4-Hour Work Week* has been called "this generation's self help guru" and "The Oprah of Audio" thanks to his hugely influential podcast?

4   Which actress's 1998 stage performance in *The Blue Room* was called "pure theatrical Viagra"?

5   Which Canadian actor divorced Scarlett Johansson in 2011 and married Blake Lively in 2012?

6   The *Druk Gyalpo* is the 'Dragon King' of which country?

7   In which type of sea creature was Green Fluorescent Protein (GFP) discovered?

8   Which future prime minister became MP for Ladywood in 1918?

9   Dethroned by the peasant Li Zicheng, Chongzhen was the last emperor of which Chinese dynasty?

10 Which astronaut was killed in the same 1967 fire as Ed White and Roger Chaffee?

11 Wolfe Island is the largest island in which of the Great Lakes?

12 Dave Ulmer launched which GPS-related recreational activity on May 3, 2000?

13 The Sleeper is one of the most common tricks performed in which hobby?

14 Distinguished by long sleeves, the furisode is a style of which garment?

15 Chesten Marchant (d.1676) is believed to have been which language's last monoglot speaker?

16 Romans get their water from which nose-shaped taps?

17 Famed for producing world-class long-distance runners, Iten is a town in which country?

18 Famed for its Masters tennis tournament, Indian Wells is a city in which US state?

19 Which horse held off Red Rum to win the 1976 Grand National?

20 Name the pictured US President, who was born in 1857 –

Answers to QUIZ 166 – General Knowledge

1 Leopold I
2 Alan Cumming
3 Filo pastry
4 Connacht
5 Thailand
6 Depression
7 Beijing's Old Summer Palace
8 Jilly Cooper
9 Dmitri Shostakovich
10 Ginger ale
11 BBC Radio Leicester
12 *Pied Beauty*
13 Fly – it is known as the Mydas fly
14 Hugh Trevor-Roper
15 *A Doll's House*
16 Antoine-Jean Gros
17 Republican Party
18 Shooting
19 John Lowe
20 Tim Berners-Lee

1 Margaret Tudor, sister of Henry VIII, married which King of Scotland?

2 The Ditchley portrait by Marcus Gheeraerts the Younger depicts which queen?

3 Which Norman king was the fourth and youngest son of William the Conqueror?

4 Which queen-consort died of a postpartum infection on her 37th birthday in 1503?

5 The Louvre owns a c.1445 or c.1450 portrait by Jean Fouquet of which French king, known as "the Victorious"?

6 Shot with the Bothwellhaugh carbine, James Stewart, 1st Earl of Moray, was which queen's half-brother?

7 Who did Ernest Augustus I succeed as king of Hanover in 1837?

8 In 1950, who married Queen Sirikit after a quiet engagement in Lausanne?

9 Argentina's former minister of agriculture, Jorge Zorreguieta, is the father-in-law of which king?

10 Why was Haydn's Symphony no.85, the fourth of his six Paris symphonies, nicknamed *La Reine*?

11 John Bradshaw was the first of 59 men to sign what document?

12 Edward of Middleham (d.1484) was which king's only legitimate child?

13 Born in 1928, Queen Fabiola is the widow of which Belgian king?

14 John Dryden's *Threnodia Augustalis* commemorated which king's death?

15 The RMS *Queen Mary* ocean liner was named after which king's wife?

16 Which mythical king of Thebes was the father of Polynices and Eteocles?

17 Who was the last Stuart monarch?

18 Olav V, King of Norway, won Olympic gold in which sport?

19 Owned by the Queen, which horse won Royal Ascot's Gold Cup in 2013?

20 The pictured man was the last king of which country?

Answers to QUIZ 167 – General Knowledge

1   *Hunky Dory*
2   Nazareth
3   Timothy Ferriss – his podcast *The Tim Ferriss Show* reached 70 million downloads in 2016
4   Nicole Kidman
5   Ryan Reynolds
6   Bhutan
7   Jellyfish – in *Aequoria victoria*
8   Neville Chamberlain
9   Ming dynasty
10 Virgil Ivan "Gus" Grissom
11 Lake Ontario
12 Geocaching
13 Yo-yoing
14 Kimono
15 Cornish
16 *Nasoni*
17 Kenya
18 California
19 Rag Trade
20 William Howard Taft

QUIZ 169 – General Knowledge

1 Which General Motors brand is the US President's official state car?

2 Paul Hindemith composed *Trauermusik* ('Funeral Music') on which king's death?

3 Tubby, Burpy and Baldy were rejected names for which Disney characters?

4 Naval engineer Richard James and his wife Betty invented which spring toy?

5 Which 1944 Billy Wilder film features the femme fatale Phyllis Dietrichson?

6 Who set his final land speed record in the *Golden Arrow* car in 1929?

7 Welsh artist Barry Flanagan was best known for his sculptures of which animals?

8 Which fantasy novelist wrote the 'Johnny Maxwell' children's book trilogy?

9 Which salad dressing is named after an archipelago in the St Lawrence River?

10 In 1937, the town of Detskoe Selo was renamed in honour of which poet?

11 The 1976 "Axe Murder Incident" saw two US soldiers killed where?

12 Which 1895 play by Oscar Wilde features Lady Bracknell?

13 Drinks magnate John Halewood derived which nickname from a light perry?

14 On his death in 2006, who had lived longer than any other US president?

15 The Royal Agricultural College is in which Gloucestershire market town?

16 With 158 stanzas, which country's national anthem is the world's longest?

17 The last, decisive phase of which war saw French victories at Patay, Formigny and Gerberoy?

18 In 1921, which Lombard city hosted the first ever Italian Grand Prix?

19 Which Prague-born tennis player won the Wimbledon men's singles title in 1954?

20 Named after a Dutch city, what early form of capacitor is pictured?

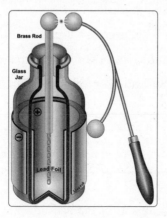

Answers to QUIZ 168 – Kings & Queens

1 James IV
2 Elizabeth I
3 Henry I
4 Elizabeth of York, wife of Henry VII
5 Charles VII
6 Mary, Queen of Scots – he was assassinated by James Hamilton in 1570
7 His brother King William IV of the United Kingdom
8 Bhumibol Adulyadej or Rama IX, king of Thailand
9 Willem-Alexander of the Netherlands, who married Zorreguieta's daughter Máxima
10 It was a favourite of the French queen Marie Antoinette
11 King Charles I's death warrant
12 Richard III
13 King Baudouin
14 Charles II
15 George V, husband of Mary of Teck
16 Oedipus
17 Queen Anne
18 Sailing (in 1928 in the 6m mixed event with his vessel, the *Norna*)
19 Estimate
20 Italy – Umberto II, nicknamed the "May King" (*Re de Maggio*), ruled for 34-days in 1946, with Italy abolishing its monarchy

QUIZ 170 – General Knowledge

1   A remix of which TV theme, composed by Mark Snow, was a 1996 no.1 single in France?

2   In Saudi Arabia, what organisation is the *Mutawa* or *Hayaa*?

3   The building of the Aswan High Dam created which lake?

4   Gougères are the savoury equivalent of which cream-filled French pastries?

5   Swedish, Thai, Hot Stone and Ayurvedic are types of what therapy?

6   Clifton James played Sheriff J.W. Pepper in which two James Bond films?

7   The 12-letter Rotokas alphabet is used where in Papua New Guinea?

8   Ben Collins appeared as which mystery man on TV for seven years?

9   What is the common name of the goat-antelope *Rupicapra rupicapra*?

10 Czar, Early Laxton and Marjorie's Seedling are varieties of which fruit?

11 Which American outlaw married his first cousin Zerelda Mimms?

12 In which country is the ski area of Soldeu?

13 Which Roman emperor began building the Colosseum in 70AD?

14 Who sings the canzone "La Donna e Mobile" in the Verdi opera *Rigoletto*?

15 What did Albert Einstein claim "is more important than knowledge"?

16 Banff National Park is which country's oldest such park?

17 Launched in the UK in 1868, what was the first advertising magazine?

18 Who was the first British black woman to win Olympic gold?

19 Which Northern Irishman was the first jockey to win BBC Sports Personality of the Year?

20 Who is the pictured American singer?

Answers to QUIZ 169 – General Knowledge

1   Cadillac
2   George V
3   Snow White's Seven Dwarfs
4   Slinky
5   *Double Indemnity* – played by Barbara Stanwyck
6   Henry Segrave
7   Hares
8   Terry Pratchett
9   Thousand Island dressing
10 Aleksandr Pushkin
11 North & South Korea's *de facto* border region (Joint Security Area)
12 *The Importance of Being Earnest*
13 "Mr Lambrini"
14 Gerald Ford – 93 years & 165 days
15 Cirencester
16 Greece
17 Hundred Years' War – in 1429, 1435, 1450
18 Brescia
19 Jaroslav Drobný
20 Leyden jar

QUIZ 171 – Business

1   Areva is which country's state-owned nuclear power company?

2   Ceasing operations in 1991, Interflug was which country's state airline?

3   Which financial services company adopted its Centurion logo in 1958?

4   Author of *Triad Power*, which Japanese business guru developed the 3C's Model?

5   Founded on the outskirts of Jaffa, which city is Israel's financial centre?

6   Which corporation is the US's largest civilian employer?

7   The publisher Simon & Schuster's logo was inspired by which French artist's 1850 painting, *The Sower*?

8   Founded in 1908, what is the leading daily French financial newspaper?

9   Which bird forms the logo of the crystal company Swarovski?

10 Which Canadian mining company is the world's largest gold producer?

11 In finance, which form of algorithmic trading is HFT?

12 Mary Wells Lawrence (b.1928) made her name in which male-dominated business?

13 Which Indian company owns Jaguar Land Rover?

14 Carole White and Chris Owen founded which model agency in 1981?

15 Which space transport services company was founded by Elon Musk in 2002?

16 Pierre Bellon founded which food services and facilities management company in 1966?

17 Which British company markets and manufactures the "original malted milk drink" Horlicks?

18 Author of *Common Sense on Mutual Funds*, which US businessman founded The Vanguard Group in 1975?

19 Which social network game company created *FarmVille* and *Mafia Wars*?

20 The pictured logo is used by which of the seven "Supermajor" oil companies?

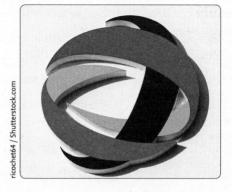

ricochet64 / Shutterstock.com

Answers to QUIZ 170 – General Knowledge

1	*The X-Files* theme	10	Plum
2	The kingdom's feared religious police	11	Jesse James
		12	Andorra
3	Lake Nasser (also called Lake Nubia)	13	Vespasian
		14	Duke of Mantua
4	Profiteroles	15	"Imagination"
5	Massage	16	Canada
6	*Live and Let Die & The Man with the Golden Gun*	17	*Exchange & Mart*
		18	Tessa Sanderson – who won the javelin event in 1984
7	Bougainville Island		
8	The Stig from *Top Gear*	19	Tony McCoy – in 2010
9	Chamois	20	Katy Perry

1 What is the largest food company in the world measured by revenues?

2 What was the high priest of the College of Pontiffs in ancient Rome called?

3 Who links the TV roles Moll Flanders, River Song and Dr. Elizabeth Corday?

4 Count Axel von Fersen the Younger was which queen's alleged lover?

5 Which 1989 film centered on the 54th Massachusetts Volunteer Infantry?

6 Which pinniped is the largest member of the order Carnivora?

7 Created by Leslie Scott, which game's name means 'build' in Swahili?

8 The Danish woodcarver, Thomas Dam, is best known for creating which dolls?

9 Dedicated in 1922, which Washington, D.C. monument was designed by Henry Bacon?

10 Which English general wrote the 1774 comedy play *The Maid of the Oaks*?

11 Eger in Hungary is famed for which red wine?

12 Which private eye employs a secretary named Effie Perine?

13 The Durand Line marks the border between which two Asian countries?

14 Opened in 1798, what is "London's oldest restaurant"?

15 Which British ceramic artist published the memoir *The Hare with Amber Eyes*?

16 The umbilicus is the medical name for which part of the body?

17 According to a Philip Larkin poem, "Sexual intercourse began" in which year?

18 Which Henley-on-Thames rowing club was founded in 1818?

19 In Spanish football, the 'Zamora' is awarded to the best player in what position?

20 What is the pictured building?

Answers to QUIZ 171 – Business

1 France
2 East Germany
3 American Express
4 Kenichi Ohmae
5 Tel Aviv or Tel Aviv-Yafo
6 Walmart
7 Jean-François Millet
8 *Les Echos*
9 Swan
10 Barrick Gold Corporation
11 High-frequency trading
12 Advertising
13 Tata Motors
14 Premier Model Management
15 SpaceX (Space Exploration Technologies Corporation)
16 Sodexo – founded as Sodexho
17 GlaxoSmithKline (GSK)
18 John C. Bogle
19 Zynga
20 Total – the French multinational

1 Which American painted *The Gross Clinic* (1875) and *The Agnew Clinic* (1889)?

2 The UK's most popular parenting network, which advice website uses the slogan "By parents for parents"?

3 What word describes a sentence that uses all the letters of the alphabet?

4 Made in Syria in the 13th century, what is 'The Luck of Edenhall'?

5 Which writer named his ideal pub *The Moon Under Water*?

6 Virginia McKenna played British secret agent Violette Szabo in which 1958 film?

7 Used to measure how expensive a stock is, what is a P/E ratio?

8 Which brand of matches is named after the Roman goddess of the hearth?

9 What is the Shindo scale used for measuring in Japan?

10 Which English cathedral has the world's oldest working medieval clock?

11 What is the world's largest landlocked country?

12 The *Chicago Tribune* ran which infamous front page headline on November 3, 1948?

13 Who first became Prime Minister at the age of 24 years and 205 days?

14 Hay-on-Wye is located within which national park?

15 Which English folk rock band released the albums *Unhalfbricking*, *Full House* and *Angel Delight*?

16 Which British mathematician invented the Game of Life in 1970?

17 What breed was the faithful Edinburgh dog Greyfriars Bobby?

18 The "Green Monster" is a left field wall at which Boston Red Sox ballpark?

19 Which athletic training method derives its name from the Swedish for 'speed play'?

20 The pictured winter hat is known by what Russian name?

Answers to QUIZ 172 – General Knowledge

1	Nestlé	**12**	Sam Spade – in *The Maltese Falcon*
2	*Pontifex maximus*		
3	Alex Kingston	**13**	Afghanistan & Pakistan
4	Marie Antoinette of France	**14**	Rules
5	*Glory*	**15**	Edmund de Waal
6	Southern elephant seal (*Mirounga leonina*)	**16**	Navel or belly button
		17	1963
7	Jenga	**18**	Leander Club
8	Trolls or Troll dolls	**19**	Goalkeeper
9	Lincoln Memorial	**20**	Scottish Parliament Building, Holyrood, Edinburgh
10	John Burgoyne		
11	Bull's Blood or *Egri Bikavér*		

1   What are the USA's "Big Three" automobile companies?

2   Which Savannah-based subsidiary of General Dynamics produces the G550 business jet?

3   Which film star died in his Porsche 550 Spyder on September 30, 1955?

4   Wilhelm Bruhn invented which device for charging fares in 1891?

5   The Davis apparatus helped submarine crews do what?

6   The Modane train crash killed more than 500 French troops during which conflict?

7   The acronym JATO refers to which type of aircraft take-off system?

8   In a 1968 musical film, which car has the number plate GEN11?

9   Martin Luther King's assassin, James Earl Ray, was arrested at which airport?

10 Published since 1952, *Christophorus* is the official magazine of which German carmaker?

11 May 20, 2016, saw the launch of which Royal Caribbean cruise ship, the largest in the world?

12 Which Arab kingdom's International Airport is on Al-Muharraq Island?

13 Which tragic transport 'first' befell Mr E.R. Sewell on February 25, 1899?

14 Which British carmaker manufactures the Mulsanne and Continental GT?

15 Which company made the DC-3, the world's first successful commercial airliner?

16 Bologna's international airport is named after which Italian electrical engineer?

17 In 1979, American Airlines Flight 191 crashed moments after takeoff from which US airport, killing all 271 people on board?

18 Owners of which sports cars make up the Octagon Club?

19 A replica of Sir Francis Drake's ship, the *Golden Hind*, is moored in which Devon fishing port?

20 Which Handley Page heavy bomber is pictured?

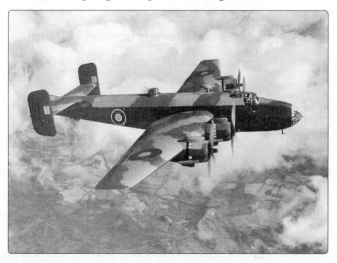

Answers to QUIZ 173 – General Knowledge

1	Thomas Eakins	11	Kazakhstan
2	Mumsnet	12	"Dewey Defeats Truman"
3	Pangram	13	William Pitt the Younger
4	A famous glass beaker or goblet	14	Brecon Beacons National Park
5	George Orwell	15	Fairport Convention
6	*Carve Her Name with Pride*	16	John Horton Conway
7	Price/earnings ratio	17	Skye Terrier
8	Swan Vesta	18	Fenway Park
9	Intensity of earthquakes	19	Fartlek
10	Salisbury Cathedral	20	Ushanka

1 Arnold Schwarzenegger played the spy Harry Tasker in which 1994 film?

2 The hard palate is located where in the body?

3 Which Peter Wyngarde TV vehicle was a spin-off of *Department S*?

4 President Coriolanus Snow is a villain in which trilogy of novels?

5 Which Czech created the artificial language Ptydepe in his play *The Memorandum*?

6 Which deputy prime minister resigned on November 1, 1990?

7 Also known as an intracranial injury, what is a TBI?

8 Which famous Oxford pub is nicknamed "The Bird and Baby"?

9 Who was the first woman to win the Booker Prize, for *The Elected Member*?

10 The Allier, Puy-de-Dôme, Cantal and Haute-Loire departments form which region?

11 Spanning 48m base pairs, what is the smallest human chromosome?

12 Which dragon was killed by the Black Arrow from the bow of Bard the Bowman?

13 Which Andrew Lloyd Webber musical takes place in the mind of the child Control?

14 In 1729, John Gay wrote a sequel, *Polly*, to which ballad opera?

15 In 1990, DNA released a hit remix of which Suzanne Vega song?

16 Dave Seville is the adoptive father and manager of which fictional trio?

17 Bradley Wiggins rode which company's Dogma 2 bike in the 2012 Tour de France?

18 Kingsholm is the home of which Aviva Premiership rugby club?

19 In 2011, Canada's Patrick Chan won which world title for the first time?

20 Name the pictured seabird –

Answers to QUIZ 174 – Transport

1   General Motors, Ford and Chrysler
2   Gulfstream Aerospace
3   James Dean
4   Taximeter
5   Helped them escape from submerged vessels – its proper name is the Davis Submerged Escape Apparatus
6   World War One (1917)
7   Jet Assisted Take-Off
8   Chitty Chitty Bang Bang
9   Heathrow (London)
10 Porsche
11 *Harmony of the Seas*
12 Bahrain
13 First driver of a petrol-driven car to die in an accident
14 Bentley
15 Douglas Aircraft Company
16 Guglielmo Marconi
17 O'Hare, Chicago – it remains the deadliest aviation accident to occur on US soil
18 MG
19 Brixham
20 The Halifax

1 *Gettin' Over You* (2010) was which DJ's first no.1 in his native France

2 The novel *A Man Without Breath* by Philip Kerr features which German sleuth?

3 The term *Waheguru* ('Wonderful Teacher') is used for God in which religion?

4 *Duden* is the equivalent of the Oxford English Dictionary in which country?

5 Which travel review website was founded by Stephen Kaufer in 2000?

6 Which Buckinghamshire farm was the hideout for the Great Train Robbers?

7 Which sci-fi theme links the films *Looper*, *12 Monkeys*, *Primer* and *Donnie Darko*?

8 Manny Bianco and Fran Katzenjammer were characters in which sitcom?

9 The highest peak in the Balkan Peninsula, Musala is in which country?

10 Zhu Zhu Pets are realistic toys that take the form of which rodent?

11 Jöchi was the eldest of which Mongolian warrior-ruler's four sons?

12 Which one-word title links songs by Blur, Travis, Ed Sheeran and Annie Lennox?

13 The Antonov AN-225 Mriya is the world's largest what?

14 The first commoner to marry into the imperial family, who is Empress of Japan?

15 Which anticyclonic storm is located 22° south of Jupiter's equator?

16 In 2007, which 88-year-old became the oldest ever Nobel Prize in Literature winner?

7   In which 1876 battle were about 268 members of the US 7th Cavalry killed?

8   Roderick George Toombs became a kilt-wearing WWF wrestler with which ring name?

9   The Barramundis are the cricket team of which country?

20 The pictured equestrian statue in Rome portrays which Roman emperor?

Answers to QUIZ 175 – General Knowledge

	True Lies	13	*Starlight Express*
2	The roof of the mouth	14	*The Beggar's Opera*
3	*Jason King*	15	*Tom's Diner*
4	*The Hunger Games*	16	Alvin and the Chipmunks
5	Vaclav Havel	17	Pinarello
6	Geoffrey Howe	18	Gloucester Rugby
7	Traumatic Brain Injury	19	World Figure Skating
8	The Eagle and Child		Championship (men's
9	Bernice Rubens – in 1970		singles)
10	Auvergne, France	20	Guillemot or Common
11	Chromosome 21		guillemot or Common
12	Smaug – in *The Hobbit*		murre (*Uria aalge*)

1 Which planet has the fastest winds seen on any planet in the Solar System, with speeds of up to 1,500 mph?

2 The Titius-Bode law was widely accepted until which discovery in 1846?

3 Comet Shoemaker-Levy 9 broke apart and collided with which planet in July 1994?

4 Discovered in 2003, which dwarf planet is named after the Hawaiian goddess of birth and fertility?

5 In 1975, NASA's Viking program sent two space probes to which planet?

6 The Hubble Deep Field is an image of a region in which constellation?

7 Who was US president at the time of the Apollo 11 moon landing?

8 Tharsis Montes is the largest volcanic region on which planet?

9 Which constellation is named after the Latin for 'hunting dogs'?

10 Named after the Latin for 'little king', what is the brightest star in Leo?

11 What is a "vyomanaut"?

12 Launched in 2009, which NASA observatory is named after a Renaissance astronomer?

13 The Eagle Nebula is an open star cluster in which constellation?

14 Which "Richter scale for cosmic collisions" was created by Richard P. Binzel and adopted in 1999?

15 Which moon rocket remains the only launch vehicle to have transported human beings beyond low Earth orbit?

16 Which comet is named after the British amateur astronomer who discovered it on November 6, 1892?

17 Which astronaut hit two golf balls on the moon with a six-iron in February 1971?

18 The coldest place in the universe found so far, the Boomerang Nebula is in which constellation?

19 Zeus put the cup bearer Ganymede in the sky as which zodiacal constellation?

20 What is the pictured space telescope?

Answers to QUIZ 176 – General Knowledge

1 David Guetta
2 Bernie Gunther
3 Sikhism
4 Germany
5 TripAdvisor
6 Leatherslade Farm
7 Time travel
8 *Black Books* – played by Bill Bailey and Tamsin Greig
9 Bulgaria
10 Hamster
11 Genghis Khan
12 *Sing*
13 Aircraft
14 Empress Michiko
15 The Great Red Spot
16 Doris Lessing
17 Battle of the Little Bighorn or "Custer's Last Stand"
18 "Rowdy" Roddy Piper
19 Papua New Guinea
20 Marcus Aurelius

1 What is the name of Han Solo's modified YT-1300 Corellian Freighter?

2 Despite being dead, Alastair Sim was John Mortimer's first choice for which role?

3 The Hornbostel-Sachs system classifies which instruments?

4 Which British star of TV's *Hannibal* is married to the US actress Claire Danes?

5 Alvin Langdon Coburn photographed a nude G. B. Shaw in the pose of which sculpture?

6 Rome's Circus Maximus was sited between the Aventine and which other hill?

7 The fashion photographer Gilles Bensimon divorced which Australian in 1989?

8 Which US TV drama centred on the ACN show *News Night with Will McAvoy*?

9 Steinmetz styles itself as "Creators of the world's finest…" what?

10 In China, Macaque peach, Hairy bush fruit and Vine pear are names for what?

11 Which postage stamp was the 1841 successor to the Penny Black?

12 *Giovanna d'Arco* is an 1845 opera by which Italian composer?

13 Which Netflix series was originally based on a 2010 prison memoir by Piper Kerman?

14 The satyr Silenus was a companion and tutor to which wine god?

15 The National Security Agency has its HQ at Fort Meade in which US state?

16 Pico da Neblina ('Mist Peak') is which country's highest mountain?

17 The German gunboat *Panther* was sent to which Moroccan port on July 1, 1911?

18 Australia's Jamie Dwyer is a multiple FIH World Player of the Year in which sport?

19 Iran's greatest Olympian, Hadi Saei won two golds and a bronze in which sport?

20 Designed by Isambard Kingdom Brunel, name the pictured ship –

Answers to QUIZ 177 – Astronomy

1	Neptune	**13**	Serpens / the Serpent
2	Discovery of the planet Neptune	**14**	Torino Scale – for categorising impact hazard associated with near-Earth objects (NEOs) such as asteroids and comets
3	Jupiter		
4	Haumea		
5	Mars		
6	Ursa Major	**15**	Saturn V
7	Richard Nixon	**16**	Comet Holmes – named after Edwin Holmes
8	Mars		
9	Canes Venatici	**17**	Alan Shepard
10	Regulus	**18**	Centaurus
11	An astronaut from India	**19**	Aquarius
12	Kepler	**20**	Hubble Space Telescope

1   The nobles known as the "Immortal Seven" invited which man to invade England?

2   Which town is home to the third oldest university in the English-speaking world?

3   Who introduced Ukridge in his first adult novel *Love Among the Chickens* (1906)?

4   Opened in 1927, the Ferens Art Gallery is located in which city?

5   Mogwai recorded the soundtrack to which French TV zombie thriller?

6   The Saint-Estèphe AOC is in which subregion of the Bordeaux wine region?

7   Capital of the state of Bahia, what is the largest city on Brazil's north-east coast?

8   Which makeup company was founded by the chemist Thomas Lyle Williams in 1914?

9   Which poet was killed after a duel with Georges d'Anthès in February 1837?

10 Which Metz museum was designed to mimic a Chinese hat by Shigeru Ban?

11 Who is the Conservative MP for North East Somerset?

12 Which building was sold by Sir Charles Sheffield to George III for £21,000?

13 Which Biblical giant was described as "six cubits and a span" tall?

14 According to legend, which Egyptian king founded the city of Memphis in c.2925 BC?

15 Truss, beam, cantilever and cable-stay are basic types of which structure?

16 The Daft Punk no.1 *Get Lucky* features which US singer's vocals?

17 The Tennessee town of Oak Ridge was built in 1942 to house which project's workers?

18 The Oscar Mathisen Award is for outstanding performances in which sport?

19 Which surname links the first three brothers to play together in Test cricket?

20 Who is the pictured celebrity chef?

Answers to QUIZ 178 – General Knowledge

1   *Millennium Falcon* – in the *Star Wars* films
2   [Horace] Rumpole of the Bailey
3   Musical instruments
4   Hugh Dancy
5   *The Thinker* by Auguste Rodin
6   The Palatine
7   Elle Macpherson
8   *The Newsroom*
9   Diamonds
10 Kiwifruit
11 Penny Red
12 Giuseppe Verdi
13 *Orange is the New Black*
14 Dionysus
15 Maryland
16 Brazil
17 Agadir
18 Field hockey
19 Taekwondo
20 SS *Great Britain*

1   Part of the Carlsberg Group, Baltika is which country's largest brewing company?

2   A Tom Collins cocktail contains lemon juice, soda water, sugar and which spirit?

3   Which brand of Swedish vodka comes in Hibiskus, Cilantro and Peppar flavours?

4   Owned by the Rothschild family, which French wine estate's name comes from a Gascon term meaning 'small hill'?

5   Which sweet dessert wine from Cyprus is the oldest named wine still in production?

6   Franconia is the only wine region in which German state?

7   A Navy Grog cocktail includes a few spoons of which 'runny' substance?

8   Noilly Prat is a French brand of which fortified wine?

9   What do you add to a Gin Fizz to get a Golden Fizz cocktail?

10   Identified by Dr. Emil Hansen, what is *Saccharomyces carlsbergensis*?

11   Also known as dextrose, which sugar derives its name from a Greek word for 'sweet wine'?

12   Launched in 1999, Hendrick's is a brand of which alcoholic spirit?

13   A Saint Clement's non-alcoholic cocktail combines which two drinks?

14   Denbies Wine Estate, England's largest single estate vineyard, i in which county?

15   Amrut is a brand of single malt whisky made in which Asian country?

16   Which gin-based cocktail was supposedly created by the Raffle: Hotel bartender Ngiam Tong Boon?

17 Owned by Pernod Ricard Winemakers, Brancott Estate wines are made in which country?

18 Named after a Colonel "Joe", what was officially named Washington DC's native cocktail in 2011?

19 What is the most famous beer made by East African Breweries?

20 Which famous Soho pub is pictured?

Thinglass / Shutterstock.com

Answers to QUIZ 179 – General Knowledge

1	William of Orange, who became King William III	**12**	Buckingham House, which became Buckingham Palace
2	St Andrews, Scotland	**13**	Goliath
3	P.G. Wodehouse	**14**	Menes
4	Hull	**15**	Bridge
5	*The Returned* or *Les Revenants*	**16**	Pharrell Williams
6	The Médoc	**17**	Manhattan Project
7	Salvador	**18**	Speed skating
8	Maybell Laboratories or The Maybelline Company	**19**	Grace – E.M., W.G. & G.F. aka Fred – who played v. Australia in 1880
9	Alexander Pushkin		
10	Centre Pompidou Metz	**20**	Gary Rhodes
11	Jacob Rees-Mogg		

QUIZ 181 – General Knowledge

1 What are the only two predominantly Christian nations in South East Asia?

2 In 1887, Menelik II founded which African capital?

3 Who is UKIP's only MP?

4 Fanny Price is the heroine of which Jane Austen novel?

5 Which German physicist (1822-88) introduced the concept of entropy?

6 A statue of which Italian composer is in the Glover Garden in Nagasaki?

7 Which 630-foot structure is the tallest man-made monument in the western hemisphere?

8 What is the most abundant metallic element in the human body?

9 Which French king was the son of Marie de' Medici and husband of Anne of Austria?

10 Where in London is the largest covered public space in Europe?

11 Born Anthony J. Mahavorick, which US self-help author published *Unlimited Power* in 1987?

12 Where was the US Bullion Depository built in 1936 to hold the bulk of America's gold reserves?

13 Who is the British author of the *Starbuck Chronicles* and the *Saxon Stories*?

14 Founded in 1841, which magazine was initially subtitled *the London Charivari*?

15 Bruce M. Kerner was the first actor to be on the receiving end of which Arnie quote?

16 The Aouzou Strip is disputed by Chad and which country?

17 Tino Sehgal cleared which NYC museum's rotunda for his 2010 artwork *This Progress*?

18 Which country won the Davis Cup by default in 1974?

19 In 1900, Margaret Abbott became the first American woman to achieve which sporting feat?

20 Name the pictured volcano, which erupted in 1991

Answers to QUIZ 180 – Booze

1 Russia
2 Gin
3 Absolut Vodka
4 Château Lafite Rothschild – from "la hite"
5 Commandaria
6 Bavaria
7 Honey
8 Vermouth
9 An egg yolk
10 A lager brewing yeast
11 Glucose
12 Gin
13 Orange juice and a lemon-flavoured drink, e.g. lemon tonic or bitter lemon
14 Surrey
15 India
16 Singapore Sling
17 New Zealand
18 The Rickey
19 Tusker
20 The Coach & Horses on 29 Greek Street

1   Which English author's only historical novel is *Helena* (1950)?

2   Written in 1958, *The Zoo Story* is the debut play by which US dramatist?

3   The 11-ship First Fleet set out for Australia during which king's reign?

4   The African continent's most northern point, Ras ben Sakka, is in which country?

5   Which 1957 hit is the only no.1 with an Elvis Presley co-writer credit?

6   Alfred Molina played the treacherous guide Satipo in which 1981 film?

7   Found in South America, the mata mata is a freshwater species of which reptile?

8   The farce *Nothing On* is the play within which 1982 Michael Frayn play?

9   Which area is given as the last item of each Shipping Forecast?

10 In 2012, Tuareg rebels declared Azawad independent from which country?

11 Which Italian sculpted the 3.4m-tall nude *Napoleon as Mars the Peacemaker* (1802-06)?

12 Pope Pius V excommunicated which English monarch?

13 Elizabeth Gaskell wrote an 1857 biography of which friend and fellow writer?

14 What is the largest arts festival in the world?

15 What is the largest lake contained wholly within Switzerland?

16 Thomas Hardy's poem *The Convergence of the Twain* described which famous event?

17 Who did Paul Holmes replace as MP for Chesterfield in 2001?

18 The Flamingo, Back Layout and Ballet Leg are positions in which Summer Olympic sport?

19 Which US golfer retired after doing the single-season Grand Slam in 1930?

20 Which New York skyscraper is pictured?

Answers to QUIZ 181 – General Knowledge

1 East Timor & the Philippines
2 Addis Ababa
3 Douglas Carswell
4 *Mansfield Park*
5 Rudolf Clausius
6 Giacomo Puccini – referencing his Nagasaki-set opera *Madama Butterfly*
7 Gateway Arch, St. Louis
8 Calcium
9 Louis XIII
10 British Museum – as in the Elizabeth II Great Court
11 Tony Robbins
12 Fort Knox
13 Bernard Cornwell
14 *Punch*
15 "I'll be back" in *The Terminator*
16 Libya
17 [Solomon R.] Guggenheim Museum
18 South Africa – India, their opponents in the final, withdrew in protest at apartheid
19 Win an Olympic gold medal – she won the women's golf event
20 Mount Pinatubo, Philippines

QUIZ 183 – Jazz

1   Which jazz bandleader (1899-1974) famously collaborated with *Lush Life* composer Billy Strayhorn?

2   Which jazz-pop musician released the albums *Twentysomething* and *Momentum*?

3   Which photographer's 1958 picture *A Great Day in Harlem* portrays 57 notable jazz musicians?

4   Which jazz venue is located at 726 St. Peter Street, New Orleans?

5   *Let's Get Lost* is a 1988 documentary about which US jazz trumpeter?

6   In which song was Heloísa Eneida Menezes Paes Pinto described as "Tall and tan and young and lovely"?

7   Which jazz pianist, composer and teacher was born Mary Elfrieda Scruggs in 1910?

8   Known as the "King of Jazz", which US bandleader (1890-1967) commissioned George Gershwin's *Rhapsody in Blue*?

9   Which US pianist formed the jazz-rock fusion group Return to Forever in 1971?

10   Which youngest child of Benito Mussolini was a successful jazz pianist?

11   Which jazz legend had a no.4 hit with *Hello, Dolly!* in 1964?

12   Nicknamed "The Brute" or "Frog", which jazz tenor saxophonist released the LPs *Soulville* and *The Warm Moods*?

13   Which jazz cornetist inspired the Kirk Douglas film *Young Man with a Horn*?

14   Formed in 1952, which jazz combo featured John Lewis, Milt Jackson, Percy Heath and Connie Kay?

15   Which alto saxophonist wrote The Dave Brubeck Quartet hit *Take Five*?

16 In 1931, which jazz bandleader recorded his most famous song, *Minnie the Moocher*?

17 Which saxophonist released the albums *The Shape of Jazz to Come* and *Sound Grammar*?

18 Which US jazz legend scored the 1958 Louis Malle film *Lift to the Scaffold*?

19 "Blood on the leaves and blood at the root / Black bodies swinging in the southern breeze" – which song?

20 Name the trumpeter in the picture –

Answers to QUIZ 182 – General Knowledge

1	Evelyn Waugh	11	Antonio Canova
2	Edward Albee	12	Elizabeth I
3	George III – in 1787	13	Charlotte Brontë
4	Tunisia	14	Edinburgh Festival Fringe
5	*All Shook Up*	15	Lake Neuchâtel
6	*Raiders of the Lost Ark*	16	The sinking of the *Titanic*
7	Turtle	17	Tony Benn
8	*Noises Off*	18	Synchronised swimming
9	South-east Iceland	19	Bobby Jones
10	Mali	20	Chrysler Building

1   Which type of air-raid shelter was named after the 1st Viscount Waverley?

2   Which American glass designer created the *Macchia* and *Persian* series?

3   Which Labour party leader was MP first for Bedwellty and then for Islwyn?

4   Which "Burgers and Fries" restaurant chain was started in 1986 by Janie and Jerry Murrell?

5   Which band was formed in 1976 by Mick Jones, Ian McDonald and Lou Gramm?

6   Which gin is based on a 1761 recipe created by English distiller Thomas Dakin?

7   The world's most remote airport, Mataveri International Airport is on which island?

8   Which architect's Home and Studio is at 951 Chicago Avenue in Oak Park, Illinois?

9   Which American cosmetics queen (1906-2004) was born Josephine Esther Mentzer?

10 Which Latin American revolutionary is the title subject of the 2013 film *The Liberator*?

11 Which supersonic transport aircraft first flew on December 31, 1968?

12 Operation Husky was the codename for which World War Two invasion?

13 The 'Ndrangheta is a mafia-style group centred in which Italian region?

14 In which French city was the Musée Fabre founded in 1825?

15 Which Roman vase was smashed by a drunken William Lloyd in 1845?

16 Murdered in Oran in 1994, Cheb Hasni was a renowned singer of which music?

17 Punto banco is a variant of which casino card game?

18 Which French driver was the 1994 World Rally Champion?

19 LeBron James wears which Cleveland Cavaliers shirt number?

20 Name the pictured American stand-up comedian –

Answers to QUIZ 183 – Jazz

1 Duke Ellington
2 Jamie Cullum
3 Art Kane
4 Preservation Hall
5 Chet Baker
6 *The Girl from Ipanema / Garota de Ipanema* – written by Antônio Carlos Jobim & Vinícius de Moraes; English lyrics by Norman Gimbel
7 Mary Lou Williams
8 Paul Whiteman
9 Chick Corea
10 Romano Mussolini
11 Louis Armstrong
12 Ben Webster
13 Bix Beiderbecke
14 The Modern Jazz Quartet (MJQ)
15 Paul Desmond
16 Cab Calloway (and his Orchestra)
17 Ornette Coleman
18 Miles Davis
19 *Strange Fruit* – first written by Abel Meeropol as a poem and published in 1937
20 Dizzy Gillespie

1   Which Romanian singer had a global hit in 2011 with *Mr. Saxobeat*?

2   Which African capital was founded in 1890 by the Pioneer Column as Fort Salisbury?

3   WhiteKnightTwo, or Eve, is the mothership and launch platform for which spacecraft?

4   Which airline is named after the Arabic word for 'union'?

5   Which one-word title links a Regina Spektor song, a Peter Gabriel album and a David Nicholls novel?

6   Zoe Sugg is the real name of which beauty vlogger and YouTube star?

7   Paul Day's 9m-tall sculpture *The Meeting Place* is in which London station?

8   The beautiful youth Endymion was loved by which Greek moon goddess?

9   Professor Isak Borg (Victor Sjöström) is the protagonist of which Ingmar Bergman film?

10 Cliff diving at La Quebrada takes place in which Mexican resort?

11 Which 1586-88 El Greco painting is displayed at the Church of Santo Tomé, Toledo?

12 Which American photographer took the 1955 picture *Dovima with Elephants*?

13 The late US Navy SEAL, Chris Kyle, wrote which 2012 autobiography?

14 Which 13th century saint was the first person said to have received the stigmata?

15 "Things fall apart; the centre cannot hold" is a line from which W.B. Yeats poem?

16 The 47-storey Beetham Tower is which English city's tallest skyscraper?

17 Introduced in 1965, the Randy 720 was the first shoe designed for which activity?

18 The "Bo Knows" Nike ad campaign featured which baseball and American football star?

19 The Dilscoop is a batting stroke named after which Sri Lankan cricketer?

20 What is the name of the pictured Arsenal FC mascot?

Answers to QUIZ 184 – General Knowledge

1	Anderson shelter – named after John Anderson, who was created Viscount Waverley in 1952	**10**	Simon Bolivar
		11	Tupolev Tu-144
		12	Allied invasion of Sicily
		13	Calabria
2	Dale Chihuly	**14**	Montpellier
3	Neil Kinnock	**15**	Portland Vase or Barberini vase
4	Five Guys		
5	Foreigner	**16**	Raï music
6	Bombay Sapphire	**17**	Baccarat
7	Easter Island	**18**	Didier Auriol
8	Frank Lloyd Wright	**19**	23
9	Estée Lauder	**20**	Bill Hicks

QUIZ 186 – General Knowledge

1   Mount Kinabalu is a sacred mountain in which country?

2   Which English chemist (1733-1804) invented soda water?

3   In 1930, who flew solo from England to Australia in the *Jason*?

4   Luke Howard proposed which nomenclature system in 1802?

5   What is the surname of *The Three Sisters* in Chekhov's play?

6   Brian Jarvis invented which miniature synthesizer in 1967?

7   Used in medieval warfare, what was a misericorde?

8   Amanda Grayson is the mother of which sci-fi character?

9   Simon Cowell was a contestant on which TV quiz in 1990?

10 In Judaism, what is the concept of *Olam Haba*?

11 Wincanton, Somerset is twinned with which fictional city-state?

12 Max Perutz determined the structure of which metalloprotein in 1959?

13 El-Aaiún is the largest city in which breakaway African state?

14 A branch of theology, soteriology is the study of the religious doctrines of what?

15 Who composed the *Tales of the Vienna Woods* waltz in 1868?

16 Which prolific American author's first novel was *The Thomas Berryman Number* (1976)?

17 The condition *medial epicondylitis* has what sporting nickname?

18 Which Greek shepherd won the first modern Olympic marathon?

19 Which Jamaican was the first black footballer to play for Celtic?

20 The pictured chocolate-covered bar dessert is named after which west coast city in Canada?

Answers to QUIZ 185 – General Knowledge

1 Alexandra Stan
2 Harare
3 Virgin Galactic's SpaceShipTwo
4 Etihad Airways
5 *Us*
6 Zoella
7 St. Pancras railway station or St. Pancras International
8 Selene
9 *Wild Strawberries* or *Smultronstället*
10 Acapulco
11 *The Burial of the Count of Orgaz*
12 Richard Avedon
13 *American Sniper*
14 St. Francis of Assisi
15 *The Second Coming*
16 Manchester
17 Skateboarding
18 Bo Jackson
19 Tillakaratne Dilshan
20 Gunneraurus Rex

QUIZ 187 – General Knowledge

1   What infamous nickname was given to October 29, 1929?

2   According to legend, Codrus was the last king of which city?

3   Hami melons come from a namesake city in which country?

4   "Sharif don't like it" is a repeated line in which song by The Clash?

5   Atlas, Pandora and Janus are moons of which planet?

6   "Daisy", "Doady" and "Trot" are nicknames of which Dickens title hero?

7   Jor-El and Lara Lor-Van are the parents of which alien?

8   Marc Quinn's gold statue *Siren* is modelled on which woman?

9   Which Italian patriot was dubbed the "Hero of the Two Worlds"?

10 Who wrote *The Day of the Turbins*, Stalin's favourite play?

11 Friedrich Bessel first used which stellar measurement in 1838?

12 What did Thomas Carlyle call "the biography of great men"?

13 The Holocron is a reference database for which fictional universe?

14 Edward Johnston created which transport system's typeface in 1913?

15 Where in North Yorkshire is Europe's largest army base?

16 Which painter's chaotic studio was at 7 Reece Mews, South Kensington?

17 In which city is the 220,000-capacity Great Strahov Stadium?

18 Which European Cup winners play home games at the Estádio do Dragão?

19 Which jockey's Derby-winning mounts included Troy and Erhaab?

20 Who is the pictured former president of Ireland?

Answers to QUIZ 186 – General Knowledge

1	Malaysia	11	Ankh-Morpork
2	Joseph Priestley	12	Haemoglobin
3	Amy Johnson	13	Western Sahara
4	Names for cloud types	14	Salvation
5	(Olga, Masha and Irina) Prozorov	15	Johann Strauss the Younger
6	Stylophone	16	James Patterson
7	A long, thin knife	17	Golfer's elbow
8	Spock (from *Star Trek*)	18	Spiridon Louis
9	*Sale of the Century*	19	Gil Heron – father of musician Gil Scott-Heron
10	The afterlife or World-to-come	20	Nanaimo, British Columbia – it is called a Nanaimo bar

1 Which Thomas Adès opera is based on the life of Margaret, Duchess of Argyll?

2 Who was aged 12 when he wrote the opera *Bastien und Bastienne* (1768)?

3 Which Russian composed the operas *The Enchantress* (1887) and *Iolanta* (1892)?

4 Which Glinka opera is based on the tale of peasant Ivan Susanin?

5 Gaston Leroux gave *The Phantom of the Opera* what first name?

6 Which Russian composer never finished his operas *Zhenitba* and *Oedipus in Athens*?

7 Benjamin Britten's last opera was based on which Thomas Mann book?

8 The opera singer Helen Porter Mitchell adopted which stage name?

9 *La Calisto* (1651) is which Italian composer's best known opera?

10 Which opera features *O welche Lust*, aka the 'Prisoners' Chorus'?

11 Which German composer's first two operas, *Guntram* and *Feuersnot*, were failures?

12 In which Spanish city did Bizet set his opera *Carmen*?

13 Which American poet wrote the operas *Le Testament* and *Cavalcanti*?

14 Which Puccini opera is based on an 1887 Victorien Sardou play?

15 Macheath is the antihero of which musical work by Kurt Weill?

16 Which composer's first opera was *Hippolyte et Aricie* (1733)?

17 *Mefistofele* (1868) was the only completed opera by which Italian composer-librettist?

18 Called "glorious John" by Walter Scott, who wrote the libretto for Purcell's 1691 "dramatick opera" *King Arthur*?

19 *Angels in America* and *Love and Other Demons* are operas by which Hungarian composer?

20 Who is the pictured Russian opera singer?

artnana / Shutterstock.com

Answers to QUIZ 187 – General Knowledge

1	Black Tuesday	11	Parallax
2	Athens	12	"The history of the world"
3	China	13	*Star Wars*
4	*Rock the Casbah*	14	London Underground
5	Saturn	15	Catterick
6	David Copperfield	16	Francis Bacon
7	Superman (Kal-El)	17	Prague
8	Kate Moss	18	FC Porto
9	Giuseppe Garibaldi	19	Willie Carson
10	Mikhail Bulgakov	20	Mary McAleese

QUIZ 189 – General Knowledge

1   Which US skin care brand was started in 1930 by Emanuel Stolaroff as a cosmetics company called Natone?

2   Pinnace, Clyde puffer, bawley and cutter are types of what?

3   Which Irish actor had a 1968 hit with the Jimmy Webb song *MacArthur Park*?

4   Which 1908 W. Somerset Maugham novel is about Oliver Haddo, a caricature of Aleister Crowley?

5   Developed from the Braunvieh, Brown Swiss is a North American breed of what?

6   Which Christian youth organisation's motto is "Sure & Steadfast"?

7   Which Italian fashion company launched the "United Colors" ad campaign?

8   Which Swiss city was destroyed by an earthquake on October 18, 1356?

9   Which Conservative served as Chancellor from 1951 to 1955?

10 Which Peter Jackson film was based on New Zealand's Parker-Hulme murder case?

11 *Fluid Concepts and Creative Analogies* was the first book ordered from which company?

12 The soft drink Inca Kola was created by José Robinson Lindley in which country in 1935?

13 Which animal features in Henri Rousseau's 1897 painting *The Sleeping Gypsy*?

14 In 1949, Narayan Apte was executed for his role in which assassination?

15 Introduced in 1976, what was the Sinclair Sovereign?

16 Which US Navy base is the world's largest naval station?

17 The Greek party, the Coalition of the Radical Left, is better known by which name?

18 Hexham Racecourse is which county's only racecourse?

19 Which World Snooker Champion is nicknamed "The Jester from Leicester"?

20 Who designed the pictured memorial?

Answers to QUIZ 188 – Opera

1	*Powder Her Face*	11	Richard Strauss
2	Wolfgang Amadeus Mozart	12	Seville
3	Pyotr Ilyich Tchaikovsky	13	Ezra Pound
4	*A Life for the Tsar*	14	*Tosca*
5	Erik	15	*The Threepenny Opera*
6	Modest Mussorgsky	16	Jean-Philippe Rameau
7	*Death in Venice*	17	Arrigo Boito
8	Nellie Melba	18	John Dryden
9	Francesco Cavalli	19	Péter Eötvös
10	*Fidelio* by Beethoven	20	Feodor Chaliapin

1   Prince George of Cambridge was born at which London hospital in 2013?

2   Which US aircraft company makes the PA-28 Cherokee and PA-34 Seneca?

3   In a Lisa Jardine biography, which natural philosopher (1635-1703) was *The Man Who Measured London*?

4   Which French pianist's real name is Philippe Pagès?

5   Wordsworth called which bird an "Ethereal minstrel!"?

6   The gastrocnemius muscle is located where on the body?

7   Native to New Zealand, what creature is a cockabully?

8   Which former talk show host owns an estate called the *Promised Land*?

9   Robbie Turner and Cecilia Tallis are doomed lovers in which Ian McEwan novel?

10 Opened in 1885, the Rudolfinum is a concert hall in which capital city?

11 Rachel Whiteread designed which capital city's Holocaust Monument?

12 Patrimonio is said to be which island's most famous wine?

13 Which US millionaire became the first space tourist in 2001?

14 Which emperor is buried at St Michael's Abbey, Farnborough in Hampshire?

15 TAROM is the flag carrier airline of which European country?

16 Who formed the Free Presbyterian Church of Ulster in 1951?

17 Which French fashion house makes the "Charlotte" pump?

18 PECOTA is a system used to forecast players' performances in which sport?

19 Played by teams of 12 players, what type of sport is kho kho?

20 Who are the pictured English fashion designers?

FashionStock.com / Shutterstock.com

Answers to QUIZ 189 – General Knowledge

1 Neutrogena
2 Boat
3 Richard Harris
4 *The Magician*
5 Dairy cattle
6 The Boys' Brigade
7 Benetton
8 Basel
9 R.A. "Rab" Butler
10 *Heavenly Creatures*
11 Amazon.com – it is a book by Douglas Hofstadter
12 Peru
13 Lion
14 Assassination of Mahatma Gandhi
15 A high-end calculator
16 Naval Station Norfolk in Virginia
17 Syriza
18 Northumberland
19 Mark Selby
20 George Gilbert Scott – it is The Albert Memorial in Kensington Gardens

1   Who assisted Charles Barry in rebuilding the Houses of Parliament?

2   What type of tower is a raised bridge on a submarine?

3   The Barton Swing Aqueduct carries which canal?

4   The Aon Center and John Hancock Center are supertall skyscrapers in which US city?

5   Which architect designed and lived in the National Trust property 2 Willow Road, Hampstead?

6   The Teatro Colón is a famous opera house in which South American city?

7   Which Baroque architect built the Sant'Ivo alla Sapienza church in Rome (1642-60)?

8   What was the birthplace of Henry VIII, Mary I and Elizabeth I?

9   Completed in 2011, which London skyscraper is also known as 110 Bishopsgate?

10   Which Chinese city's Yuexiu Park features the Zhenhai Tower and the city emblem, the Five Rams Sculpture?

11   Germany's most heavily used railway bridge, the Hohenzollern Bridge crosses the river Rhine in which city?

12   Which city in Castile-La Mancha is famed for its *Casas Colgadas* (Hanging Houses)?

13   In 1941, German spy Josef Jakobs became the last person to be executed at which fortress?

14   Completed in 27 AD, the palace Villa Jovis was built by which emperor on Capri?

15   Which 2013 Pritzker architecture prize winner designed the Sendai Mediatheque and the White U and Silver Hut houses?

16   Which Paris building surpassed the Tour Montparnasse as France's tallest skyscraper in 2011?

17 Which 18th century Scottish architect designed the country house Luton Hoo for the 3rd Earl of Bute?

18 La Citadelle Laferrière is a mountaintop fortress in which Caribbean country?

19 The 156m-tall skyscraper One Churchill Place serves as the HQ of which 'Big Four' bank?

20 Which historic house is pictured?

Answers to QUIZ 190 – General Knowledge

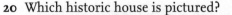

1   St. Mary's Hospital
2   Piper Aircraft
3   Robert Hooke
4   Richard Clayderman
5   Skylark
6   (Calf of the) leg
7   Small freshwater fish
8   Oprah Winfrey
9   *Atonement*
10 Prague
11 Vienna
12 Corsica
13 Dennis Tito
14 Napoleon III of France or Louis-Napoléon Bonaparte
15 Romania
16 Ian Paisley
17 Yves Saint Laurent
18 Baseball
19 A tag sport, like kabaddi
20 Katie Hillier (on left of picture) and Luella Bartley (on right of picture)

1   Ronald Wayne is which tech company's oft-forgotten third founder?

2   Japan's first Nobel laureate, Hideki Yukawa predicted the existence of which subatomic particle in 1935?

3   Launched in 1931, which effervescent antacid and pain reliever was developed by chemist Maurice Treneer?

4   Which 1772 Haydn symphony ends with the musicians leaving one by one?

5   Which Biblical figure founded a city that he named after his son Enoch?

6   Which British sitcom featured Lieutenant Gruber and General Von Klinkerhoffen?

7   Boston, Bull, Tibetan and Patterdale are breeds of which dog?

8   The jukebox musical *Beautiful* tells the story of which female songwriter?

9   Which "Edinburgh of the South" is home to the University of Otago?

10 Which Zimbabwean-born author wrote the 2015 thriller *The Girl on the Train*?

11 Which poet married the "Mauchline Belle", Jean Armour, in 1788?

12 The sinister duo Goldberg and McCann appear in which 1958 play?

13 What term describes angles smaller than a right angle?

14 Which English-born Australian singer had a no.1 single with *Lovesick Blues* in 1962?

15 Which Norwegian explorer is the subject of Tony Harrison's play *Fram*?

16 Invented by Hero of Alexandria, what device is an *aeolipile*?

17 The Voiturette Type A (1898) was the first car made by which company?

18 In which sport might you perform a Dragulescu, Amanar or Cuervo?

19 What was the wood-related nickname of All Blacks rugby legend Colin Meads?

20 Which species of duck is pictured?

Answers to QUIZ 191 – Structures

1 Augustus Pugin

2 Conning tower

3 Bridgewater Canal (over the Manchester Ship Canal)

4 Chicago

5 Ernő Goldfinger

6 Buenos Aires

7 Francesco Borromini – original name Francesco Castelli

8 Palace of Placentia or Greenwich Palace

9 Heron Tower

10 Guangzhou or Canton

11 Cologne

12 Cuenca

13 The Tower of London – he was shot by military firing squad

14 Tiberius

15 Toyo Ito

16 Tour First

17 Robert Adam

18 Haiti

19 Barclays Bank

20 Blenheim Palace

1   Which police detective was killed off in the novel *The Remorseful Day*?

2   Abkhazia is a breakaway region in which former Soviet republic?

3   Which guitar company was founded as the Ro-Pat-In Corporation in 1931?

4   Which Polish composer wrote the *St. Luke Passion* in 1966?

5   What number comes next in this sequence: 8, 28, 496, ...?

6   Which US underwear company invented the first men's Y-front brief in 1934?

7   The theatre director Lewis Casson married which British actress, for whom G.B. Shaw specially wrote *Saint Joan*, in 1908?

8   Which US critic wrote the history of 20th century music, *The Rest is Noise*?

9   *Begin the Beguine* first featured in which 1935 Cole Porter musical?

10 What punctuation mark is called a *point-virgule* in French?

11 Which woman artist and film director published the 2004 photographic book *Crying Men*?

12 What is the literal meaning of the Thai dish *Mee krob*?

13 The late Saparmurat Niyazov ruled which former Soviet republic?

14 Which Scottish king consort fathered King James I of England?

15 Ahmet Ertegun and Herb Abramson founded which record label in 1947?

16 Which twin-brothers wrote the screenplay for *Casablanca* with Howard Koch?

17 In online gaming, what does the abbreviation PSW stand for?

18 Which Spanish cyclist won the 1988 Tour de France and Vuelta a España in 1985 and 1989?

19 Which Japanese figure skater is the 2014 men's Olympic champion?

20 Which Polish castle, the world's largest by surface area, is pictured?

Answers to QUIZ 192 – General Knowledge

1 Apple Computer – the others being Steve Jobs and Steve Wozniak
2 Meson
3 Alka-Seltzer
4 Farewell Symphony or Symphony no .45
5 Cain
6 'Allo 'Allo!
7 Terrier
8 Carole King
9 Dunedin
10 Paula Hawkins
11 Robert Burns
12 *The Birthday Party* by Harold Pinter
13 Acute
14 Frank Ifield
15 Fridtjof Nansen
16 Steam engine or simple bladeless radial steam turbine
17 Renault
18 Gymnastics – they are all types of vault
19 "Pinetree"
20 Muscovy duck (*Cairina moschata*)

1   Who dedicated his long poem, *The Age of Anxiety* (1947), to John Betjeman?

2   "A Bandersnatch swiftly drew nigh / And grabbed at the Banker" in which Lewis Carroll poem?

3   Which US poet began her poem, *Poetry*, with the words: "I, too, dislike it"?

4   Which Mahler symphony set six poems taken from Hans Bethge's translations of Tang Dynasty poetry?

5   The world's most expensive coloured gemstone, the Sunrise Ruby, is named after a poem by which 13th century Persian poet?

6   Which Roman poet's surviving work consists of 16 satires divided among five books (though Satire 16 is incompletely preserved)?

7   Which poet is the subject of the *Newbattle portrait* (c.1595)?

8   Which Britten opera is based on George Crabbe's poem *The Borough*?

9   Who commemorated Arthur Hugh Clough in his 1867 poem *Thyrsis*?

10 Which Scottish poet wrote the collections *Landing Light* (2003) and *Rain* (2009)?

11 Paul Verlaine shot which fellow French poet in 1873?

12 The poet Leopold Senghor was which African country's first president?

13 Which poet was *Making Cocoa for Kingsley Amis* in 1986?

14 Which poet wrote that "Kind hearts are more than coronets"?

15 Which poem begins: "Had we but world enough, and time"?

16 The phrase "paths of glory" comes from which Thomas Gray poem?

17 Walter Scott's poem *Marmion* recounts which battle?

18 In 1924, while in prison, who wrote his last major poetic work, the 17-canto *In Excelsis*?

19 *Requiem* (1935-40) is which Russian poet's tragic masterpiece about the Stalinist terror?

20 Name the Russian poet in the picture –

Answers to QUIZ 193 – General Knowledge

1	Inspector Endeavour Morse	**12**	'Crispy noodles'
2	Georgia	**13**	Turkmenistan
3	Rickenbacker	**14**	Lord Darnley or Henry Stuart, Duke of Albany
4	Krzysztof Penderecki	**15**	Atlantic Records
5	8128 – they are perfect numbers	**16**	Philip G. & Julius J. Epstein
6	Coopers, Inc., now called Jockey International	**17**	Persistent State World
		18	Pedro Delgado
7	Sybil Thorndike	**19**	Yuzuru Hanyu
8	Alex Ross	**20**	Malbork Castle or *Ordensburg Marienburg* or or Castle of the Teutonic Order in Malbork
9	*Jubilee*		
10	Semicolon		
11	Sam Taylor-Wood, later Sam Taylor-Johnson		

1   Born in 1935, which US musician is famously associated with the Tijuana Brass?

2   Which Swedish industrialist patented the smokeless gunpowder Ballistite?

3   Castries is the capital of which Caribbean country?

4   Extracorporeal shockwave lithotripsy is a non-invasive treatment of which problem?

5   The Ken Russell film *Song of Summer* (1968) is about which English composer?

6   The 2600 and Giulia TZ were made by which Italian car manufacturer?

7   Which artist (c.1421-97) frescoed the Magi Chapel in the Medici Palace, Florence?

8   Derbyshire Blue John is a semi-precious form of which mineral?

9   Nicko McBrain became which heavy metal band's drummer in 1982?

10 Which Irish island group includes Inishmore, Inishmaan and Inisheer?

11 Which 1916 naval battle is known in German as the *Skagerrakschlacht*?

12 Which Portuguese-born painter married the British artist Victor Willing in 1959?

13 Which society was founded in 1924 as The Fellowship of the White Boar?

14 Having as many as six horns, what is a Manx Loaghtan?

15 Which Whig was Prime Minister from 1743 until his death in 1754?

16 Pirithous was famed for his friendship with which mythical Greek hero?

17 Yukigassen is a Japanese name for what type of fighting competition?

18 How many cards is each player dealt in Omaha hold 'em poker?

19 Egypt's Abdelfattah Amr, aka F.D. Amr Bey, dominated which sport in the 1930s?

20 Name the pictured hairstyle –

Answers to QUIZ 194 – Poetry

1 W.H. Auden
2 *The Hunting of the Snark*
3 Marianne Moore
4 *Das Lied von der Erde* or *The Song of the Earth*
5 Rumi
6 Juvenal
7 John Donne
8 *Peter Grimes*
9 Matthew Arnold
10 Don Paterson
11 Arthur Rimbaud
12 Senegal
13 Wendy Cope
14 Alfred Lord Tennyson
15 *To His Coy Mistress* by Andrew Marvell
16 *Elegy Written in a Country Churchyard*
17 Flodden Field
18 Lord Alfred Douglas
19 Anna Akhmatova
20 Alexander Pushkin

1 What is the largest African river to discharge into the Indian Ocean?

2 Which Icelandic band sings in the language Volenska, also known as Hopelandic?

3 Who is the US author of *The Hunters* (1956) and *All That Is* (2013)?

4 Refined in 1920s Shanghai, what type of garment is the qipao?

5 Which traditional gunpowder ingredient is also known as potassium nitrate?

6 The 18th century MP John Elwes reputedly inspired which Dickens character?

7 Gustave Flaubert's 1862 historical novel *Salammbô* is set in which ancient city?

8 Which womanising *Lawrence of Arabia* producer was nicknamed "the velvet octopus"?

9 What shellfish is the main ingredient of the Scottish soup Partan Bree?

10 Which charity was founded by Chad Varah "to befriend the suicidal and despairing"?

11 Which terrorist separatist group is led by a committee known as the Zuba?

12 Which musical by Harvey Fierstein and Jerry Herman is based on a 1973 Jean Poiret play?

13 Which "master gland" is housed in the sella turcica of the sphenoid bone?

14 The Battle of Königgrätz or Sadowa was the decisive clash in which 1866 war?

15 Which ousted Cuban dictator died in Guadalmina, near Marbella, in 1973?

16 Which billionaire describes his fellow business magnate Charlie Munger as "my partner"?

17 Elwood, Revend, Attacc and Radar are styles of jeans made by which Dutch company?

18 Which Formula 1 mogul married the model Slavica Radić in 1985?

19 Which tennis player is nicknamed "The Tower of Tandil" after his Argentine hometown?

20 Which French encyclopedist, philosopher and David Cameron lookalike is pictured?

Answers to QUIZ 195 – General Knowledge

1	Herb Alpert	11	Battle of Jutland
2	Alfred Nobel	12	Paula Rego
3	Saint Lucia	13	The Richard III Society
4	Kidney stones and gallstones	14	Sheep breed
5	Frederick Delius	15	Henry Pelham
6	Alfa Romeo	16	Theseus
7	Benozzo Gozzoli	17	Snowball-fighting (it means 'snow battle')
8	Fluorite or fluorspar	18	Four
9	Iron Maiden	19	Squash
10	Aran Islands	20	French twist [braid]

1 Which American magazine calls itself "The Capitalist Tool"?

2 The humourist Gelett Burgess coined which publishing term in 1906?

3 Associated Press photographer Joe Rosenthal took which Pulitzer Prize-winning picture on February 23, 1945?

4 Zanny Minton Beddoes is the 17th and first female editor-in-chief of which magazine?

5 Robert B. Silvers has served as editor of which biweekly magazine since 1963?

6 "Independent since 1920", *Cherwell* is a student newspaper of which university?

7 The US journalist Ernie Pyle was killed during which 1945 Second World War battle?

8 Launched in 2003, *Fakt* is the top-selling newspaper in which country?

9 Nicholas Burns played which "self-facilitating media node" in a 2005 TV comedy?

10 Opened in 1983, the National Media Museum is in which city?

11 The American, Ron Gallela (b.1931), is known as a pioneer in which journalistic field?

12 Which aviator was *Time* magazine's first Man of the Year?

13 Mark Lemon and Henry Mayhew were joint editors of which magazine from 1841?

14 Founded in 1903, *ABC* is the oldest newspaper still operating in which European capital?

15 Tim Keck and Chris Johnson founded which satirical newspaper in Madison, Wisconsin, in 1988?

16 Which journalist wrote *Anatomy of Britain* (1962) and *The New Anatomy of Britain* (1971)?

17 Nicknamed *La Rosa*, what is the most read Italian newspaper?

18 *France Football* magazine writer Gabriel Hanot conceived which award in 1956?

19 Which Irish *Sunday Times* journalist was called a "little troll" by Lance Armstong?

20 Name *The Insider* –

RoidRanger / Shutterstock.com

Answers to QUIZ 196 – General Knowledge

1 Zambezi

2 Sigur Rós

3 James Salter

4 A one-piece dress with a fitted, high-necked bodice

5 [Ordinary] saltpetre

6 Ebenezer Scrooge

7 Carthage

8 Sam Spiegel

9 Crab

10 The Samaritans

11 ETA (Euskadi Ta Askatasuna – "Basque Homeland and Liberty")

12 *La Cage aux Folles*

13 Pituitary gland

14 Seven Weeks' War or Austro-Prussian War

15 Fulgencio Batista

16 Warren Buffett

17 G-Star RAW

18 Bernie Ecclestone

19 Juan Martin del Potro

20 Denis Diderot

1   The Abbey of Abingdon's Axe brewery was the earliest known building to have stood on the site of which London street?

2   The Gothic-turreted Spasskaya (Saviour) Tower is the official entrance to which citadel?

3   What is the biggest opera house in Italy?

4   What is by far the biggest ballet company in the world?

5   Which Anton Chekhov play opens on a muggy autumn afternoon in the garden of Professor Serebryakov's estate?

6   Cubital Tunnel Syndrome is a condition that involves pressure or stretching of which nerve?

7   Inspired by the hovercraft, Karl Dahlmen invented what garden device?

8   Operation Corporate was launched to regain which islands?

9   Tracy Reed (playing a mistress named Miss Scott) was the only woman to appear in which Stanley Kubrick film?

10 Which British novelist wrote the plays *Sheppey* and *The Constant Wife*?

11 Star of the films *The Four Poster* (1952) and *The Story of Anastasia* (1956), which German actress divorced Rex Harrison in 1957?

12 Star of the films *Genevieve* and *Les Girls*, which wife of Rex Harrison died of myeloid leukaemia aged just 32?

13 Which music hall song was allegedly written for a 5-shilling bet in Stalybridge on January 30, 1912, and performed the next night at the local music hall?

14 Who was Texas congressman Matt Santos' predecessor as US president?

15 Acqua Panna bottled water gets its name from the Villa Panna in the hills of which Italian region?

16 The human Sir Anduin Lothar and orc Durotan are lead characters in which 2016 film?

17 The most prolonged drought ever – 400 years – in the world in recorded history occurred in which desert?

18 Charlie Saikley, who died in 2005 aged 69, has been called the "Godfather" of which Olympic sport?

19 Which heavyweight boxing champion told Billy Conn: "He can run, but he can't hide"?

20 Which Scottish explorer and missionary is pictured?

Answers to QUIZ 197 – Media

1	*Forbes*	13	*Punch*
2	Blurb	14	Madrid
3	*Raising the Flag on Iwo Jima*	15	*The Onion*
4	*The Economist*	16	Anthony Sampson
5	*New York Review of Books*	17	*La Gazzetta dello Sport*
6	University of Oxford	18	Ballon d'or / European
7	Battle of Okinawa		Footballer of the Year
8	Poland	19	David Walsh
9	Nathan Barley	20	Piers Morgan – author of
10	Bradford		*The Insider: The Private*
11	Paparazzo-style photography		*Diaries of a Scandalous*
12	Charles Lindbergh		*Decade* (2005)

1   Patented in 1862, Parkesine is the trademark for the first man-made what?

2   The Lagoon Nebula is in which zodiacal constellation?

3   Alfonso XI of Castile was the only monarch to be killed by which 14th century event?

4   The first Ku Klux Klan was founded in Pulaski in which US state?

5   Whernside is the highest point in which national park?

6   Calasparra rice is particularly associated with which dish?

7   What type of drinks bottle was invented in 1884 by Dr. Hervey D. Thatcher of Potsdam, New York?

8   Which former MP for Redditch was the first ever female Home Secretary?

9   Pigeon blood red is the most valued form of which gemstone?

10 Reuben and Rose Mattus founded which ice cream brand in the Bronx in 1961?

11 Featuring Jay-Z, *The Devil is a Lie* was the lead single from which US rapper's sixth studio album, *Mastermind* (2013)?

12 In a 1993 novel, who owns a musical instrument named *Antonia*?

13 Matsya (Sanskrit for 'fish'), who rescued the first man, Manu, from a great deluge, was the first avatar of which Hindu god?

14 Who wrote the Caroline era history play *Perkin Warbeck* and tragedy *The Broken Heart*?

15 How would you hear the sounds of Korotkov?

16 Who were the two female founding members of the Royal Academy (in 1768)?

17 The Barry Burn is found on which Scottish golf course?

8 Which Norwegian speed skater was the only triple gold medallist at the 1936 Winter Olympics?

9 Which baseball star's brother Mack won the 200m silver behind Jesse Owens by 0.4 seconds at the Berlin Olympics?

o Name the pictured British actress –

nswers to QUIZ 198 – General Knowledge

Downing Street
Moscow Kremlin
Teatro Massimo, Palermo
The Bolshoi Ballet
Uncle Vanya
Ulnar nerve aka "funny bone" nerve
Flymo or hovercraft lawnmower
The Falkland Islands
Dr. Strangelove
o W. Somerset Maugham
1 Lilli Palmer (born Lilli Marie Peiser)

12 Kay Kendall
13 *It's a Long Way to Tipperary*
14 Josiah "Jed" Bartlett – in *The West Wing*
15 Tuscany
16 *Warcraft: The Beginning* – based on the namesake video game series
17 Atacama Desert, Chile
18 Beach volleyball
19 Joe Louis
20 David Livingstone

1   Which US inventor of FM radio jumped to his death from a 13th floor window in 1954?

2   Played on film by Jennifer Lawrence, who invented the self-wringing Miracle Mop and Huggable Hangers?

3   Richard Drew invented which US company's masking and clear cellophane tapes?

4   Which magician invented the Chinese Water Torture Cell and patented a 1921 diving suit?

5   Seth Boyden never legally protected his process for making which glossy form of coated leather?

6   English inventor James Starley (1831-81) has been called the father of which transport industry?

7   Which German scientist invented the ophthalmoscope in c.1850?

8   First sold in 1923, which yeast spread was invented by Cyril P. Callister of Fred Walker & Co.?

9   Invented by Dean Kamen, what type of device is the iBOT?

10 Patented in 1873, a scrapbook with adhesive pre-applied to pages was invented by which US writer?

11 The Power Drencher was the original name of which toy water gun, the invention of nuclear engineer Lonnie Johnson?

12 Bill O'Brien and Harry Norville founded which sandwich toaster maker in 1932?

13 A 1973 Chevrolet Impala sedan was the first car to be mass-produced with what GM safety system?

14 Which Englishman invented the wedge hairstyle in 1974?

15 In 1867, which form of wire was first patented in the US by Lucien B. Smith?

16 Which inventor was issued the patent on the phonograph on February 19, 1878?

7 John Shore invented which two-pronged instrument in 1711?

8 Which elastic hair band was patented by Rommy Revson in 1987?

9 Created by Tony Horton and launched in 2003, what is P90X?

10 What is the pictured device?

Answers to QUIZ 199 – General Knowledge

Plastic (it is nitrocellulose)
Sagittarius
The Black Death (or the Great Plague of 1350)
Tennessee
Yorkshire Dales National Park
Paella
Milk bottle
Jacqui Smith
Ruby
Häagen-Dazs
Rick Ross

12 Captain Antonio Corelli (*Captain Corelli's Mandolin* by Louis de Bernières)
13 Vishnu
14 John Ford
15 By placing a stethoscope over an artery
16 Mary Moser and Angelica Kauffman
17 Carnoustie
18 Ivar Ballangrud
19 Jackie Robinson
20 Natalie Dormer

1 Which pantomime dame was born George Wild Galvin in 1860?

2 Digby is the faithful batman of which "Pilot of the Future"?

3 The tycoon Richard Tompkins introduced which stamps in 1958?

4 The French version of which children's game is called *jouer à saute-mouton*?

5 Loplop is a bird-man alter ego that recurs in prints, collages and paintings by which German surrealist artist?

6 The Siq is the main entrance to which ancient city in southern Jordan?

7 *Bad Boys* is a 1987 song by which Jamaican reggae group?

8 In Greek mythology, which Titan fathered Helios, Selene and Eos?

9 Which "Father of the Atom" appears on New Zealand's $100 note?

10 In America, which butterfly (*Nymphalis antiopa*) is known as the Mourning Cloak?

11 Which physician described "paralysis agitans" in his *Essay on the Shaking Palsy* (1817)?

12 The fictional character Dan Humphrey was revealed to be which titular blogger?

13 During their childhood, which siblings created the imaginary worlds of Gondal and Angria?

14 The Greek town Galaxidi's Clean Monday festival involves the throwing of what?

15 Which Swiss artist published the book *Necronomicon* in 1977?

16 Which US lawyer defended Leopold and Loeb in the 1924 "Trial of the Century"?

17 Which Egyptian Pharaoh signed the world's oldest surviving peace treaty in around 1258 BC?

8 Which Kentucky company makes the famed Louisville Slugger baseball bat?

9 Gabe Polsky's 2014 documentary *Red Army* is about which sports team?

10 The pictured type of knife is named after which defender of The Alamo?

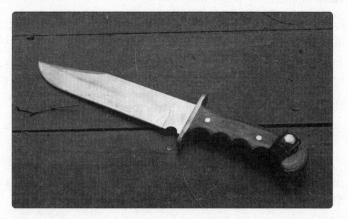

Answers to QUIZ 200 – Inventions

Edwin Armstrong	**12**	Breville – which started as the business Breville Radio
Joy Mangano – subject of the film *Joy*	**13**	Air Cushion Restraint system or front airbags
3M	**14**	Trevor Sorbie
Harry Houdini	**15**	Barbed wire
Patent leather	**16**	Thomas Edison
Bicycle industry	**17**	Tuning fork
Hermann von Helmholtz	**18**	Scrunchie
Vegemite	**19**	A home exercise regimen or workout programme
Stair-climbing wheelchair		
10 Mark Twain aka Samuel L. Clemens	**20**	Self-balancing scooter or electric hoverboard
1 Super Soaker		

QUIZ 202 – General Knowledge

1 Started in 1818 as a family business, what is America's oldest clothing retailer?

2 Who directed the films *Down Terrace*, *Kill List*, *Sightseers* and *High-Rise*?

3 Which architect's firm is the largest practice in Britain?

4 In *Les Misérables*, Cosette falls in love with which young lawyer?

5 The Suri and Huacaya are breeds of which South American camelid?

6 The Shrine of Hazrat Ali is in which city, the fourth largest in Afghanistan?

7 Which West African country's 15 counties include Maryland, Bong and Nimba?

8 In 1968, Samuel W. Alderson created the first example of which test device?

9 The online retailer Rakuten is which country's largest internet company?

10 Which holiday company opened its first village at Sherwood Forest in 1987?

11 In 1859, Thomas Austin introduced into Australia 24 of which animals?

12 Nicknamed "Lo Spagnoletto", who painted *The Martyrdom of St Philip* (1639)?

13 The 13-year-old Ukrainian "Eugene Goostman" apparently passed which test?

14 Which Starbucks drinks size comes between Tall and Venti?

15 Which character was Dr. David Keel's (Ian Hendry) assistant in the first series of *The Avengers*?

16 From 1940 to 1957, which Russian city was named Molotov?

17 Invented by Mandy Haberman, what was the world's first totally non-spill cup?

18 The 2014 film *United Passions* stars Tim Roth as which dynamic football administrator?

19 Which South African fast bowler features in a cameo in the Adam Sandler film *Blended*?

20 The world's largest nocturnal primate, which lemur is pictured?

Answers to QUIZ 201 – General Knowledge

1 Dan Leno
2 Dan Dare
3 Green Shield Stamps
4 Playing leap-frog (it means "to play leap-sheep")
5 Max Ernst
6 Petra
7 Inner Circle
8 Hyperion – with his sister and Titaness, Theia
9 Ernest Rutherford
10 Camberwell Beauty
11 James Parkinson – the disorder became known as Parkinson's disease

12 Gossip Girl
13 The Brontës (Charlotte, Branwell, Emily & Anne)
14 Flour – in a "flour war"
15 H.R. Giger or Hans Rudolf "Ruedi" Giger
16 Clarence Darrow
17 Rameses II or Ramses the Great – who signed the Egyptian-Hittite peace treaty
18 Hillerich & Bradsby
19 Soviet Union ice hockey team
20 Jim Bowie – it is a "Bowie knife"

QUIZ 203 – Crime Literature

1   Who was originally called Sheridan Hope?

2   Peter Davison played which Leslie Thomas creation in *The Last Detective*?

3   Which sleuth first appeared in the Alexander McCall Smith novel *The Ladies' No. 1 Detective Agency*?

4   Set in Melbourne, Australia, which 1886 book by Fergus Hume was the best-selling crime novel of the 19th century?

5   Which 19th century French writer penned the 11-novel *Les Habits Noirs* criminal saga over a 30-year period?

6   Which future First Lady detects in 1770s Massachusetts in books by Barbara Hambly?

7   Which Australian author introduced the detective, the Honourable Phryne Fisher (b.1900), in the 1989 novel *Cocaine Blues*?

8   Which US author's "alphabet mysteries" feature the former policewoman Kinsey Millhone?

9   Which US mystery novelist wrote the police procedural *Last Seen Wearing...* (1952)?

10 Who does the detecting in *The Silent World of Nicholas Quinn* (1977), *The Wench is Dead* (1989) and *The Daughters of Cain* (1994)?

11 *The Last Scholar* (2013) is the fourth Lord Peter Wimsey novel to be written by who?

12 Edmund Crispin's 1946 comic crime novel *The Moving Toyshop* features which detective and Oxford don?

13 Which Japanese woman wrote the 1997 crime novel *Out*?

14 The detective TV series *Vera* is based on the works of which crime author?

15 In which Agatha Christie novel does Poirot investigate the murder of heiress Linnet Ridgeway Doyle?

16 Which master of the locked-room mystery wrote *The Hollow Man* (1935)?

17 Which private eye encounters Moose Malloy, Mrs Lewin Lockridge Grayle, the psychic Jules Amthor and drug dealer Dr. Sonderborg in a 1940 novel?

18 Which *Sun on Sunday* columnist writes crime novels about DC Max Wolfe?

19 *Even Dogs in the Wild* (2015) is the 20th book in which series of crime novels?

20 Which English crime writer is pictured?

Answers to QUIZ 202 – General Knowledge

1 Brooks Brothers
2 Ben Wheatley
3 Norman Foster
4 Marius Pontmercy
5 Alpaca (*Vicugna pacos*)
6 Mazar-i-Sharif
7 Liberia
8 Crash test dummy
9 Japan
10 Center Parcs UK
11 Rabbit – leading to environmental disaster
12 José (Jusepe) de Ribera – the nickname means 'the Little Spaniard'
13 Turing Test, "he" is a computer program that imitates a teenager
14 Grande
15 John Steed (Patrick Macnee)
16 Perm
17 Anywayup Cup
18 Sepp Blatter
19 Dale Steyn
20 Aye-aye (*Daubentonia madagascariensis*)

1   Pleasant Island is a former name of the Pacific Republic of where?

2   Baiji is home to the biggest oil refinery in which country?

3   Who created the graphic novels *Jimmy Corrigan: The Smartest Kid on Earth* and *Building Stories*?

4   Ian Fleming International Airport is located in Boscobel in which country?

5   Which bone is formed by the manubrium, gladiolus and xiphoid process?

6   The Battle of Dakar, aka Operation Menace, took place during which war?

7   Which tourist attraction is the London equivalent of the Museé Grévin in Paris?

8   The fashion companies Acne Studios and Nudie Jeans were founded in which country?

9   Which Spanish author won the first Nadal Prize for her 1944 debut novel *Nada*?

10 Which lip balm was invented by Dr. Charles Browne Fleet in the 1880s?

11 Which Hayao Miyazaki film tells the story of Mitsubishi A6M Zero designer Jiro Horikoshi?

12 The Dalmatian is the largest of which long beaked-water birds?

13 Which event started at noon on July 6 with the launch of the *chupinazo* rocket?

14 The artist Francesco Vezzoli created *Trailer for a Remake of Gore Vidal's* what?

15 Who was Tsar of Russia during the Battle of Waterloo?

16 Which female Egyptian pharaoh's Mortuary Temple is at Deir el-Bahari?

17 Full Moon Parties originated at Haad Rin beach on which Thai island?

18 Which 2003 book by Michael Lewis is subtitled *The Art of Winning an Unfair Game*?

19 Argentina's Amadeo Carrizo was the first footballer to use which protective wear?

20 Who created the pictured *Lobster Telephone*?

Answers to QUIZ 203 – Crime Literature

1 Sherlock Holmes
2 DC "Dangerous" Davies
3 Precious Ramotswe
4 *The Mystery of a Hansom Cab*
5 Paul Féval, père
6 Abigail Adams
7 Kerry Greenwood
8 Sue Grafton
9 Hillary Waugh
10 Morse
11 Jill Paton Walsh
12 Gervase Fen
13 Natsuo Kirino

14 Ann Cleeves – as in the DI Vera Stanhope novels
15 *Death on the Nile*
16 John Dickson Carr
17 Philip Marlowe – in *Farewell, My Lovely* by Raymond Chandler
18 Tony Parsons – Wolfe features in *The Murder Bag* and *The Slaughter Man*
19 Inspector Rebus series by Ian Rankin
20 Dorothy L. Sayers

1   Arthur C. Clarke's third law states that any sufficiently advanced technology is what?

2   Which Persian king's forces won the 480 BC Battle of Thermopylae?

3   Betteridge's law of headlines is "Any headline which ends in a a question mark can be..." what?

4   Which European river is the title subject of a 1986 book by scholar Claudio Magris?

5   The oldest religious structure ever found, Göbekli Tepe is in which country?

6   Who composed the film scores for *The Bride of Frankenstein*, *Rebecca* and *Rear Window*?

7   Which designer named her signature Reva ballet flats after her mother?

8   Which province of Pakistan contains more than half the country's total population?

9   Which Italian singer is perhaps best known for her 1986 song *Bello e Impossibile*?

10 In June 2015, which amphibious assault ship, the Royal Navy's sole Landing Platform Helicopter, became the fleet flagship?

11 Simon Brenner is the hero of crime novels by which Austrian writer?

12 The 2013 Filipino film *Norte, the End of History* reworks which classic Russian novel?

13 Which Japanese artist self-published 500 copies of her book *Grapefruit* in 1964?

14 Frédéric Bartholdi finished which monumental red sandstone animal sculpture in 1880?

15 Ida Siekmann was the first to die trying to cross which "anti-fascist rampart"?

16 Which French perfume house makes Jicky, L'Heure Bleue and Mitsouko?

17 The Swedish company SKF is best known for manufacturing which items?

18 Which Ukrainian billionaire founder of System Capital Management (SCM) owns the football club Shakhtar Donetsk?

19 Vikersundbakken in Modum, Norway, is the world's largest type of which hill?

20 Name the pictured band, formed in London in 1963 –

Answers to QUIZ 204 – General Knowledge

1 Nauru
2 Iraq
3 Chris Ware
4 Jamaica
5 Sternum or breastbone
6 World War Two (in 1940)
7 Madame Tussauds wax museum
8 Sweden
9 Carmen Laforet
10 ChapStick
11 *The Wind Rises*
12 Pelican

13 Festival of San Fermin or the Running of the bulls in Pamplona
14 *Caligula*
15 Alexander I
16 Hatshepsut – meaning 'Foremost of Noble Ladies'
17 Koh Phangan or Koh Pha-Ngan
18 *Moneyball*
19 Goalkeeper gloves
20 Salvador Dali

1 Which red deer subspecies is the only member of the deer family that is native to Africa?

2 Also called the güiña, what is the smallest cat in the Americas?

3 What is the name of the large, inflatable sac a male dromedary camel extrudes from his mouth when in rut to assert dominance and attract females?

4 What is the largest living deer species?

5 Which wild goat subspecies, known as *geyik* to Anatolian locals possess the world's longest horns in relation to body weight?

6 The neurosurgeon Dr. Robert J. White was infamous for which animal transplants?

7 What is thought to be the world's most abundant wild bird species?

8 The drop-earred variety of which toy dog breed is called the Phalène (French for 'moth')?

9 What is the largest fish family and the largest vertebrate animals family in general, with about 3,000 living and extinct species in about 370 genera?

10 *Nasua nasua* is the South American or ring-tailed species of which raccoon family member?

11 What is by far the largest living non-mammalian vertebrate?

12 The mad cow-like chronic wasting disease (CWD) is nearly always lethal to which mammals?

13 In 2015, what was voted the National Bird in UK's biggest ever nature poll?

14 Which Danish artist and amateur zoologist wrote the 1926 book *The Origin of Birds*?

15 Which vulture, whose Latin name is *Aegypius monachus*, is believed to be the largest true bird of prey in the world?

16 The great grey (*Strix nebulosa*), with the largest facial disc of any raptor, is a species of which bird?

17 Black-tailed, white-tailed, Gunnison's, Utah and Mexican are the five species of which burrowing rodent?

18 Nicknamed the "lady of the stream", which salmon family fish is *Thymallus thymallus*?

19 The largest extant wild equid, what is the largest and most endangered species of zebra?

20 The 'Giant' species of which fish – the world's longest bony fish – is pictured?

Answers to QUIZ 205 – General Knowledge

1 Indistinguishable from magic
2 Xerxes I
3 Answered by the word *no*
4 Danube (*Danubio*)
5 Turkey
6 Franz Waxman
7 Tory Burch
8 Punjab
9 Gianna Nannini
10 HMS *Ocean*
11 Wolf Haas
12 *Crime and Punishment* by Dostoevsky
13 Yoko Ono
14 *Lion of Belfort*
15 Berlin Wall
16 Guerlain
17 Ball and roller bearings
18 Rinat Akhmetov
19 Ski jumping hill or ski-flying hill
20 The Kinks

1 The lawyer Gabriel John Utterson investigates the events of which 1886 novella?

2 Mendoza is which Latin American country's largest wine region?

3 As worn by David Cameron, the Sebastian polo shirt is made by which swimwear label?

4 Who composed the first known opera, *Dafne* (1598)?

5 The Kant-Laplace nebular hypothesis explains the formation of what?

6 The Two Towers (both leaning) are the symbol of which Italian city?

7 Which pianist became the prime minister of newly independent Poland in 1919?

8 Who considered John Amery to be the bravest man he ever hanged?

9 Which 1961 album by John Coltrane is named after a song from *The Sound of Music*?

10 Who did Lúcia dos Santos and Jacinta and Francisco Marto reportedly see in 1917?

11 Which sculpture is Michelangelo's only signed work?

12 The Maya deity Kukulkan is a plumed form of which creature?

13 What links Aldwych, Blake Hall, British Museum, Lord's and York Road?

14 Designed by Andrew Higgins and used in the Second World War, what was an LCVP?

15 In a 1973 film, which Walter Matthau title character is "The Last of the Independents"?

16 *Purgatorio* is the second movement of which symphony by Franz Liszt?

17 Which 1982 film featured the fictional soap opera *Southwest General*?

18 Camogie is the female version of which Irish men's sport?

19 Which club beat Wolves 3-2 on aggregate to win the first UEFA Cup in 1971-72?

20 Name the pictured musical instrument –

Answers to QUIZ 206 – Wildlife

1 Atlas deer or Barbary stag (*Cervus elaphus barbarus*)

2 Kodkod (*Leopardus guigna*)

3 Dulla

4 Moose or Eurasian elk (*Alces alces*)

5 Bezoar ibex or Anatolian Bezoar Ibex (*Capra aegagrus aegagrus*) – it is the main progenitor of the modern domestic goat

6 Living monkey head transplants

7 Red-billed quelea or red-billed weaver or red-billed dioch (*Quelea quelea*)

8 Papillon

9 Cyprinidae or cyprinids or "carp family" or "minnow family"

10 Coati or coatimundi

11 Whale shark (*Rhincodon typus*)

12 Deer and elk

13 Robin

14 Gerhard Heilmann

15 Cinereous vulture or Eurasian black vulture or black vulture or monk vulture

16 Owl

17 Prairie dog (genus *Cynomys*)

18 Grayling

19 Grévy's zebra (*Equus grevyi*)

20 Giant oarfish (*Regalecus glesne*)

1   Who are you most likely to have seen wearing a Custodian helmet?

2   Mount Korab is the highest mountain in Albania and which other country?

3   On which island is the Pitch Lake, the world's largest natural deposit of asphalt?

4   Which "Spanish Caravaggio" painted a trussed-up lamb in *Agnus Dei* (1635-40)?

5   Assassinated in 1589, Henri III was the last French king of which dynasty?

6   Which Indian writer (1906-2001) set most of his stories in the fictional town of Malgudi?

7   In 1940, Eleanor Lambert founded which famous annual list?

8   The paratroopers Jan Kubiš and Jozef Gabčík assassinated which high-ranking Nazi?

9   On January 6, 1957, Elvis Presley made his third and final appearance on which show?

10 *Storm of Steel* (1920) is a World War One memoir by which German officer?

11 Which actor links the TV series *Jekyll*, *Murphy's Law*, *The Missing* and *Babylon*?

12 The stars Alnilam, Mintaka and Alnitak form an asterism known by what name?

13 Which saint (1887-1968) was born Francesco Forgione?

14 Creator of the first lyre, which Greek god was born in a cave on Mount Cyllene?

15 Charles Krug is the oldest winery in which American wine region?

16 The 1883 Pony Track is the simplest route of ascent for which mountain?

17 Built by Gustave Eiffel, the Maria Pia railway bridge crosses which river?

18 Which endocrine gland in the brain produces melatonin?

19 Nicknamed "The Munchkin of Munich", which gymnast won Olympic team, balance beam and floor exercise golds in 1972?

20 What is the pictured football ground?

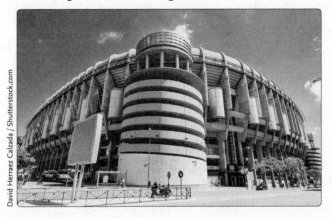

David Herraez Calzada / Shutterstock.com

Answers to QUIZ 207 – General Knowledge

1   *Strange Case of Dr. Jekyll and Mr. Hyde* by Robert Louis Stevenson
2   Argentina
3   Orlebar Brown
4   Jacopo Peri
5   The Solar System
6   Bologna
7   Ignacy Paderewski
8   Albert Pierrepoint
9   *My Favorite Things*
10 Visions of Our Lady of Fátima, i.e. the Virgin Mary, or the Lady of the Rosary – in Portugal
11 The *Pietà*
12 Serpent or snake
13 They are disused London Underground stations or 'ghost stations'
14 Higgins boat or Landing craft, vehicle, personnel
15 Charley Varrick
16 *Dante Symphony*
17 *Tootsie*
18 Hurling
19 Tottenham Hotspur
20 Euphonium

1   Who wrote the motorcycle travel book *Jupiter's Travels* (1980)?

2   Which title links singles released in the 1980s by Joy Division and Russ Abbot?

3   Which film studio first published its RenderMan software in 1988?

4   Joan Quigley found fame as which woman's astrologer in the '80s?

5   Which British singer last had a UK no.1 single with *Baby Jane* (1983)?

6   In 1986, Davina Thompson became the first transplant patient of what type?

7   Having left *Tatler* in 1983, Tina Brown went on to edit which American magazine in 1984?

8   Which comedian co-authored the 1983 book *Families and How to Survive Them* with psychiatrist Robin Skynner?

9   Which violinist recorded the 1989 album *Vivaldi: The Four Seasons* with the English Chamber Orchestra?

10 In 1984, Liu Chuanzhi founded which computer company in a Beijing guard house?

11 The book *As You Wish* by Cary Elwes is a memoir of which 1987 film?

12 Which European Space Agency mission flew by and studied Halley's Comet in 1986?

13 Which 1982 record is the best-selling album of all time?

14 Which Japanese firm released the TB-303 bass synthesizer in 1982?

15 Which actor-director co-founded the Renaissance Theatre Company with David Parfitt in 1987?

16 Meryl Streep won an Oscar for her role in the 1982 film of which William Styron novel?

17 Who is the US star of the stand-up comedy concert films *Delirious* (1983) and *Raw* (1987)?

18 Which Scottish darts player won his second BDO world championship in 1989?

19 Which Mexican WBC featherweight champion, aged 23, was killed while driving his Porsche 928 on August 12, 1982?

20 Name the chart topping pop group –

Jaguar PS / Shutterstock.com

Answers to QUIZ 208 – General Knowledge

1   Male police constables or sergeants in England and Wales
2   Macedonia
3   Trinidad
4   Francisco de Zurbarán
5   Valois
6   R.K. Narayan
7   The International Best-Dressed List – now seen in *Vanity Fair*
8   Reinhard Heydrich
9   *The Ed Sullivan Show*
10 Ernst Jünger

11 James Nesbitt
12 Orion's Belt or the Three Kings
13 Padre Pio or St. Pio of Pietrelcina
14 Hermes
15 Napa Valley
16 Ben Nevis
17 Douro
18 Pineal gland or conarium or epiphysis cerebri
19 Olga Korbut
20 Santiago Bernabéu Stadium – home of Real Madrid

1   Which social networking site styles itself as the "world's largest professional network"?

2   Which choreographer adapted *The Nutcracker* into *The Hard Nut* (1991)?

3   Which *Parks and Recreation* star wrote the autobiography *Yes Please*?

4   Sugaar and Mari are the supreme god and goddess in which European people's mythology?

5   *Be Right Back, White Bear* and *15 Million Merits* are episodes of which anthology TV series?

6   Which dwarf planet is the largest asteroid in the Solar System?

7   Who wrote about "atomic bombs" in his 1914 novel *The World Set Free*?

8   Surrounding the Kaaba in Mecca, what is the largest mosque in the world?

9   The 1914 Christmas Truce inspired which 1990 song by The Farm?

10 Who are the only siblings to have won Best Actress Oscars?

11 Lazzaroni, Di Estasi and Luxardo are brands of which almond-flavoured liqueur?

12 Which country features Fish River Canyon, the largest canyon in Africa?

13 Who was the last sovereign to be buried in Westminster Abbey?

14 Which Estonian composer wrote the 1978 piece *Spiegel im Spiegel*?

15 In which city is the Antica Pizzeria Port'Alba, reputedly the world's first pizzeria?

16 In 1464, who became the first commoner in history to marry an English king?

17 Which *Breaking Bad* TV character was originally named James M. McGill?

18 Which French businessman founded the cycling team La Vie Claire in 1984?

19 Riding a Yamaha motorcycle, Cyril Neveu became which rally's first winner in 1979?

20 The pictured Harley-Davidson motorcycle is the 2016 Ultra Classic version of which model?

Answers to QUIZ 209 – The 1980s

1 Ted Simon
2 *Atmosphere*
3 Pixar
4 Nancy Reagan
5 Rod Stewart
6 Heart-lung-liver or triple transplant – at Papworth Hospital, Cambridge (she died aged 47 in 1998)
7 *Vanity Fair*
8 John Cleese
9 Nigel Kennedy
10 Lenovo – founded as Legend Holdings
11 *The Princess Bride*
12 Giotto
13 *Thriller* by Michael Jackson
14 Roland
15 Kenneth Branagh
16 *Sophie's Choice*
17 Eddie Murphy
18 Jocky Wilson
19 Salvador Sánchez
20 Culture Club

1. Founded in 1693, what is the oldest gentlemen's club in London?

2. Which British fashion magazine was launched by Terry and Tricia Jones in 1980?

3. Which US sitcom featured the *Doctor Who* parody *Inspector Spacetime*?

4. In Japan, which occupational problem is known as *karoshi*?

5. Which money transfer service was initially founded in 1998 as Confinity?

6. What has the *Wall Street Journal* called Britain's "biggest contribution to gastronomy"?

7. Christopher Wren is a hotel guest in which Agatha Christie play?

8. Which US pop star wrote the music and lyrics for the musical *Kinky Boots*?

9. Which US poet began a sonnet: "Thou are not lovelier than lilacs, -no"?

10. In Chinese mythology, the Great Race between the animals determined which order?

11. Jane Turner and Gina Riley played the title roles in which Australian sitcom?

12. Saleswoman Brownie Wise developed the "party plan" system of marketing which products?

13. In the film *Cool Hand Luke*, Paul Newman's title character is jailed for which crime?

14. Château Musar is a winery in which Middle Eastern country?

15. Known in Irish as *Port Láirge*, what is Ireland's oldest city?

16. Which musical and film is about a "slip of a girly boy" who was born Hansel Schmidt?

17. Which British-Nigerian artist created *Mr. and Mrs. Andrews without their Heads* (1998)?

18 Which South African was the 1996 women's 100m and 200m breaststroke Olympic champion?

19 Who won the first of five Monaco Grands Prix in 1963?

20 What is the pictured vegetable?

Answers to QUIZ 210 – General Knowledge

1 LinkedIn

2 Mark Morris

3 Amy Poehler

4 Basque

5 *Black Mirror*

6 Ceres

7 H.G. Wells

8 Masjid al-Haram

9 *All Together Now*

10 Olivia de Havilland & Joan Fontaine

11 Amaretto

12 Namibia

13 King George II

14 Arvo Pärt

15 Naples

16 Elizabeth Woodville, who married Edward IV

17 Saul Goodman, the title lawyer in the spin-off *Better Call Saul*

18 Bernard Tapie

19 Dakar Rally, formerly Paris-Dakar Rally

20 Electra Glide

1   Rolex calls which of its products "the iconic divers' watch since 1953"?

2   Equivalent to starch in plants, what is the principal storage form of glucose in animals?

3   Robert A. Caro's book *The Power Broker* is a biography of which New York master builder?

4   Which Mendelssohn oratorio features a trio of angels singing *Lift Thine Eyes*?

5   Which manager was born Andreas Cornelis van Kuijk in 1909?

6   Percy Bysshe Shelley called which country "Thou Paradise of exiles"?

7   Judi Dench won a Tony for her role as Esme Allen in which 1997 David Hare play?

8   Which Umbrian town hosts Italy's top arts festival, the *Festival dei Due Mondi* (Festival of the Two Worlds)?

9   Which US poet wrote: "Life, friends, is boring. We must not say so."?

10 Which TV soap began with the line: "Cor, stinks in 'ere, dunnit?"?

11 In the film *Three Men and a Baby*, which actor's character Jack Holden is the biological father?

12 What is, historically, the oldest brandy distilled in France?

13 During the Second World War, Field Marshal Bernard Montgomery wore a beret made by which Cumbrian firm?

14 The church, Crathie Kirk, is close to which royal residence?

15 Which college is the principal training centre for London's Metropolitan Police?

16 A Jacksonville, Florida gym teacher inspired which Southern rock band's name?

ANSWERS ON PAGE **439**

17 Which two nations share the world's largest gas field, the South Pars / North Field?

18 Argentina's Luciana Aymar (b.1977) became known as the "Maradona" of which sport?

19 Which Briton won the Three-Day Eventing individual world title in 1986?

20 Who is the pictured 19th century novelist?

Answers to QUIZ 211 – General Knowledge

1 White's
2 *i-D*
3 *Community*
4 It is death from overwork
5 PayPal
6 The sandwich
7 *The Mousetrap*
8 Cyndi Lauper
9 Edna St. Vincent Millay
10 The order of the 12 animals as they appeared in the Chinese zodiac
11 *Kath & Kim*
12 Tupperware
13 Knocking the heads off parking meters
14 Lebanon
15 Waterford
16 *Hedwig and the Angry Inch*
17 Yinka Shonibare
18 Penny Heyns
19 Graham Hill
20 Swede or rutabaga

1   Mao Zedong was born the son of a farmer in Shaoshan in which south-central province of China?

2   The civil execution of which man remains the only time Israel has enacted a death sentence?

3   Paso de Mercedes, Lomas Valentinas and Tuyutí were battles in which 1864-70 war?

4   Richard I began building which 'Saucy Castle' above the Seine in 1196?

5   Which conflagration ended at a spot called Pye Corner on Giltspur Street?

6   Who was the only President of the United Arab Republic (Egypt & Syria)?

7   Who married Julius Caesar's only child, Julia, in 59 bc?

8   The Battle of Ligny on June 16, 1815, was which man's final military victory?

9   Which war began with the Battle of Gonzales on October 2, 1835?

10 Who was elected MP for Fermanagh & South Tyrone in April 1981?

11 Which Union Army general was victorious at the 1863 Battle of Gettysburg?

12 Who was proclaimed Queen of England on July 10, 1553?

13 Which 1942 parliamentary report identified five "Giant Evils" plaguing society?

14 Which son of the emperor Claudius and Messalina was poisoned by Nero in 55 AD?

15 Which explorer (c.1554-1618) founded the Roanoke Colony in what is now Dare County, North Carolina?

16 On June 10, 1190, which Holy Roman Emperor drowned in the Saleph river?

17 Watching the Chasseurs d'Afrique charge to immortality, Wilhelm I exclaimed: "Ah! Les braves gens!" at which battle?

18 Which Mexican revolutionary (1878-1923) was born José Doroteo Arango Arámbula?

19 Which nurse said: "I realise that patriotism is not enough. I must have no hatred or bitterness towards anyone"?

20 The picture features which Frenchman?

Answers to QUIZ 212 – General Knowledge

1 Submariner
2 Glycogen
3 Robert Moses
4 *Elijah*
5 'Colonel' Tom Parker – of Elvis Presley fame
6 Italy
7 *Amy's View*
8 Spoleto
9 John Berryman in *Dream Song 14*
10 *EastEnders*
11 Ted Danson
12 Armagnac
13 Kangol
14 Balmoral Castle
15 Hendon Police College
16 Lynyrd Skynyrd – named after Leonard Skinner
17 Iran & Qatar
18 Women's field hockey
19 Virginia Leng
20 George Eliot aka Mary Anne Evans

1 Which consort of Brahma is the Hindu goddess of learning, wisdom and the arts?

2 Which Dutch-born American abstract expressionist painter began his *Woman* series in 1950?

3 Which "father of immunology" was also the first person to describe the brood parasitism of the cuckoo?

4 The deepest section of which metro system is 74m underground at Park Pobedy station?

5 Stephen Fry, Hugh Laurie and Emma Thompson won the Perrier Award as part of which revue?

6 Who remains the longest-ever serving leader of the Labour Party?

7 Doug Kenney, Henry Beard and Robert Hoffman founded which American humour magazine in 1970?

8 The 24-year-old "Runner" Faith Connors is the protagonist of which 2008 video game?

9 Which New York Dolls frontman performs as the lounge singer Buster Poindexter?

10 "Hot dog, jumping frog, Albuquerque" is the chorus of which 1988 Prefab Sprout hit?

11 Which king of the Lapiths was bound by Zeus to a fiery wheel in Tartarus for trying to seduce Hera?

12 Horatio Nelson lost the use of his right eye at which 1794 siege?

13 Alexia is a form of aphasia marked by loss of the ability to do what?

14 The Cuban composer Enrique Jorrín created which ballroom music style?

15 Who played the title roles in the films *Lili* (1953), *Gigi* (1958) and *Fanny* (1961)?

16 Who did Sir Thomas Knyvett and Edmund Doubleday find in the House of Lords' basement?

17 Produced by the Solingen firm Wester & Co., the *Modell 1890* was the first official iteration of which multi-tool?

18 Which tycoon bought Turnberry golf course from Leisurecorp in 2014?

19 In 1924, who became the first Italian winner of the Tour de France?

20 Which London venue is pictured?

Answers to QUIZ 213 – History

1	Hunan	12	Lady Jane Grey
2	Adolf Eichmann	13	Beveridge Report or the
3	War of the Triple Alliance or		report on Social Insurance
	Paraguayan War		and Allied Services
4	Château Gaillard	14	Britannicus
5	Great Fire of London of 1666	15	Sir Walter Raleigh
6	Egypt's Gamal Abdel Nasser	16	Frederick I Barbarossa
	(president: 1958-61)	17	Sedan – in 1870
7	Pompey [the Great]	18	Pancho Villa
8	Napoleon Bonaparte	19	Edith Cavell
9	Texas Revolution or Texas	20	Cardinal Richelieu or
	War of Independence		Armand Jean du Plessis,
10	Bobby Sands		Cardinal-Duke of Richelieu
11	George G. Meade		and of Fronsac

1   Which US documentary filmmaker interviews people using his invention, the Interrotron?

2   Which Coen brothers film starred Gabriel Byrne as the gangster Tom Regan?

3   The Ingmar Bergman film *Smiles of a Summer Night* inspired which Sondheim musical?

4   Prince Hans of the Southern Isles and the Duke of Weselton are villains in which Disney film?

5   Who played Juror #8 in the 1957 film *12 Angry Men*?

6   Which 2015 film tells the story of artist Einar Wegener who became Lili Elbe?

7   Who scored the films *Aliens*, *Field of Dreams*, *Glory*, *Apollo 13* and *Braveheart*?

8   Who played the conductor Sir Alfred de Carter in the 1948 Preston Sturges film *Unfaithfully Yours*?

9   Which US comedian wrote, directed and starred in the 2014 film *Top Five*?

10 Which US sound rerecording mixer holds the record for most Oscar nominations without a win (20)?

11 Played by Joel McCrea, what is Johnny Jones's job in the title of a 1940 Alfred Hitchcock film?

12 Which French actress made her directorial debut with the 2000 film *Le Goût des autres* or *The Taste of Others*?

13 *Dracula* star Bela Lugosi made his final appearance on film in which notoriously bad 1959 movie?

14 Which Frenchman directed the 12-hour, 53-minute film *Out 1: Noli Me Tangere* (1971)?

15 What is the name of the boy at the centre of the custody battle in the film *Kramer vs. Kramer*?

16 In 1940, which "Brazilian Bombshell" made her first Hollywood film, *Down Argentine Way*?

17 Which Spielberg film tells the Cold War story of Brooklyn lawyer James B. Donovan (Tom Hanks)?

18 Playing the columnist J.J. Hunsecker, Burt Lancaster says "Match me, Sidney" in which film?

19 Who was revealed to be John James Preston in a 2008 film?

20 Which Japanese director of such cult films as *Audition* and *Ichi the Killer* is pictured?

marcello farina / Shutterstock.com

Answers to QUIZ 214 – General Knowledge

1   Saraswati
2   Willem de Kooning
3   Edward Jenner
4   Moscow Metro
5   1981 Cambridge Footlights Revue, titled 'The Cellar Tapes'
6   Clement Attlee
7   *National Lampoon*
8   *Mirror's Edge*
9   David Johansen
10 *The King of Rock 'n' Roll*
11 Ixion
12 Calvi in Haute-Corse, Corsica
13 Read or understand written language
14 Cha-cha-chá
15 Leslie Caron
16 Guy Fawkes
17 Swiss Army knife
18 Donald Trump
19 Ottavio Bottecchia
20 Alexandra Palace

Quizzes by subject

Art	18, 216
Astronomy	82, 366
Booze	372
Business	136, 234, 354
Classical Music	70, 210
Crime Literature	418
Fashion	94, 258
Film	30, 148, 326, 442
First	118
Food & Drink	64, 190
France	240
General Knowledge	14, 16, 20, 22, 26, 28, 32, 34, 38, 40, 44, 46, 48, 50, 54, 56, 60, 62, 66, 68, 72, 74, 78, 80, 84, 86, 90, 92, 96, 98, 102, 104, 108, 110, 114, 116, 120, 122, 126, 128, 132, 134, 138, 140, 144, 146, 150, 152, 156, 158, 162, 164, 168, 170, 174, 176, 180, 182, 186, 188, 192, 194, 196, 198, 202, 204, 208, 212, 214, 218, 220, 224, 226, 230, 232, 236, 238, 242, 244, 248, 250, 254, 256, 260, 262, 266, 268, 272, 274, 278, 280, 284, 286, 288, 290, 294, 296, 300, 304, 306, 310, 312, 316, 318, 322, 324, 328, 330, 334, 338, 340, 344, 346, 350, 352, 356, 358, 362, 364, 368, 370, 374, 376, 380, 382, 384, 386, 390, 392, 396, 398, 402, 404, 408, 410, 414, 416, 420, 422, 426, 428, 432, 434, 436, 440
Geography	166, 314
History	36, 154, 302, 438
Inventions	412
Jazz	378
Kings & Queens	348
Landmarks	282
Literature	24, 142, 298
Media	406
Mountains	276
Mythology	124, 342
Olympics	292
Opera	388
Poetry	400
Politics	106, 252
Popular Music	42, 178, 320
Religion	88, 246
Sciences	130, 206, 332
Sport	76, 222
Structures	160, 394
Technology	264
The 1980s	430
The One and Only...	308
Theatre	112, 200, 336
Transport	100, 228, 360
TV	52
USA	172
War	270
Wildlife	58, 184, 424

Image Credits

Quiz 1 – General Knowledge	Tom Roche / Shutterstock.com
Quiz 2 – General Knowledge	Helga Esteb / Shutterstock.com
Quiz 3 – Art	shalunts / Shutterstock.com
Quiz 4 – General Knowledge	Kobby Dagan / Shutterstock.com
Quiz 5 – General Knowledge	f8grapher / Shutterstock.com
Quiz 6 – Literature	Abbey of Kells / Public Domain
Quiz 7 – General Knowledge	Zoltan Katona / Shutterstock.com
Quiz 8 – General Knowledge	Steven Frame / Shutterstock.com
Quiz 9 – Film	Naomi Goggin / News Syndication
Quiz 10 – General Knowledge	Brent Hofacker / Shutterstock.com
Quiz 11 – General Knowledge	Charles01 / CC-BY-SA-3.0 and others
Quiz 12 – History	Everett Historical / Shutterstock.com
Quiz 13 – General Knowledge	Times Newspapers Ltd
Quiz 14 – General Knowledge	Ev. Safronov / Shutterstock.com
Quiz 15 – Popular Music	Avis De Miranda / Shutterstock.com
Quiz 16 – General Knowledge	Evikka / Shutterstock.com
Quiz 17 – General Knowledge	Yury Dmitrienko / Shutterstock.com
Quiz 18 – General Knowledge	Jac. de Nijs / Anefo / CC-BY-SA-3.0 (Netherlands)
Quiz 19 – General Knowledge	Mauvries / Shutterstock.com
Quiz 20 – TV	Featureflash Photo Agency / Shutterstock.com
Quiz 21 – General Knowledge	Ben Gurr / News Syndication
Quiz 22 – General Knowledge	Rocky Grimes / Shutterstock.com
Quiz 23 – Wildlife	davemhuntphotography / Shutterstock.com
Quiz 24 – General Knowledge	ermess / Shutterstock.com
Quiz 25 – General Knowledge	Helga Esteb / Shutterstock.com
Quiz 26 – Food & Drink	Alex Staroseltsev / Shutterstock.com
Quiz 27 – General Knowledge	Jack Baker / News Syndication
Quiz 28 – General Knowledge	Featureflash Photo Agency / Shutterstock.com
Quiz 29 – Classical Music	DavidGraham86 / Shutterstock.com
Quiz 30 – General Knowledge	Featureflash Photo Agency / Shutterstock.com
Quiz 31 – General Knowledge	Travel Stock / Shutterstock.com
Quiz 32 – Sport	Author unknown / Public Domain
Quiz 33 – General Knowledge	Nils Versemann / Shutterstock.com
Quiz 34 – General Knowledge	magicinfoto / Shutterstock.com
Quiz 35 – Astronomy	NASA, modified by Chmee2 / Public Domain
Quiz 36 – General Knowledge	Bamboofurniture / CC-BY-SA-3.0
Quiz 37 – General Knowledge	Throwawayhack / CC-BY-SA-4.0 and others (assumed based on copyright claims) Note – photo of a replica.
Quiz 38 – Religion	Arena Photo UK / Shutterstock.com
Quiz 39 – General Knowledge	Alessandro Colle / Shutterstock.com
Quiz 40 – General Knowledge	Everett Historical / Shutterstock.com
Quiz 41 – Fashion	Eric Koch / Anefo / CC-BY-SA-3.0
Quiz 42 – General Knowledge	Nadar (1820–1910) / Public Domain
Quiz 43 – General Knowledge	julie deshaies / Shutterstock.com
Quiz 44 – Transport	Kosarev Alexander / Shutterstock.com
Quiz 45 – General Knowledge	Mat Hayward / Shutterstock.com
Quiz 46 – General Knowledge	Sergey Uryadnikov / Shutterstock.com
Quiz 47 – Politics	Unknown / CC-BY-SA-3.0 (Netherlands)
Quiz 48 – General Knowledge	Mbalotia / CC-BY-SA-3.0
Quiz 49 – General Knowledge	Anna Sedneva / Shutterstock.com
Quiz 50 – Theatre	Steve Bowbrick / CC-BY-2.0
Quiz 51 – General Knowledge	Marsyas (assumed based on copyright claims) / CC-BY-SA-3.0 and others
Quiz 52 – General Knowledge	GDAE2015 / Shutterstock.com
Quiz 53 – First	Everett Historical / Shutterstock.com
Quiz 54 – General Knowledge	Ekaterina Pokrovsky / Shutterstock.com
Quiz 55 – General Knowledge	zhekoss / Shutterstock.com
Quiz 56 – Mythology	GhostKnife / Shutterstock.com
Quiz 57 – General Knowledge	Erin Cadigan / Shutterstock.com
Quiz 58 – General Knowledge	Justin Black / Shutterstock.com
Quiz 59 – Sciences	NATIONAL LIBRARY OF MEDICINE/ SCIENCE PHOTO LIBRARY
Quiz 60 – General Knowledge	Anna Jedynak / Shutterstock.com
Quiz 61 – General Knowledge	Warut Chinsai / Shutterstock.com
Quiz 62 – Business	mtkang / Shutterstock.com
Quiz 63 – General Knowledge	sailko / CC-BY-SA-3.0
Quiz 64 – General Knowledge	Veniamin Kraskov / Shutterstock.com
Quiz 65 – Literature	David Bebber / News Syndication
Quiz 66 – General Knowledge	Oleg Znamenskiy /Shutterstock.com
Quiz 67 – General Knowledge	Christian Bertrand / Shutterstock.com
Quiz 68 – Film	Jaguar PS / Shutterstock.com
Quiz 69 – General Knowledge	Migel / Shutterstock.com
Quiz 70 – General Knowledge	Triff / Shutterstock.com
Quiz 71 – History	Sir Benjamin Stone / Public Domain
Quiz 72 – General Knowledge	Pyty / Shutterstock.com
Quiz 73 – General Knowledge	belizar / Shutterstock.com
Quiz 74 – Structures	Paul McKinnon / Shutterstock.com
Quiz 75 – General Knowledge	David Bebber / News Syndication
Quiz 76 – General Knowledge	Lukasz Miegoc / Shutterstock.com
Quiz 77 – Geography	macumazahn / Shutterstock.com
Quiz 78 – General Knowledge	fi1photo / Shutterstock.com
Quiz 79 – General Knowledge	Royal Society / CC-BY-SA-3.0
Quiz 80 – USA	Debby Wong / Shutterstock.com
Quiz 81 – General Knowledge	Mihai-Bogdan Lazar / Shutterstock.com
Quiz 82 – General Knowledge	Alejandro Linares Garcia / CC-BY-SA-4.0 and others
Quiz 83 – Popular Music	Featureflash Photo Agency / Shutterstock.com
Quiz 84 – General Knowledge	leungchopan/ Shutterstock.com
Quiz 85 – General Knowledge	Francesca Moscatelli / Shutterstock.com
Quiz 86 – Wildlife	Sainam51 / Shutterstock.com
Quiz 87 – General Knowledge	Valentyna Chukhlyebova / Shutterstock.com
Quiz 88 – General Knowledge	Everett Historical / Shutterstock.com
Quiz 89 – Food & Drink	Margoe Edwards / Shutterstock.com
Quiz 90 – General Knowledge	Lee Sie / CC-BY-SA-2.0
Quiz 91 – General Knowledge	Gamegfx / Shutterstock.com
Quiz 92 – General Knowledge	Amanda Lucidon / White House / Public Domain
Quiz 93 – General Knowledge	Luxerendering / Shutterstock.com
Quiz 94 – Theatre	Times Newspapers Ltd
Quiz 95 – General Knowledge	ErickN / Shutterstock.com
Quiz 96 – General Knowledge	Edmund Lowe Photography / Shutterstock.com
Quiz 97 – Sciences	A. BARRINGTON BROWN, GONVILLE AND CAIUS COLLEGE/SCIENCE PHOTO LIBRARY
Quiz 98 – General Knowledge	Linn Currie / Shutterstock.com
Quiz 99 – Classical Music	Mezzofortist / CC-BY-SA-3.0
Quiz 100 – General Knowledge	ARENA Creative / Shutterstock.com
Quiz 101 – General Knowledge	Kenneth William / CC-BY-2.0
Quiz 102 – Art	Kielnhofer / Public Domain
Quiz 103 – General Knowledge	Reinhold Leitner / Shutterstock.com
Quiz 104 – General Knowledge	Semmick Photo / Shutterstock.com
Quiz 105 – Sport	Dim50 / CC-BY-SA-3.0
Quiz 106 – General Knowledge	Featureflash Photo Agency / Shutterstock.com
Quiz 107 – General Knowledge	In Green /Shutterstock.com
Quiz 108 – Transport	72Dino / CC-BY-SA-3.0
Quiz 109 – General Knowledge	Margaret Smeaton / Shutterstock.com
Quiz 110 – General Knowledge	kozer / Shutterstock.com
Quiz 111 – Business	s_bukley / Shutterstock.com
Quiz 112 – General Knowledge	Chris Harris / News Syndication
Quiz 113 – General Knowledge	Chris Harris / News Syndication
Quiz 114 – France	Nadar (1820–1910) / Public Domain
Quiz 115 – General Knowledge	Nicole Ciscato / Shutterstock.com
Quiz 116 – General Knowledge	VICTOR TORRES / Shutterstock.com
Quiz 117 – Religion	Pierre Leclerc / Shutterstock.com
Quiz 118 – General Knowledge	Sinead Lynch / News Syndication
Quiz 119 – General Knowledge	Everett – Art / Shutterstock.com

Quiz 120 – Politics	Tiglath-Pileser IV / Public Domain
Quiz 121 – General Knowledge	totajla / Shutterstock.com
Quiz 122 – General Knowledge	ChrisO / CC-BY-SA-3.0
Quiz 123 – Fashion	Featureflash Photo Agency / Shutterstock.com
Quiz 124 – General Knowledge	Mike Peel (www.mikepeel.net) / CC-BY-SA-4.0
Quiz 125 – General Knowledge	Tomas Kotouc / Shutterstock.com
Quiz 126 – Technology	Mikael Hjerpe / Shutterstock.com
Quiz 127 – General Knowledge	Chris Harris / News Syndication
Quiz 128 – General Knowledge	Chris Smith / News Syndication
Quiz 129 – War	George Charles Beresford (1864–1938) / Public Domain
Quiz 130 – General Knowledge	Frank Hermann / News Syndication
Quiz 131 – General Knowledge	Soloviev Andrey / Shutterstock.com
Quiz 132 – Mountains	Aleksandar Kamasi / Shutterstock.com
Quiz 133 – General Knowledge	Georgios Kollidas / Shutterstock.com
Quiz 134 – General Knowledge	chrisdorney / Shutterstock.com
Quiz 135 – Landmarks	Sergey Dzyuba / Shutterstock.com
Quiz 136 – General Knowledge	Tamara Kulikova / Shutterstock.com
Quiz 137 – General Knowledge	Zoran Veselinovic / CC-BY-SA-2.0
Quiz 138 – General Knowledge	360b / Shutterstock.com
Quiz 139 – General Knowledge	Viacheslav Lopatin / Shutterstock.com
Quiz 140 – Olympics	Joshua C. Millage / CC-BY-SA-3.0
Quiz 141 – General Knowledge	Nick Ray / News Syndication
Quiz 142 – General Knowledge	LianeM / Shutterstock.com
Quiz 143 – Literature	Allan Glenwright / News Syndication
Quiz 144 – General Knowledge	KGBOxford / CC-BY-SA-3.0
Quiz 145 – History	Author unknown / Public Domain
Quiz 146 – General Knowledge	HildaWeges Photography / Shutterstock.com
Quiz 147 – General Knowledge	United States Department of Energy / Public Domain
Quiz 148 – The One and Only...	Helga Esteb / Shutterstock.com
Quiz 149 – General Knowledge	Charles Haynes / CC-BY-SA-2.0
Quiz 150 – General Knowledge	Boudewijn Sluijk / Shutterstock.com
Quiz 151 – Geography	ollirg / Shutterstock.com
Quiz 152 – General Knowledge	Atlaspix / Shutterstock.com
Quiz 153 – General Knowledge	Sean Pavone / Shutterstock.com
Quiz 154 – Popular Music	Christian Bertrand / Shutterstock.com
Quiz 155 – General Knowledge	Andrew Burgess / Shutterstock.com
Quiz 156 – General Knowledge	Jack Taylor / News Syndication
Quiz 157 – Film	NY89 / CC-BY-SA-4.0
Quiz 158 – General Knowledge	yxm2008 / Shutterstock.com
Quiz 159 – General Knowledge	R Sones / CC-BY-SA-2.0
Quiz 160 – Sciences	John D. and Catherine T. MacArthur Foundation / CC-BY-4.0 Int
Quiz 161 – General Knowledge	OlegD / Shutterstock.com
Quiz 162 – Theatre	Almotional / Shutterstock.com
Quiz 163 – General Knowledge	antgirl / CC-BY-SA-2.0
Quiz 164 – General Knowledge	Stewart Williams / News Syndication
Quiz 165 – Mythology	Paul Brady Photo / Shutterstock.com
Quiz 166 – General Knowledge	drserg / Shutterstock.com
Quiz 167 – General Knowledge	Everett Historical / Shutterstock.com
Quiz 168 – Kings & Queens	Tanner (Capt), War Office official photographer / Public Domain
Quiz 169 – General Knowledge	Fouad A. Saad / Shutterstock.com
Quiz 170 – General Knowledge	Brad Wakefield / News Syndication
Quiz 171 – Business	ricochet64 / Shutterstock.com
Quiz 172 – General Knowledge	Angelina Dimitrova / Shutterstock.com
Quiz 173 – General Knowledge	PHILIPIMAGE / Shutterstock.com
Quiz 174 – Transport	No author listed / Public Domain

Quiz 175 – General Knowledge	Martin Mecnarowski / Shutterstock.com
Quiz 176 – General Knowledge	Bill Perry / Shutterstock.com
Quiz 177 – Astronomy	MarcelClemens / Shutterstock.com
Quiz 178 – General Knowledge	David Woolfenden / Shutterstock.com
Quiz 179 – General Knowledge	Mecca Ibrahim from Richmond, UK / CC-BY-2.0
Quiz 180 – Booze	Thinglass / Shutterstock.com
Quiz 181 – General Knowledge	audioscience / Shutterstock.com
Quiz 182 – General Knowledge	Rafael Xavier / Shutterstock.com
Quiz 183 – Jazz	Van Vechten Collection at Library of Congress / Public Domain
Quiz 184 – General Knowledge	Angela Davis (Angela D.) from Austin, TX, USA / CC-BY-2.0
Quiz 185 – General Knowledge	cjmac / Shutterstock.com
Quiz 186 – General Knowledge	Simone van den Berg / Shutterstock.com
Quiz 187 – General Knowledge	Niall Marshall / News Syndication
Quiz 188 – Opera	artnana / Shutterstock.com
Quiz 189 – General Knowledge	nhtg / Shutterstock.com
Quiz 190 – General Knowledge	FashionStock.com / Shutterstock.com
Quiz 191 – Structures	Neil Mitchell / Shutterstock.com
Quiz 192 – General Knowledge	EGG90 / Shutterstock.com
Quiz 193 – General Knowledge	fotorince / Shutterstock.com
Quiz 194 – Poetry	iryna1 / Shutterstock.com
Quiz 195 – General Knowledge	Stilfehler / CC-BY-SA-3.0 and others
Quiz 196 – General Knowledge	No author listed / Public Domain
Quiz 197 – Media	RoidRanger / Shutterstock.com
Quiz 198 – General Knowledge	Everett Historical /Shutterstock.com
Quiz 199 – General Knowledge	Andrew Sims / News Syndication
Quiz 200 – Inventions	dantess / Shutterstock.com
Quiz 201 – General Knowledge	ARENA Creative / Shutterstock.com
Quiz 202 – General Knowledge	Anna Veselova / Shutterstock.com
Quiz 203 – Crime Literature	Times Newspapers Ltd
Quiz 204 – General Knowledge	James Glossop / News Syndication
Quiz 205 – General Knowledge	No author listed / Public Domain
Quiz 206 – Wildlife	Wm. Leo Smith / Public Domain
Quiz 207 – General Knowledge	Boris Medvedev / Shutterstock.com
Quiz 208 – General Knowledge	David Herraez Calzada / Shutterstock.com
Quiz 209 – The 1980s	Jaguar PS / Shutterstock.com
Quiz 210 – General Knowledge	William Crochot / CC-BY-SA-4.0
Quiz 211 – General Knowledge	Picasa user Seedambassadors / CC-BY-SA-3.0
Quiz 212 – General Knowledge	Author unknown / Public Domain
Quiz 213 – History	National Gallery / Pubic Domain
Quiz 214 – General Knowledge	iolya / Shutterstock.com
Quiz 215 – Film	marcello farina / Shutterstock.com